Working with Men 1

Praise for this book

'This is an extremely interesting and timely book, given the pressing need to ensure the realisation of substantive gender equality as a cornerstone of social justice and sustainable development. Drawing on diverse examples from initiatives around the world, the book highlights both the potential for and importance, or indeed necessity, of involving men and boys, alongside women and girls, in addressing gender inequalities and promoting and ultimately achieving gender equality, for the good of all.'

Helen Longlands, UCL Centre for Education and International Development (CEID), UCL Institute for Education, University College London

Working with Men for Gender Equality

Edited by
Caroline Sweetman

Published by Practical Action Publishing in association with Oxfam GB

Practical Action Publishing Ltd
27a Albert Street, Rugby, Warwickshire, CV21 2SG, UK
www.practicalactionpublishing.org

A catalogue record for this book is available from the British Library.
A catalogue record for this book has been requested from the Library of Congress.

ISBN 978-1-78853-048-4 Paperback
ISBN 978-1-78853-047-7 Hardback
ISBN 978-1-78044-936-4 Ebook
ISBN 978-1-78044-866-4 Library PDF

Citation: Sweetman, C. (eds) (2019) *Working with Men for Gender Equality*, Rugby, UK: Practical Action Publishing and Oxford: Oxfam GB http://dx.doi.org/10.3362/9781780448664.

Since 1974, Practical Action Publishing has published and disseminated books and information in support of international development work throughout the world. Practical Action Publishing is a trading name of Practical Action Publishing Ltd (Company Reg. No. 1159018), the wholly owned publishing company of Practical Action. Practical Action Publishing trades only in support of its parent charity objectives and any profits are covenanted back to Practical Action (Charity Reg. No. 247257, Group VAT Registration No. 880 9924 76).

Oxfam is a registered charity in England and Wales (no 202918) and Scotland (SC 039042). Oxfam GB is a member of Oxfam International.

Oxfam GB,
Oxfam House, John Smith Drive,
Oxford, OX4 2JY, UK
www.oxfam.org.uk

Cover photo shows children from Dharavi, Mumbai.
Credit: Tash McCarroll with Ojos Nuevos and Luis Alberto Amaya ProCo, winners of the UN Women India Freedom from Violence Photo Competition, 2014
Printed in the United Kingdom

Contents

http://dx.doi.org/10.3362/9781780448664.000

About the editor

Caroline Sweetman is Editor of the international journal *Gender & Development* and works for Oxfam GB.

Working in Gender and Development

The *Working in Gender and Development series* brings together themed selections of the best articles from the journal *Gender & Development* and other Oxfam publications for development practitioners and policy makers, students, and academics. Titles in the series present the theory and practice of gender-oriented development in a way that records experience, describes good practice, and shares information about resources. Books in the series will contribute to and review current thinking on the gender dimensions of particular development and relief issues.

Other titles in the series are available from www.developmentbookshop.com and include:

Gender-Based Violence
HIV and AIDS
Climate Change and Gender Justice
Gender and the Economic Crisis
Gender, Faith and Development
Gender, Monitoring, Evaluation and Learning
Gender, Business and Enterprise
Gender, Development and Care
Gender and Inequalities

For further information on the journal please visit www.genderanddevelopment.org

CHAPTER 1

Introduction: Working with men for gender equality

Caroline Sweetman

There are compelling reasons – both pragmatic and principled – to work with men as allies to achieve lasting transformation in gender relations benefiting both women and men. In late 2012, the author and commentator Naila Kabeer wrote on the website Open Democracy about the grief and rage sweeping India in response to the death of 'Nirbhaya', the young Indian woman gang-raped and murdered in Delhi in late 2012. She observed that the spectacle of widespread public protest showed that women's rights and gender equality have become causes 'seared into the public consciousness and put onto the public agenda,…breaking through class and gender barriers' (Kabeer 2012, no page number). Naila Kabeer particularly noted the presence of men standing shoulder to shoulder with women in protest about the death, arguing: '…such male support is critical. Without it, the question of sexual violence will remain ghettoized as a woman's issue and efforts to eradicate it remain ineffective' (ibid.).

Six years after the murder of Nirbhaya in Delhi, the extent of male violence against women – and its role in keeping patriarchal elites in power, to the detriment of most of humanity – is being revealed. We live in a turbulent political era, where #MeToo and other campaigns around the world exist parallel to rising misogynistic violence and abuse, in wealthy and poor countries alike. Yet as fast as new forms of online violence and abuse are emerging, feminist activists are mobilizing against them. Feminist men (sometimes called 'pro-feminist men') are joining women in these struggles. Many are realizing that the structures of patriarchy can oppress men and boys too, as well as LGBTQI individuals, and people whose race, caste, or other identity means they fail to make the grade as 'Alpha males'. While men will always be differently positioned in relation to these issues, they can consciously choose to become allies in the struggle, rejecting harmful stereotypes of what it means to be a man.

This book – first published as an issue of the journal, *Gender & Development* – focuses on the progress made over the past two decades in working with men to achieve gender equality. It is a follow-up to a pioneering 1997 issue, titled Men and Masculinity. Authors in that issue mapped out the terrain, considering the connections between gender and development as a field of activism and research, along with insights from researchers and activists working on

http://dx.doi.org/10.3362/9781780448664.001

'masculinities' – that is, men's gender identities, interests and needs. Currently the notion of working with men for gender equality has become much more widespread, and debates are under way about how this should be done in future. Is it, as some argue, an issue which needs to be integrated into 'gender and development', which has until now focused on working with women? Or are there reasons for seeing this work as separate and complementary? During the planning of this new issue, authors from policy and practice backgrounds, as well as academic researchers, were asked to share their experience of feminist work with men, with these questions in mind.

Chapters in this issue come from researchers exploring gender issues in particular contexts and focusing on both women and men's interests and needs; from development and humanitarian organisations working on gender justice and women's rights; and from feminist organisations specifically working with men. They highlight various kinds of work undertaken with men, in relation to violence, sexual and reproductive rights and health, fatherhood, and women's economic empowerment.

Authors here are convinced of the need to work in partnership with feminist men, focusing on challenging negative ideas and modes of behaviour associated with 'being a man'. They see transformative work to help men struggling with these issues as an essential adjunct to channelling resources to women and supporting feminist organising.

Gender and development: a little history

Gender and development, as a field of research, policymaking and practice has its roots in second-wave feminism which, from the 1970s, pushed the issues of discrimination and marginalisation of women onto the agenda of development organisations and governments. Feminists working within these organisations and in the women's movements outside – in both the global South and North – lobbied them to adjust their ways of thinking about women's contribution to economic growth, their key role in ensuring family survival, and – crucially – their understanding of 'development' itself.

However, the Women in Development (WID) projects which initially resulted came in for criticism (Moser 1989). Typically, WID projects focused on supporting women as producers, giving them small loans and training, but failed to consider the implications for women of greater workloads, in the context of an unequal and rigid gender division of labour at home. Working in comparatively small projects with women left the mainstream of development and humanitarian policy and spending largely untouched. WID could have limited impact on the side of larger 'mainstream' development which failed to integrate a gender analysis of women's and men's different interests and needs. Another criticism came from Southern feminists: WID was pilloried for imposing a liberal feminist agenda on the more complex realities of women living in poverty in the global South, whose realities were shaped by race, class, and other aspects of identity – not only by gender. 'Western' feminists were accused of stereotyping Southern women as passive victims of Southern men (Mohanty 1991).

These critiques resulted in a shift in rhetoric from *including* women in development, to *reforming* development by adopting a focus on gender inequality, which attained global visibility at the UN Fourth World Conference on Women in Beijing in 1995. Gender and development as a field of research, policy and practice starts from a gender analysis of power relations shaping the lives of poor women and men in different contexts in the global South and North.

Feminists with left-wing political perspectives who formed the field of research and activism that grew up around gender and development went far further, arguing that gender and development as a movement is founded on an understanding of gender, race and class-based inequalities intersecting with each other (Sen and Grown 1987). This complex inequality creates and perpetuates a global system reliant on the labour of women, the poor, and populations in the global South, who are denied a voice in political and economic decision-making, and lack the choices and freedoms enjoyed by the development policymakers who shape their realities. What is needed is a transfer of resources and support from development organisations to women in the global South, to enable them to put their own agendas and priorities into action and challenge the current top-down, male-biased model of global development.

Gender, women, and men

Gender and development approaches in development and humanitarian work have remained, for the most part, focused on working directly with women to channel resources to them, and support their activism. The justification is the fact that the big picture is still a world order which requires radical action to advance gender justice, challenge the conservative forces which threaten to roll back progress on women's rights, and empower women in the global South.

Feminist practice focuses on supporting women to organise around shared priorities arising out of an analysis of gender inequality. At best, development and humanitarian agencies have responded to the requests of women for support and resourcing to enable them to further their own agendas. Work has spanned a vast range of concerns: reproductive and sexual rights and health; political participation and leadership; economic leadership; the eradication of gender-based violence from the point of view of working with women survivors and with women peace-builders, and more.

There is other less ambitious work too. For many organisations, programmes undertaken in the name of 'gender mainstreaming' have not travelled too far from the politically conservative WID approaches which were critiqued by Southern feminists. Since the microfinance craze crescendoed a couple of years after Beijing, the rubric of 'women's economic empowerment' has become ubiquitous, and the powerful concept of the empowerment of women in the global South has been diluted by development organisations focusing on promoting women's entrepreneurship. Assessments of the impact of projects focusing on challenging power relations between women and men have shown that they can leave some women, in some contexts, with a series of new problems, including escalating male violence at home and in communities. If men see gender relations challenged, the impact on women may be negative, at least in the short-term (Kabeer 1998).

For some, this demonstrates a pressing need to focus more on the male side of gender analysis, understanding how men's lives are constrained by gender norms relating to masculinity. While these differ from culture to culture, the majority stress men's role as community leaders, household heads, and primary providers, in a globalised world in which traditional ideas of gender relations have now blended with Western-influenced globalised values.

Concepts of men and masculinities: patriarchy, resistance and social progress

This 'big picture' of female subordination to men is the backdrop to thinking on men and masculinities in development, which has been shaped by various social science traditions. However, thinkers on men and masculinities emphasise, just like feminist researchers, that individual people interpret and play out gender norms differently. A small minority of men are able to play out the role of the 'ideal man', who displays what the influential researcher R.W. Connell referred to as 'hegemonic masculinity' (1987). This refers to the kind of man who is a leader of society. Their wealth enables them to own high-status property – be this a smart car or designer clothes. They are heterosexual, able to make alliances with young and beautiful women. They are looked up to by other men, playing a highly visible public role – as a politician, an international footballer, a media star.

Patriarchy is a select group of elite men leading and dominating society economically, socially and politically. It is their way of being 'male' that defines the ideal of masculinity in a particular context. Hegemonic masculinity is about performance and status. It is partly attained by a show of superior strength and intelligence at the expense of women. Norms of masculinity stress male power to protect and decide on behalf of women and children. To be a successful man requires a woman to provide a contrast, behaving in ways which permit a demonstration of male power. This in turn requires women to play a 'feminine' role, characterised by being in need of protection and patronage, compliant and delicate.

Thinking critically about men and masculinities starts from consideration of the relationship between patriarchy (as a social system in which men have power over women), and individual men's experience of life in different contexts throughout the world. Gender norms constrain both sexes to behave in socially-expected ways, despite the wishes and capacities of individuals to behave otherwise; and reinforce inequality between women and men.

For the majority of men, there is a level of anxiety around living up to ideals of masculinity. Lack of education and employment opportunities lead men to struggle to provide for their families – or even to form a family at all. Aspects of some men's identity including race, class or sexuality lead them to 'fail' as men. If men are, quite simply and literally, unable to 'man up' and become the successful breadwinners, family heads and leaders of wider society which stereotypes of masculine power and success demand of them, they come under stress. Tensions around masculinities aggravate socially-condoned violence and abuse of women and girls. A key part of male gender identity concerns the ability to lead and dominate. Failure can often lead to increased violence against the people over whom a man does have power: the women and children within his household.

Many factors push men into crisis. The loss of work in heavy industry, as economic changes sweep away 'male' opportunities in the job market; armed conflict, pushing men into militias and training young boys to become desensitised to violence by coercing them into becoming the perpetrators of deviant acts of violence. Other changes come about as a result of planned development and social policy. The focus on the empowerment of women in the global South is a positive change which can have unplanned negative impact on women – at least in the short-term, as gender norms are thrown into crisis by economic realities shifting and challenging the roles of women and men in marriage and the family.

It is clear that there is a potential agenda here for development and humanitarian workers to address. Ultimately, work with men aims to support them to evolve ways of behaving that support women's rights and gender equality, and will actually benefit men themselves, freeing them up from limiting gender norms which create pain and conflict.

Desiree Lwambo's chapter provides an example of a gender analysis in a particular context which shows the tensions between gender norms, crises and changes in surrounding society which challenge those norms, and the responses of NGOs and other actors seeking to support the women, men and children living in a particular region. Her chapter focuses on local understandings of masculine identity and its impact on the lives of men, women and children in North Kivo District, in the eastern region of the Democratic Republic of Congo. Her analysis of this conflict zone highlights the failure of men to be able to live up to the ideals of masculinity in the region, and norms of gender inequality. These are important – though partial – explanatory factors for the endemic sexual and gender-based violence in the area. Desiree Lwambo argues that current approaches to supporting the female survivors of sexual and gender-based violence need to be complemented by other activities aiming at breaking the cycle of violence, by focusing on how men are socialised, and the messages about gender roles and power relations they are given. These norms need to be re-formed, around an ideal of non-violence, building a sense of male pride and dignity based on progressive, gender-equitable ideals.

Challenging gender norms and working for transformation

Chapters featured in this issue focus on the work of men who see challenging oppressive ideas of masculinities, and gender inequality, as an essential part of feminist action, complementing the work of women's movements and organisations. In addition, by focusing on working with men to reduce violence, promote responsible fatherhood, or address unmet reproductive or sexual health and rights, they aim to improve the wellbeing and happiness of men themselves. Development projects working with men on gender equality typically follow a similar pattern to traditional feminist organising with women. They start by creating an opportunity for men to build solidarity, discover common interests and needs, and evolve the conviction that they need to change.

Working on violent masculinities as part of women's empowerment projects

Common sense – and much evidence – suggests that seeing a wife, daughter or mother offered a loan and starting a business as part of an NGO's work on gender equality (while no such loan is offered to men) can have a very major impact on women's relationships with their husbands. A similar impact is felt beyond the world of planned development, in families where daughters can get work in call centres or factories while fathers find no market for their own labour.

A key focus for many authors in this issue is the 'economic empowerment' of women, and the need to protect women participants in microfinance and other progrmmes supporting them as producers. Development organisations working to support women's livelihoods may find grassroots women requesting them to take an additional step and work with men to persuade them to accept changes which challenge gender norms.

Henny Sleigh, Gary Barker, Augustin Kimonyo, Prudence Ndolimana and Matt Bannerman focus on a pilot project in Rwanda linked to CARE-Rwanda's Village Savings and Loan programme. This project started where many analyses of economic empowerment and its impact on marital relationships leave off – at the point where the risk of friction and male resentment are identified. Projects focusing on challenging power relations between women and men can leave some women, in some contexts, with a series of new problems, including escalating male violence at home and in communities, as men's sense of themselves as leaders and providers for families is further undermined; a reduction in men's own contribution to household income leaving women with a disproportionate responsibility for children and other dependents; less time, less sleep and less voice in marital relationships than ever. The pilot project discussed by Henny Sleigh *et al.* worked with men to get them to deliberately question their ideas about successful manhood and power dynamics between them and their wives.

Work to challenge male violence in marital relationships has been questioned by some feminists who believe that women should be supported to leave violent relationships, rather than stay in them. However, the wish of some women is to stay and to ensure their menfolk are 'taken along' with the agenda of women's empowerment, and accept changes to gender relations which they would otherwise resist. Options to leave abusive men are not easy in societies in which lone women with children face deepening poverty or violence from men beyond the family.

Rhoda Mitchell's chapter presents experience from an Oxfam Quebec-supported project, Construction of Violence-Free Masculinities (CJMT), run by the Peruvian women's centre, Centro Mujer Teresa de Jesus. This project aims to eradicate violence against women by working with violent men. Once more, this strategy was developed as a result of the feedback of the women whose interests and needs the centre serves. The centre runs activities aiming to empower women that are wider than the 'economic empowerment' focus which is currently so widespread, featuring support to enable them to develop personal and leadership skills also. Women involved in the project reported increased violence as a result of men responding with hostility to their wives' increased self-esteem, undermining their perception of themselves as sole family providers. Programme staff at the CJMT initially assumed that the appropriate approach to the problem involved supporting an affected woman to separate from her intimate partner, but economic realities meant many women could not consider this, and the activities aiming to support women economically were being boycotted, despite desperate need. In this context, responding to need meant working with men.

In their chapter, Tu-Anh Hoang, Trang Thu Quach and Tam Thanh Tran discuss an initiative in Vietnam encouraging men to develop a positive, non-violent version of masculinity. The Responsible Men Club is a pilot programme developed between 2010 and 2012 in a coastal area of Vietnam, by the Center for Creative Initiatives in Health and Population (CCIHP). It works with male perpetrators of violence against women, to change their attitudes towards women and girls by promoting new values about manhood and masculinities. The chapter focuses on the method used with men to encourage change, arguing that empowerment approaches used in gender and development to support women can help men to understand that gender equality actually empowers both sexes to behave democratically and with integrity in marital relationships.

Supporting men to be responsible husbands and fathers

Work with men can start from the vantage point of aiming to change behaviour in intimate sexual relationships, marriage and the family.

In their chapter, Wessel van den Berg, Lynn Hendricks, Abigail Hatcher, Dean Peacock, Patrick Godana, and Shari Dworkin focus on a programme, One Man Can, set up to work with black South African men to enhance their ideas of themselves as caring fathers and help them change their behaviour to their families, ending abuse and violence. South African men today are one generation removed from the apartheid system, which inflicted state-sanctioned violence on black South Africans of both sexes. Today's adult men grew up in households where their own fathers were absent, forced to migrate for low-paid work in heavy industry and agriculture. This policy affected men and women in very distinct and gendered ways, denying men their lives with their families, and rendering women and children economically dependent on male wages, weakening women's voice within marriages, reinforcing stereotypes of male household headship and women as junior partners in marriage. One Man Can was implemented by Sonke Gender Justice, a well-known South African NGO set up in 2006 in order to support men and boys to take action to promote gender equality and prevent both violence against women, and HIV and AIDS.

A chapter focusing on working with husbands as a way of improving sexual and reproductive health comes from Lisa MacDonald, Lori Jones, Phaeba Thomas, Le Thi Thu, Sian FitzGerald, and Debra Efroymson. They discuss the experience of Healthbridge International in working with men to promote their involvement in family planning in Vietnam and India. Interestingly, this experience focuses on persuading men to take up *male* methods of contraception. In the past there has been much feminist concern about reproductive health interventions using men's participation to lend weight to their efforts to promote female methods, in relationships where gender inequality meant women were not able to articulate independent choices about use of methods which affected their health and future options. In contrast, this work aimed to promote higher rates of male uptake of condoms (also to prevent sexually-transmitted infections, including HIV), and vasectomy, as an option alongside female-centred methods, and to work with men in a transformative way, to reduce stigmas and misconceptions around contraceptive use in general.

Working with adolescents

Two chapters here focus on working with young adolescents to change their attitudes to gender norms. Rebecka Lundgren, Miranda Beckman, Surendra Prasad Chaurasiya, Bhawna Subhedi, and Brad Kerner focus on Save the Children's Choices programme, supporting young adolescent girls and boys in Nepal to explore alternative views of masculinities and femininities, to take into adulthood. The long-term aim is to achieve improved sexual and reproductive health in the future. They observe, 'men who use caring words instead of violence, and who are equal partners in nurturing their children, are not formed overnight'.

Stephanie Baric's chapter focuses on working with adolescent boys to enlist their support for girls' education and leadership. She focuses on the work of the Power To Lead Alliance, a project implemented by CARE in Honduras, Yemen, India, Malawi, Tanzania and Egypt. Leadership activities offered to girls in vulnerable communities ended up attracting 30 per cent participation from boys, and work was piloted with these boys to challenge gender norms and attitudes, enlisting their support for girls' education and leadership.

Concerns about working with men

Pro-feminist men argue, with women, that gender justice and equal rights for women are a key part of transforming a global system benefiting a tiny elite into one where social, economic and political power are shared more equitably across gender, race and class divides. Yet there remains some scepticism on the part of feminists working in development about this work. This section briefly raises some of the concerns.

Legitimacy and location

What legitimacy do men have in struggles for gender equality? Change movements – for example, anti-racist movements – are all concerned with the question of identity politics. The influential writer on men and masculinities, R.W. Connell, coined the extremely helpful notion of the 'patriarchal dividend', to open up space for men to participate in challenging gender inequality, while not losing sight of their different location in this struggle. The patriarchal dividend refers to the advantage that all men have in a society that, openly or otherwise, favours males, maleness, or masculinity (see www.australianhumanitiesreview.org/archive/Issue-Dec-1996/connell.html, last checked 20 February 2013). Individual men can either choose to press this advantage, or opt, whenever possible, not to. Women have no such advantage, which means a very different position in relation to feminist struggle.

From a pragmatic perspective, men's participation adds to the range of strategies available to feminist movements. This can be seen as 'using the master's tools', which for some is very positive and a pragmatic way of advancing a cause. For example, men command attention in male-dominated institutions, in ways women do not. If a male gender advisor from an NGO can command the attention of senior male government officials in a way that could not occur with a woman, due to prejudice, then the work of changing short-term agendas and getting things done will go ahead more quickly. But this presents clear dilemmas. In the long-term, male representation of female voices and interests – if this means space is taken up by a man rather than a woman – can work against challenging and transforming gender norms.

An interesting reflection on the role of male political leaders in promoting gender equitable laws and policies in parliament is offered by Sonia Palmieri in her chapter in this issue. She uses qualitative data from the Inter-Parliamentary Union to present some of the strategies that have persuaded male parliamentarians to take up the cause of gender equality, from countries across the world.

In their chapter on Sonke Gender Justice mentioned above, Wessel van den Berg *et al.* usefully discuss the ethics underlying Sonke's work, as a feminist organisation working with men. Sonke works in progressive coalitions with women's organisations, emphasising the gains to the vast majority of women and men of recognising the costs of gender, race and class based oppression. The losers would be a tiny elite (among whom gender inequality still exists, and still costs women their independence, and often their health, happiness and right to live free from domination and violence).

What gets lost in translation when you turn from 'women' to 'gender' to 'men'?

In conversations in development circles over the past decade and a half, feminists from different contexts have voiced their scepticism about widening the gender and development agenda to include working with men. A widespread concern is that this can derail good transformative work on gender equality, because of the complexity of the message. That is, the message that we work with men for *gender equality* becomes heard as, 'gender work of all kinds must always involve working with men'. The logic runs that male bias in the culture of organisations can hook into narratives of gender being about relations between men and women, and before you know it, strange things have happened to programmes and projects aiming to support women's rights and gender justice.

Evidence of this is mainly anecdotal, but persuasive. In a research study of gender mainstreaming in South Africa, a director of a legal support organisation had found her donors interpreted a shift from working on women's rights to gender equality in the following ways:

> ... you have men at a meeting as well as women. And it also means you have to have men's sector views on all sorts of things. So if you are going to talk about things like violence against women, women is no longer the correct term because it means you aren't recognising that men also get raped and the men also experience domestic violence.
>
> (South African practitioner, quoted by Mannell 2012, 428).

In their chapter, Sandy Ruxton and Nikki van de Gaag discuss the findings of a study commissioned by a Swedish organisation, Men for Gender Equality, to map the many different organisations and individuals working on men's gender equality issues in the 27 states of the European Union (EU). In countries in which relative progress has been made on reforming laws – in particular, family laws – to promote the rights of women, and where universal access to education has resulted in relatively high female attainment, there is a popular belief on the part of some that the pendulum has swung too far in women's favour.

Sandy Ruxton and Nikki van der Gaag discuss the rise of a conservative approach to the family and gender relations, which is allied to the emergence of 'men's rights' and 'father's rights' groups. They argue that 'Although they embrace a variety of points of view, these groups tend to come together around core arguments that men are as powerless relative to women as women are to men, that women or feminism are to blame for men's plight, and that men are now the real victims within current gender relations'. This point about perceptions of the negative effect of gender equality agendas takes us back to the idea of gender power relations as being about zero-sum gains. It is clearly a misconception which is both dangerous to gender equality work in Europe, and to gender and development in the global South, since such misconceptions can be one more factor in staff resistance to gender equality agendas.

Resourcing work with men

A second issue that requires resolution is the question of how work with men should be resourced. This may seem unnecessarily pedantic to those who do not work as policymakers and practitioners in development organizations, but it is a critical issue to all who face the battle to obtain sufficient resources to work on women's rights and gender justice. The small amount of funding available to channel to women's organisations and for spending on integrating gender perspectives into anti-poverty and humanitarian work cannot be diverted from this aim; instead, additional funding needs to be found for working with men. While this concern takes little space here to raise, the climate of reduced funding for feminist work worldwide makes it a very sensitive issue for feminists working in development and humanitarian organisations.

Working on men and masculinities in post-industrialised countries

Gender-, race- and class-based inequalities are clearly present in all societies, creating what has been termed a 'South in the North'. In their chapter, Sandy Ruxton and Nikki van de Gaag discuss the ways in which gender work with men in the EU plays out differently in different regional, national and local contexts. Their chapter features the voices of participants in the research about the obstacles to involving men further in gender equality work, and their perceptions of the benefits of involving men. Finally, the chapter outlines interviewees' views of possible ways to take this work forward. Gender issues are commonly seen as a 'women's issue'. The role of the media and social leaders, including political leaders, in providing positive images of alternative ways of being a man, are among important issues raised.

Conclusion: integrating these concerns into policy and practice

Gender inequality exists as a social, economic, and political reality in most societies, to women's detriment. However, the space available for individual women and men to subvert or challenge gender norms of female submission to male leadership is vastly different for individuals, not only due to their own characteristics but also depending on where they are in the world, and the changes taking place which challenge or reinforce gender norms. Being female or male in a given time and place is mitigated and complicated by a range of other factors. For some men in some contexts, these factors lead them to 'fail' as men: they are, quite simply and literally, unable to 'be a man' and become the successful breadwinners, family heads and leaders of wider society which stereotypes of masculine power and success demand of them.

Authors in this issue argue that there is considerable need for gender and development practitioners and policymakers to work with men to challenge the ideas which have led to the oppression of women, and raise their awareness of how masculinities actually negatively affect all men who could not aspire to being a member of the elite few who shape society and the global economy. Critically, this work should not take the scant resources available to work with women and women's organisations; rather, alliances and coalitions need to be built with feminist men's organisations, and additional funds allocated from central funds of large development organisations. It makes economic sense to do so, since male resistance to progressive change in gender roles and relations can present a major barrier to the goals of development and humanitarian work, as well as presenting very real risks to women, children and wider society.

Gender equality work with men involves changing hearts and minds – not only of men, but of women: not only among traditionalists, but among progressives. It involves considering where the resources will come from for this wider agenda of work; how alliances might be built between feminist women and feminist men, and how the line might be held against dilution or co-option of the agenda of gender equality.

Maybe above all, working with men on gender inequality involves challenging the categories of 'us' and 'them', and understanding the complicated ways in which individual human beings invoke different aspects of their identities and experiences to advance their own interests and either disempower, or stand in solidarity with, others. Insights can be drawn from gender and development's origins as a field of research and activism which considers not only gender, but race and class, as aspects of identity which shape our experience; opening up space to work with men on gender inequality, just as women from the global South and North are working together in solidarity to challenge unsustainable development models.

Note

1.   See Caroline Moser 1989 for her classic typology of WID policy approaches.

References

Connell, R.W., (1987), *Masculinities*, Polity Press: Oxford

Kabeer Naila, (1998), *Money Can't Buy Me Love? Re-evaluating Gender, Credit and Empowerment in rural Bangladesh*, IDS Discussion Paper 363, University of Sussex: Brighton

Kabeer, Naila, (2012), 'Grief and rage in India: making violence against women history?', http://opendemocracy.net/5050/naila-kabeer/grief-and-rage-in-india-making-violence-against -women-history last checked 20 February 2013

Mannell, Jenevieve, 'It's Just Been Such A Horrible Experience' Perceptions of Gender Mainstreaming by Practitioners In South African Organisations', in *Gender and Development* Vol 20 No 3, pp. 423–434

Mohanty, Chandra, (1991), 'Under Western Eyes: Feminist Scholarship and Colonial Discourses', in *Feminist Review 30* pp.61–88

Molyneux, Maxine, (1985), 'Mobilisation Without Emancipation? Women's Interests, The State and Revolution in Nicaragua', in *Feminist Studies,* Vol 11, No 2, pp. 227–254

Moser, Caroline, (1989), 'Gender Planning In The Third World: Meeting Practical and Strategic Gender Needs', *World Development*, Vol 17 No 11, pp. 1799–1825

Sen, Gita, and Grown, Caren, (1987), *Development Crises and Alternative Visions: Third World Women's Perspectives*, Monthly Review Press: New York

About the author

Caroline Sweetman is Editor of the international journal *Gender & Development* and works for Oxfam GB.

CHAPTER 2

'I can do women's work': reflections on engaging men as allies in women's economic empowerment in Rwanda

Henny Slegh, Gary Barker, Augustin Kimonyo, Prudence Ndolimana and Matt Bannerman

Abstract

The benefits of women's economic empowerment are well-known and documented in the development literature. Few studies and interventions, however, have explored how men react or can be engaged to enhance such interventions. This chapter presents an evaluation of a pilot project in Rwanda in collaboration with CARE Rwanda's Village Savings and Loan (VSL) programme that deliberately engaged men as partners of women beneficiaries of the micro-credit programme. Preliminary results affirm the importance of engaging men in a deliberate questioning of gender norms and power dynamics, so that they can embrace better co-operation and sharing of activities at the household level; and that a 'do-no-harm' approach to women's economic empowerment should involve activities to engage men at the community level in questioning and ending gender-based violence – building on those interventions that have shown evidence of changes in men's attitudes and behaviours related to gender-based violence.

Key words: women's economic empowerment; household gender dynamics; engaging men; Rwanda

Introduction

Most livelihood and 'economic empowerment' initiatives in the global South currently focus on women, and with good reason. At the global level, achieving income parity for women is one of the urgent, unachieved goals of gender equality. The recent *World Development Report* affirmed that women now represent 40 per cent of the world's paid workforce, and 43 per cent of the agricultural labour force (World Bank 2012, 3). While there have been significant gains in women's employment and earnings in the past 20 years, women's income continues to lag behind those of men everywhere in the world, even when women perform the same tasks or functions. In addition,

http://dx.doi.org/10.3362/9781780448664.002

women typically find that only a limited number of alternative means of earning income are open to them.

Women's 'economic empowerment' also brings benefits to their families and wider society. Numerous studies have shown that increased female control over income and spending decisions in the household translates into better outcomes for children and households (Bruce *et al.* 1995). Increased control over material resources can lead on to women having an enhanced ability to act and choose (Kabeer 2009). The idea is that greater female contribution to household income can result in women having stronger bargaining power within marital relationships and the family. In this way, 'economic empowerment' has been linked to women having a stronger voice in negotiating sexual relations and hence reducing their risk of HIV infection; to reductions in violence from male partners; and to increased social status and mobility outside the home. Awareness of these links has led development policymakers and practitioners to target women widely as beneficiaries of interventions including microfinance initiatives.

However, research in various contexts focusing on low-income couples in the global South has shown that links between women's greater role in productive activities outside the household, their 'economic empowerment', and the wider project of women's rights and gender equality, cannot be assumed. Some of this research has highlighted the fact that men react in very diverse ways when their wives are beneficiaries of microcredit programmes (e.g. Ahmed 2008). Men do not uniformly 'fall into line' and accept gender equality when their female partners gain more income.

Some interventions have found that women's risk of violence decreases as a result of participation in such groups as they are able to renegotiate power dynamics in their interactions with men in the household, or that stress on the household reduces as women's incomes rise (Hadi 2005; Schuler *et al.* 1996). For example, individual interviews and focus group discussions with men and women in 20 savings and credit groups in rural Bangladesh suggested reduced levels of domestic violence (Kelkar *et al.* 2004). Research in South Africa showed that women who participated in microcredit programmes together with group social support activities experienced 52 per cent less violence than women in a control group who did not participate in such activities (Kim *et al.* 2008).

However, other researchers have found that increases or decreases in violence against women as a result of programmes aiming to empower them economically are very context-specific (Koenig *et al.* 2003). Some research has suggested that violence may escalate soon after women receive credit but reduce as women participate in skills training and employment, and as some male partners see that they also benefit from improved household income (Ahmed 2005). Women's participation in economic empowerment activities often changes household dynamics and can result in increased gender-based violence or stress within couples, but these patterns are not uniform.

In spite of this diversity and complexity in men's reactions to their female partners' income gains, few efforts have been made to engage men as allies or partners in women's economic empowerment, to explore and promote co-operation between couples – and even fewer of these efforts have been evaluated. In settings where men have not fully accepted the principles of women's rights and gender equality, it may be an illusion to think that men will embrace the new role that women take on as providers, and that this will translate into wider positive change in gender relations, unless development policymakers and practitioners also engage men in deliberate and targeted efforts to change their attitudes, and unless we understand women's partici-pation in these initiatives in the context of their couple relationships (that is, their intimate relationships with men, including marital relationships).

Care work, and the way it is divided between women and men, is a key issue which shows it is high time to engage with men as allies around wom-en's economic empowerment initiatives. Women themselves affirm that as they do more paid work outside their home, their time burden of care work in the home often remains unchanged. Data from both low-income and upper-income settings find that as the gap between the time women and men spend on paid work has reduced, the gap between the time spent on unpaid care work has not reduced nearly as much (and in some places hardly at all) (World Bank 2012).

How can men can be engaged as partners or allies in women's economic empowerment, and what kinds of interventions will work to engage them as allies for their female partners, so that economic empowerment becomes something wider and more socially transformative for women, both as individ-uals and collectively? This chapter presents findings from a pilot intervention with couples and men in Rwanda, including baseline research and an evalua-tion, aiming to explore the potential to develop a method of working which engages with the realities of male attitudes to women's economic empower-ment, and couples' strategies for negotiating changes to their relationships, in the context of CARE Rwanda's Village Savings and Loan (VSL) programme.

Our message, in short, is that women participants in micro-credit pro-grammes need to be supported by improved and better programming which engages with men in deliberate and structured ways, including promoting greater male involvement in care work. Our second key message is that in some settings, solely focusing on women may lead to negative effects for women, both in the short and long term.

CARE's work in Rwanda on women's economic empowerment

CARE Rwanda works to promote vulnerable women's access to the financial services and products they need, to build their skills in enterprise develop-ment, and to link women entrepreneurs to functioning markets and val-ue-chains, enabling their enterprises to grow and prosper. It also works to promote women's awareness of their rights, and ensure they know of ways to gain access to information that enables them to exercise those rights.

CARE's VSL approach was pioneered in Niger in 1991, and is the cor-nerstone of CARE International's economic empowerment programming across the global South. CARE Rwanda began VSL in Rwanda in 1999, and is currently implementing VSL activities in 23 districts, reaching more than 175,000 clients in 6,000 VSL associations. By the end of 2013, CARE Rwanda plans to reach 350,000 clients. CARE began to link VSL groups to formal financial institutions in 2003, and to private microfinance institutions in 2010. CARE has found that VSL groups meet the need for savings and credit at the very bottom rung of the economic ladder by creating a platform from which the poor can navigate the market for the more sophisticated financial services that they typically begin to demand as their resources, skills and confidence grow (Maes 2007).

VSL groups build their success entirely on member savings and interest from loans paid by members from the profits on their small business ventures; they receive no direct capital investment from CARE. Members receive a year of intensive training from CARE in group dynamics and governance, and in money-management. This training enables the groups to become self-supporting, to flourish, and even to establish and train other groups. The training package provided to VSL group members during the intensive period of mobilisation and group formation includes modules on financial literacy and on the selection, planning and management of income-generating activities. These training sessions aim to build VSL group members' basic skills in the identification and selection of economic activities and their management.

CARE's VSL programming in Rwanda has highlighted the importance of the kinds of social and cultural norms highlighted by the IMAGES-Rwanda research discussed later, in determining the extent to which women members of VSL groups can fully realise their potential as savers, investors and entrepreneurs. For example, views about women's and men's roles in the family are linked to culturally sanctioned differences between businesses thought suitable for women and those suitable for men: women tend to be involved in petty trading, which can be combined with caring for the family and home – at least in principle – while larger-scale businesses are considered the province of men as primary earners. Gendered divisions of domestic labour limit women's ability to invest time in their growing businesses.

In 2010, CARE Rwanda assessed men's attitudes about their female partners' participation in VSL groups, and found a mixture of responses from men. There were some indications of positive links between women's increasing role in income generation and wider change to marital relationships, with associated impact on patterns of decision-making. Some men were supportive of their wives' involvement, and appreciated the economic benefits to their wives and households, and some apparently reduced their use of gender-based violence, because of reduced economic stress. However, other men continued to dominate household decision-making. Some responded to their wives earning more by keeping more of their own income for personal use, arguing that they were the boss of the family and that women have to obey them. A number of men apparently increased the use of gender-based violence, as household dynamics and power balances shifted. Finally, some men said they believed their wives had received the extra income through selling sex, in turn increasing conflict and violence (Barker and Schulte 2010).

Our research and intervention

These findings led CARE Rwanda to partner with Promundo[1] and Rwandan Men's Resource Centre (RWAMREC), to explore ways to engage men in the hope of enhancing the confirmed benefits of VSL to empower women, reduce poverty and achieve gender equality at the household level. The pilot intervention aimed first to research what men thought about women's participation in women's economic empowerment initiatives;[2] second, to develop and test an intervention to engage men in a couple-focused process designed to respond to doubts and resistance; and thirdly, to evaluate the results.

First, we conducted baseline research with women and men in two rural settings in Rwanda where CARE implements VSL. In one of the sites – referred to as the intervention site – we then ran 16 weeks of group-education activities in one site where VSL is running – referred to as 'the training'. The intervention site was in Huye District in the Southern Province of Rwanda. Here, we identified 30 couples to participate from vulnerable households (the usual criteria for membership of VSL). We worked with men on their own, and with couples, to engage them in discussions about household dynamics, health and gender-based violence in one site. We developed a manual and training process for engaging men (in some men-only sessions and in couple sessions) in discussions about household dynamics, health and gender-based violence. In this site we also used a pre- and post-test questionnaire with 30 couples and men, to assess changes in their attitudes after the training.

Baseline research included a survey with 130 questions for males (aged 20–76) and females (aged 21–61); five focus group discussions (two men's groups, two women's groups, and one group with couples); and ten in-depth individual interviews with five women and five men. The majority of the survey questions were adopted from the 2010 IMAGES study in Rwanda. This was undertaken in 2010 as part of the International Men and Gender Equality Survey (IMAGES).[3]

The IMAGES-Rwanda study (a nationally representative household sample) had found traditional attitudes and perceptions prevailed among both men and women about gendered household and social roles (Slegh and Kimonyo 2010). At the same time, the study found that several major factors associated with the genocide and the post-genocide period have led to changes in men's and women's practices in Rwandan society. The IMAGES study affirmed that gender relations are undergoing a tremendous transformation in Rwanda, particularly in the aftermath of the genocide and the resulting migration, displacement and loss of livelihoods. With the loss of husbands and families, women have taken on new responsibilities. They have also gained more rights, thanks to new laws and policies. Even in the face of these changes, however, the social norms transmitted through informal institutions (including family, school, and church) remain out of tune with the modernisation and new gender equality policies in place in Rwanda. It seems that much progress has been made in Rwanda on the empowerment of women from a legal and policy perspective, yet comparatively less appears to have changed in popular attitudes to gender roles and power relations.

IMAGES-Rwanda found that 73 per cent of Rwandan men, and 82 per cent of women, said that a woman's most important role is to take care of her family. More than 95 per cent of women were taught to carry out household duties as children, in contrast to just 49 per cent of men. More than 50 per cent of women and 57 per cent of men said that men *should* earn more than women. Seventy-five per cent of Rwandan women interviewed said that their husbands dominate household decision-making, while 57 per cent of men interviewed said they dominate household decision-making. About 17 per cent of men regularly abuse alcohol. Nearly 40 per cent of Rwandan men reported having carried out physical violence at least once in their lives against a female partner.

IMAGES-Rwanda found that men who witnessed or were directly affected by the genocide (which was nearly 80 per cent of all men) had higher rates of reported use of violence against their female partners, as did men who reported witnessing violence by their fathers against their mothers in their household of origin. The IMAGES research found that the vast majority of Rwandan men (more than 96 per cent) believe that the current Rwandan law on gender-based violence is too harsh toward men. This view suggests that men misunderstand the law, and perhaps also indicates that they know at some level that the law has reduced the impunity with which gender-based violence can be committed. In other words, Rwandan men may be defensive in knowing that some traditional male privileges have been taken away. These findings reflect the importance of understanding the roots of men's attitudes and practices, and in particular their resistance to gender equality, even as Rwandan law and public institutions have made major strides toward achieving gender equality.

Our own research drew on the IMAGES original questions as pre- and post-test questions with an emphasis on the impact of women's VSL participation on household management and partner relations. A baseline and follow-up study was also carried out with a comparison group in the Kirehe District, in the Eastern Province of Rwanda, to provide a control. In this site VSL was operating with women in the conventional way (with savings groups for women, and no involvement of husbands/partners). Here, a sample of 30 married couples – 30 men (aged 22–75) and 30 women (aged 21–53) – was studied using the same questionnaire for men and women; three focus group discussions: one with men, one with women and one with couples; and six individual in-depth interviews: three with women and three with men.

All the quotations in the findings sections which follow come from research and programme participants.

The baseline study findings

Baseline study results found in both the experimental and comparison group that norms about traditional gender roles dominate the way VSL benefits are used. The women are 'instructed' by their husbands about the use of loans, and the husbands help to pay back the loans, with the majority of household financial decisions made by men.

The impact on gender-based violence

According to most men and women in the baseline, the VSL programmes as currently carried out (with no specific involvement of male partners/husbands) have contributed to a reduction of gender-based violence. However, these findings contradicted responses about family conflicts as well as the accounts of key informants among the CARE staff, who reported persistent use of multiple forms of gender-based violence by men, in the form of physical violence as well as economic and sexual violence.

These findings are interesting when compared against the previous IMAGES research into gender-based violence in Rwanda. Bearing in mind our concern about the relationship of gender-based violence to women's economic role as producers, IMAGES found that women who are more economically advantaged were more likely to experience gender-based violence. This suggested a complex relationship between women's income and experiences of intimate partner violence. Research in some settings has found that as women become more economically empowered, some men react negatively, and their use of violence increases (Rahman 1999). It is possible also that women who have relatively higher levels of material resources feel more able to disclose violence. IMAGES-Rwanda results did not find a correlation between men's income and their self-reported use of violence, which implies that men who commit violence against partners may be found at all income levels.

The main sources of conflict reported in our baseline research between partners were money, men's alcohol abuse and sexual relations. Women reported more couple conflicts than men did. Interestingly, men's general health was reported to be worse than women's, as reported by both men and women. Furthermore, men seem to cope differently with stress and problems – they reported drinking and talking with friends in bars – while women more frequently reported praying, talking to friends and seeking health services. Men said they would like more information about the VSL programme and income generation, reasoning that this would enable them to collaborate with their wives to increase family income. Women said they wanted their husbands to be better informed about their VSL work in order to make them more collaborative. The women also wanted their husbands to be educated about gender laws, family planning and gender-based violence.

As stated earlier, based on the findings of the baseline research, the authors designed a training manual that includes structured group discussion and training activities on business skills (including sessions focusing on negotiation and decision-making between women and men); health and well-being (including practical information about general health, reproductive health, sexuality, alcohol consumption and coping strategies; and gender-based violence, including information on the relevant laws, in addition to wider laws and policies promoting gender equality in Rwanda).[4] Ten sessions using the manual were carried out with men only in weekly group sessions lasting approximately two and a half hours, and the remaining were carried out with couples.

The impact of the training

The pilot study of the impact of the training was evaluated as outlined above. The findings provide evidence of the positive impact of the group educational training undertaken with couples and men, on both household-level poverty and on the incidence of partner relations and family dynamics.

Economic improvement of poor households

Interviews and focus group discussions with male and female participants in the experimental group indicated that the economic situation of participating families improved even more when the group sessions with men were combined with standard VSL activities (for women). The economic improvement is reflected in an income increase among the families with the lowest income levels – which was nearly double those of the gains achieved in the control group families.

In terms of qualitative results, several husbands in the experimental group said that they now acknowledge that their wives' activities in the VSL are valuable for bringing in additional income to the family, and have led to sharing of the role of breadwinner, which in turn changed their views of the worth of women's economic role and contribution to the family. Several men said they had started to collaborate with their wives to repay loans, seeing the loan as being their responsibility as well. One man commented: 'We divided the work: I sell bananas and she sells drinks. We could buy electricity in house and now we are charging phones. With that money, we bought goats and I bought a *panje* [skirt] for my wife'.

Care work

Patterns of sharing care work also changed. Men from the experimental group said they also collaborated more after the cycle of workshops in household activities. One man said, 'I learned that I can do women's work, and my wife can do man's work'. Participants in group sessions thought men were more positively engaged in sharing household activities and taking care of children, and had more positive relations with their wives. A woman recalled: 'Yesterday, I was in VSL and my husband washed the clothes and prepared the food'.

A man who now does care work commented that he thought these individual changes were affecting general attitudes to the gender division of labour:

> *Our culture has changed. The assignment I got was to clean outside the house with a broom. But when the neighbours came, I was hiding the broom. They asked me what are you doing? I told them that I am not poisoned. And I kept on doing it.*

Partner relations, decision-making, and family dynamics

Couples in the experimental group said that the basic knowledge on planning and budgeting provided in the workshops encouraged and enabled them to increase their incomes by thinking and planning as a couple within the 16-week period of the training. A woman described this change: 'Before, my husband took decisions and I could not say anything. Now we make decisions together. When husband sells a cow, we discuss how to spend that money. I am very happy, everything has changed'. Another woman stated: ' My husband always took VSL money and drank [it] all in the bar. Now he discusses what to do with the money. Now I take VSL loans and my husband helps to pay back the loans'. In comparison, in the control group, positive changes were seen in women's income generation, but the changes were not as extensive, were not owned as a couple or linked to men's input or activities, and did not seem to have an impact on as many areas or aspects of the women's lives as in the experimental group.

In addition to these changes, some men became more supportive of family planning and many men became more involved in child-care activities – changes that were not seen in the control group. One man commented, 'Family planning enables us to improve economically, and my wife made a good decision'.

Reported changes in family dynamics included a reduction in conflict between partners, which were reported by the women and men involved but were sometimes observed by neighbours also. A woman commented: 'My in-laws ask[ed], "what is happening in your house? Normally you always came to complain about violence and your husband, and now you don't come any more"'. The reduction in violence was reported to have a positive impact on children and family life. One father of four small children stated: 'My youngest son asked me last week: papa and mama are not fighting anymore: what happened?'

Both women and men showed greater knowledge about different forms of violence, and the laws related to gender equality. A father stated, 'I told my daughters that they have rights and that they should protect themselves when a boy wants to make sex'.

The training appeared to have raised men's awareness about acts that had not previously been considered as violent. A woman highlighted this in her comment, 'He had sex with me as if he were a savage ... now he is careful, saying nice words. We talk about family planning'.

Both men and women reported that men coped better with stress after the workshops, which in turn they related to men's reduced abuse of alcohol and reduced use of violence against women. One of the sessions for men included a presentation and discussion with a doctor about basic health issues – something that the men in particular reported they had never had before.

The new insights into gender equality that the workshops aimed to give men have, according to women and men participants, resulted in greater male acceptance and implementation of the laws in Rwanda that promote gender equality.

How did these changes happen? Pathways to change

Overall, these changes were considered by participants in the group sessions to be likely to lead households out of poverty and towards an improved family life. Men and women seem to be ready to discover alternative ways in managing their households and partner relations. They seem genuinely motivated to create greater peace at home and women realise that their male partners should collaborate more as the way to escape the daily hardship of extreme poverty. The control group did also report improved household dynamics, but the changes were not nearly as far-reaching as those in the experimental group.

Our evaluation of our pilot project does suggest the potential of scaling up the engagement of men as partners in women's economic empowerment in ways that bring benefits to children, women and men themselves. It also suggests that it is possible to maintain a focus on women's empowerment while also taking into account men's expressed needs (e.g. their health needs) in ways that do not have to be oppositional. In other words, women's and men's lives can improve at the same time.

The following quotes from men offer some overall insights on the pathways to change. First, the trainers offered a role model to the men of an alternative way to be,which in turn carried economic benefits:

> The trainers made change possible; they facilitated the speed [of the change]. They told us how they do things at home; they clean and cook and wash children. Then I thought, they are rich, well doing well, why could I not do what they do? So I tried.

It is clear that change requires courage from individual men, but over time, and as more and more men join in, a tipping point is reached beyond which change becomes easier for individuals by seeing the same practices happening in other households:

> It was like a war. When I started with women's activities the neighbours were laughing and joking. I kept on doing it, and now the neighbours don't joke anymore. They start to implement the changes in their own houses because they see we are doing well now.

Change was facilitated by training sessions which encouraged the active participation not only of men as individuals, but of couples, thus encouraging change at the couple or household level and not just men or women as individuals:

> *Change is also facilitated by the active participation in homework and exercises. In one of the sessions my wife had to lead me with my eyes closed. I had to trust her and she did it well. I realised that my wife can be a leader and now she is the manager of a banana beer shop and we are doing well.*

At the same time, the results confirm the continuing challenge of changing deeply held gender norms. The quote that is used in the title of this chapter affirms that even when men take on care or domestic work, they often view this as a 'favour' to women and continue to classify domestic work or care work as women's work. Even couples that reported changes sometimes affirmed the limits of that change, as the following quotation illustrates:

> *One of my neighbours said that my wife had poisoned me* [to make me do her work]. *So, the problem is not the activity as such but rather what people think of you when they see you doing the activity.*

There was also a question remaining about whether or not changes in the gender division of labour were connected in any substantive way to changes in ideas about leadership of the family and household headship. One man stated: 'To be honest I realise that the families of those men who are involved in VSL together with their wives are well off; they are bosses'.

A woman concurred, laughing, in one of the focus groups:

> *When I share the money and manage well the income, he is happy. But the husband is the boss. If you show him that you as a wife are the boss and gain money, he will mistreat you and take the money.*

Fundamentally, change to gender relations is a long-term project. Participation in the VSL, even with the additional activities aiming at making men allies in this change, did not substantially always change people's ideas about gender relations, which are rooted deeply in culture and continue to support the patriarchal notion that men are in charge:

> *You have to respect a husband. He could sell the goat and eat all the money alone. For the security of the family, you have to accept. A woman has to be flexible and dynamic. This is also in the bible, as Eve came from the bone of Adam.*

Conclusions

We have argued that there is an urgent need to understand men as gendered beings – that is, as shaped by social norms and institutions that influence their perceptions of what it means to be men and their related behaviour.

This diversity of men (and of couples) and men's responses to their partners' involvement in microfinance programmes must be our starting point in our attempts to ensure that these programmes are as empowering as possible to women as individuals, and as a collective marginalised group.

While results are too preliminary to confirm a reduction in intimate partner violence, the group education activities we designed and evaluated in our pilot programme were based on the same principles of participatory group education that have been used in other settings with women and men to change norms associated with violence. Some of these include Stepping Stones, Program H, Men As Partners (MAP), and others, that have been found in impact evaluation studies to change the attitudes of men related to gender-based violence (Peacock and Barker 2012). Evidence of reduced use of violence by men against women in such interventions is still lacking in such research, but the consistent attitude changes in the application of such interventions across settings are nonetheless promising. The conclusion then is that adding such evidence-based gender-based violence prevention activities – both in the form of group education and community-based campaign activism – can be relatively easily combined with women's economic empowerment activities when adequate resources and training for staff are available.

While we do not have enough evidence to affirm existing anecdotal reports, the other limited research that we do have suggests that, at the very least, programmes aiming to empower women economically should be attentive to the issue that men who perceive themselves to be economically vulnerable or marginalised are already, in some settings, more likely to commit gender-based violence. If economically marginalised men view their traditional roles as 'heads' of households being eroded by women's income-generating activities, there is a need to engage them in a deliberate questioning of such roles so that they can embrace better co-operation and sharing of activities at the household level. In sum, a do-no-harm approach to women's economic empowerment would suggest that activities to engage men at the community level in questioning and ending gender-based violence should be part of *all* women-focused activities – building on those interventions that have shown evidence of changes in men's attitudes and behaviours related to gender-based violence.

In addition to gender-based violence prevention, our experience also suggests that engaging men in activities that promote their roles as caregivers and in care work are also a necessary addition to efforts to engage men, and that both women and men (and children) perceive benefits when men take on more and different kinds of care work. This experience also suggests that men, understandably, were often more attracted to group discussions when issues that they perceived as interesting to them were included – such as their relationships with their children, better relationships with their partners (including sexual relationships), their own health needs, and their needs in terms of income and employment.

Constant dialogue with women, engaging men as partners (and including men's own needs as appropriate) and listening to the voices of children all need to be part of such interventions. Furthermore, we need to move beyond a zero-sum approach and attitude that views women's increases as men's losses. Gender equality does mean that some men will have to give up a lot of privilege, and all men some kinds of privileges. But as this experience shows, there are men who fully appreciate the gains that come from gender equality, and from income gains achieved by their wives. As economic transitions occur, these men take on more caregiving, and they embrace, albeit slowly, the full potential of their female partners to be co-producers, co-workers, co-leaders, and full partners in family, political and economic life, and they see that their lives and their family's lives improve as a result.

Finally, other complementary possibilities exist for making men's involvement a common feature of women-focused economic empowerment, which should be explored. These include community campaigns targeting men, and the training of government and non-government organisation staff who currently implement micro-finance, conditional cash transfer programmes and other programmes focused on women, on ways to engage men as partners (and ways to promote a couple-based approach). Change is needed in policy formulation in the health and employment sectors also, to promote men's role as caregivers. Fauzia Ahmed (2008) argues that women's economic empowerment initiatives can 'use men to change other men', by identifying those men who are supportive of women's empowerment, and to empower those men as change agents to reach other men in the community and to change community norms. All these approaches, together with advocacy at the policy level, should be part of the mix to advance couple-based approaches to achieving gender equality and economic empowerment.

Acknowledgements

The authors wish to thank Alexa Hassink, Peter Pawlak and Beth Kenyon of Promundo for their contributions to the project. Thanks also to CARE Norway for financial and technical support on the research project.

Notes

1. Promundo is an international organisation with offices in Rio de Janeiro, Brazil; Washington, DC, USA; and Kigali, Rwanda, that carries out research, programme development and advocacy in men, masculinities and gender equality. For more information, see www.promundo.org.br/eng.
2. These include savings and credit, in addition to insurance, financial education and literacy.
3. IMAGES is a multi-country study of men's attitudes and practices related to gender equality – along with women's opinions and reports

of men's practices. Topics included: gender-based violence; health and health-related practices; household division of labour; men's participation in caregiving and as fathers; men's and women's attitudes about gender and gender-related policies; transactional sex; men's reports of criminal behaviour; and quality of life. IMAGES was co-ordinated globally by Promundo, and the International Center for Research on Women (Barker *et al.* 2011). From 2009 to 2010, household surveys were administered to more than 8,000 men and 3,500 women aged 18–59 in Brazil, Chile, Croatia, India, Mexico, and Rwanda. For more information, see www.promundo. org.br/en/wp-content/uploads/2011/01/Evolving-Men-IMAGES-1.pdf.

4. Such information could include sexual and reproductive health and rights, rights to life free of violence, understanding HIV and its prevention, the rights of people living with HIV/AIDS, political rights, civic education, rights to information – budget plans, district development plans, and relevant policies.

References

Ahmed, Fauzia (2008) 'Microcredit, men and masculinity', *NWSA Journal* 20(2): 122–155

Barker, Gary, Juan Manuel Contreras, Brian Heilman, Ajay Singh, Ravi Verma, and Marcos Nascimento (2011) 'Evolving Men: Initial Results from the International Men and Gender Equality Survey (IMAGES)', Washington, DC: International Center for Research on Women; Rio de Janeiro: Instituto Promundo

Barker, Gary and Jennifer Schulte (2010) 'Engaging Men as Allies in Women's Economic Empowerment: Strategies and Recommendations for CARE Country Offices', prepared for CARE Norway, Washington, DC: International Center for Research on Women

Bruce, Judith, Cynthia Lloyd, and Ann Leonard (1995) 'Families in Focus: New Perspectives on Mothers, Fathers and Children', New York: Population Council

Hadi, Abdullahel (2005) 'Women's productive work and marital violence in Bangladesh', *Journal of Family Violence* 20(3): 181–9

Kabeer, Naila (2009) 'Women's economic empowerment: key issues and policy options', SIDA background paper, Brighton: Institute of Development Studies

Kelkar Govind, Dev Nathan, and Rownok Jahan (2004) 'We Were in Fire, Now We Are in Water: Micro-credit and Gender Relations in Rural Bangladesh', New Delhi: IFAD-UNIFEM Gender Mainstreaming Programme in Asia

Kim, Julia, Charlotte Watts, James Hargreaves, Luceth Ndhlovu, Godfrey Phetla, Linda Morrison, Joanna Busza, John Porter and Paul Pronyk (2008) 'Understanding the impact of a microfinance-based intervention on women's empowerment and the reduction of intimate partner violence in South Africa', *American Journal of Public Health* 97: 1794–802

Koenig, Michael, Saifuddin Ahmed, Mian Hossain and A.B.M. Khorshed Alam Mozumder (2003) 'Women's status and domestic violence in rural

Bangladesh: individual and community level effects', *Demography* 40(2): 269–88

Maes, Jan (2007) 'Linkages Between CARE's VS&LAs with Financial Institutions in Rwanda', Atlanta, GA: CARE USA Economic Development Unit

Peacock, Dean and Gary Barker (2012) 'Working with Men and Boys to Promote Gender Equality: A Review of the Field and Emerging Approaches', Bangkok: UN Women

Rahman, Aminur (1999) *Women and Microcredit in Rural Bangladesh: An Anthropological Study of the Rhetoric and Realities of Grameen Bank Lending*, Boulder, CO: Westview Press

Schuler, Sidney Ruth, Syed Hashemi, Ann Riley and Shireen Akhter (1996) 'Credit programs, patriarachy and men's violence against women in rural Bangladesh', *Social Science and Medicine* 43: 1729–42

Slegh, Henny and Augustin Kimonyo (2010) 'Masculinities and Gender-based Violence in Rwanda: Experiences and Perceptions of Men and Women', Kigali, Rwanda: Rwanda Men's Resource Centre

World Bank (2012) *World Development Report: Gender Equality and Development*, Washington, DC: World Bank, http://siteresources. worldbank.org/INTWDR2012/Resources/7778105-1299699968583/ 7786210-1315936222006/Complete-Report.pdf

About the authors

Gary Barker, President and CEO, Promundo-US. Email: g.barker@promundo. org.br

Henny Slegh, Senior Fellow Promundo-US. Email: h.slegh@promundo global.org

Augustin Kimonyo, Gender Consultant, Kigali, Rwanda. Email: akimonyo@yahoo.com

Prudence Ndolimana, CARE Rwanda. Email: prudencen. rw@co.care.org

Matt Bannerman, Assistant Country Director, CARE Rwanda. Email: mattb.rw@co.care.org

CHAPTER 3

Promoting male involvement in family planning in Vietnam and India: HealthBridge experience

Lisa MacDonald, Lori Jones, Phaeba Thomas, Le Thi Thu, Sian FitzGerald and Debra Efroymson

Abstract

In many developing countries, gender inequality contributes to the continued problem of unwanted pregnancies and unmet contraception needs. The majority of family planning programmes in Asia target only women; however, women's lack of decision-making power, even with regard to their own health, hinders their ability to practise family planning. This chapter describes successes and lessons learned in India and Vietnam from a HealthBridge programme which facilitated male involvement in reproductive health, particularly in family planning and in the use of male-centred contraception. The experience shows that, given the right role models and enabling environments, men are willing to be more fully and positively engaged in reproductive health matters.

Key words: gender equality; contraception; engaging men; family planning; sexual and reproductive health

Introduction

Family planning is one of the most basic and essential health practices. In addition to the well-known positive effects of birth spacing on the health of mothers and children, family planning reduces the risk of unwanted pregnancy, and creates smaller, more economically viable families. A recent estimate suggests that contraceptive use may prevent as many as 272,000 maternal deaths annually worldwide (Ahmed *et al.* 2012, 123).

In many Asian countries, however, unequal gender relations contribute to the continued problem of unwanted pregnancies and unmet contraception needs. Women's lack of power relative to men provides them with little to no input in decisions that directly affect their health and well-being, including deciding when to have children, how many to have, whether to use contraception or protection from sexually transmitted infections, and when and where to seek health care. Gender inequality means that women receive

http://dx.doi.org/10.3362/9781780448664.003

less education and have poor knowledge of health-promoting practices; it is also thought to be a root cause of violence against women. Research conducted in 2005 by HealthBridge and its partners on causes of violence in Bangladesh, India, and Vietnam found that 'since women usually did not hold a paying job and inherited little or no land, they were considered weak and worthless. Men felt that since they earned a living, women should always be subservient to them' (Efroymson *et al.* 2006, 6). Thus, when men see women as contributing very little to the household, it is easier for them to mistreat women.

Between 2004 and 2008, the HealthBridge Foundation of Canada (HealthBridge) implemented the programme 'Promoting Male Responsibility Towards Greater Gender Equality' in three countries in South and Southeast Asia: India, Vietnam, and Bangladesh. The programme was partially funded by the Canadian International Development Agency. It sought to encourage positive male involvement and responsibility in a range of family matters including sexual and reproductive health (which includes family planning), violence against women, and domestic responsibilities and child rearing.[1] These matters – perhaps most of all, sexual and reproductive health – are stereotypically regarded as the 'female's domain'. Within the context of the programme, HealthBridge's approach to gender equality promoted equal opportunities, value, and freedom from negative stereotypes for both sexes.

This chapter focuses on HealthBridge's work in India and Vietnam to facilitate male involvement in reproductive health, particularly in family planning and in the use of male-centred contraception.

Our approach: engaging men and valuing women

HealthBridge's guiding principle is 'engaging men and valuing women', and, in this particular programme, it focused on promoting greater access to, and use of, *male*-centred methods of contraception. Most of the contraceptives currently available in Asia are for use by women, and the majority of sexual and reproductive health programmes in the region target only women. However, women's lack of decision-making power in their families, even with regards to their own health, means that their desire to practise family planning may not result in its actual use.

There is increasing recognition that for family planning to be implemented and effective, both men and women must be engaged (Oppenheim Mason and Smith 2000; Sternberg and Hubley 2004). Besides being less effective, interventions that only target and engage women – and thereby fail to address underlying gender inequities – may actually do more harm than good (Bawah *et al.* 1999). Decision-making processes that involve both partners promote shared responsibility for contraception, lessening the burden on women, and encourage inter-spousal communication.

Engaging men

While there are a number of safe and reliable female contraceptive methods available, HealthBridge's work in India and Vietnam during this programme focused on encouraging male-centred contraceptive methods, specifically condoms and vasectomy. As the heterosexual transmission of HIV and other sexually transmitted infections is an increasing problem in Vietnam and India, particularly amongst youth, it was deemed crucial to address the stigma and misconceptions that exist around condom use (Roth *et al.* 2001; Kaljee *et al.* 2007). In addition, male-centred contraceptive methods require active male involvement, thus promoting shared responsibility against pregnancy and the transmission of disease.

The intention in our programme was, therefore, not to discourage the use of female-centred methods, but, rather, to promote their use alongside transformative work to address the stigmas and misconceptions around contraceptive use in general. The programme sought to promote the benefits of male-centred methods in particular as safe and reliable options which can be used together with female-centred methods, or as an alternative to them. The project's baseline surveys clearly demonstrated that although men often said that they believed in sharing responsibility for fertility control with their partners, in practice only a small proportion actually did so. Thus, in their very nature, male-centred methods would ensure that men could and would play an active role in family planning.

Valuing women

Also central to HealthBridge's approach is addressing one of the root causes of gender inequality and its many consequences: the fact that women are not valued. For their health to be made a priority, women themselves must be valued: by their families, their communities, and their service providers. It is becoming increasingly evident that health interventions that fail to address underlying gender inequities are less effective than those that do (Barker *et al.* 2007). Furthermore, addressing the relative value of women is necessary to counter issues such as son preference, and male dominance in decision-making. HealthBridge has challenged the undervaluation of women in other work: notably by calculating, and increasing awareness of, the social and economic value of women's unpaid work in Bangladesh, India, Nepal, Pakistan, and Vietnam. Such unpaid, and typically domestic, work is often used to justify husband authority and preferential treatment of sons because it does not produce a tangible income. However, this overlooks its significant, if intangible, contribution to the family and society. HealthBridge worked with local organisations to demonstrate the value of domestic work traditionally performed by women, parallel to addressing family planning and reproductive health.[2]

The India programme

The context

In India, despite the significant advances towards gender equality achieved among the elite, the majority of women still suffer from the effects of extreme inequality, which causes ill-health, violence, and early death. Although there are national population control policies in place, and near-universal knowledge about family planning, as many as 44 per cent of couples do not use any form of contraception (International Institute for Population Sciences and Macro International 2007, 56). Female sterilisation dominates active contraceptive use, accounting for 66 per cent of all contraception. There are high discontinuation rates for non-permanent contraceptive methods, limited use of male- or couple-dependent methods, and negligible use of any methods amongst married couples and unmarried adolescents. Dependence on permanent contraceptive methods means that many married couples do not practise any form of family planning until they reach their desired family size (typically after a son is born). This means that spacing between siblings is unplanned, with many women giving birth too frequently in too short a period of time. While men are the chief decision-makers in the home and exert a strong influence over women, reproductive health matters are still considered 'women's responsibility', and men's involvement is very limited. For example, in one family visited during the project, the woman had delivered a child in the morning, by herself, and in the afternoon was cooking for her family. The husband was not even aware that she had given birth. The notion that reproductive health is only a women's concern is reinforced by the many family planning programmes that target only women, even though women have little to no power to purchase or actually use contraception without the approval of their husbands.

The programme

The programme in India was implemented primarily by HealthBridge's local partner, the Evangelical Social Action Forum (ESAF), in the locality of Bhuj, in the state of Gujarat. Project activities included public awareness-raising, support to government reproductive health programmes, and fostering direct community discussion of, and participation in, decision-making about the type of reproductive health services that were needed and how they should be provided. The project consisted of several distinct yet complementary components: research, media engagement, government engagement, capacity building, and networking. These activities are discussed in more detail below. While engaging men in family planning and reproductive health was the primary focus, basic education about gender issues and women's rights was also provided.

Qualitative and quantitative research was conducted on the existing roles and responsibilities of men in family life, including contraception. Based on the research results, ESAF developed mass media materials to promote positive male responsibility for reproductive health and family planning, including a message telecasted on a local TV channel to nearly 35,000 houses about male responsibilities in the family. ESAF also worked with broad circulation newspapers to improve and increase media coverage of sensitive gender issues, including contraception and family planning. The local media proved to be eager for information, and printed all the articles that ESAF provided. Articles published in multiple newspapers addressed issues such as dowry, child marriage, and 'missing girls', which in turn led to an increase in local, community-level awareness of the problems that such traditions pose for women, and discussions about them. The project's research results were also published in a local newspaper, with a special focus on the lack of physicians able to perform vasectomies.

ESAF established linkages with women journalists who had participated in a five-day tour of Europe as part of an exchange programme. As a result of the relationships built, All India Radio broadcasted a special episode on gender issues, using a script supplied by ESAF.

In addition to engaging media, the programme sought to improve government-provided reproductive health services by working closely in partnership with existing programmes at provincial and national levels, rather than establishing separate, and possibly competing, programmes. ESAF conducted a series of awareness-raising and capacity-building activities with government staff and media workers. Integrated Child Development Services (ICDS) officials subsequently took the initiative to target fathers through child-care centres. Training programmes were designed and implemented for community health workers, particularly on the subjects of gender, sex, and social inequalities. ESAF also lobbied government officials to recruit male health workers (locally known as animators) to improve the reach of reproductive health programmes.

To foster community engagement, ESAF organised community information sessions about family planning, sterilisation, gender bias in family life (stereotypes in the way that children are raised), immunisation, tuberculosis, and HIV/AIDS. Additionally, men's and women's core groups were organised to increase awareness of the benefits to be gained from men being positively involved in family life, through group discussion, counselling, videos, and poster shows. While the project generally focused on men, women's core groups were supported in the recognition that women, as primary child-rearers, play an important role in implanting and reinforcing gender stereotypes in the young.

Another key element in the project was the creation and management of a community-based condom bank, through which a female health worker supplied condoms to a local man who in turn agreed to serve as a local distributor from his home. This meant that men in the community could have access to free condoms, without the embarrassment of requesting them from a female health worker, or having to purchase them at a shop.

Lastly, links were successfully made with nearby communities and with local government bodies, at times by helping them to achieve other (albeit related) goals. This, in turn, resulted in positive changes in sexual and reproductive health practices. For example, ESAF helped local communities to get birth certificates for their children, so that they could be admitted to government-run schools. After this, community members made a commitment to change their long-accepted norms of female harassment and killings for monetary gain (that is, dowry deaths). In addition, by providing training opportunities for ICDS staff on gender issues and the importance of male involvement in reproductive health issues, HealthBridge was able to gain the support of government officials to staff sexual and reproductive health worker positions locally.

Successes

The India programme made some noteworthy achievements related to gender equality and male engagement in sexual and reproductive health. As a result of the media activities, public enquiries about gender issues increased and media attention continued to snowball. For example, the Urban Family Welfare Department requested articles and messages about gender roles and relations, and inequality, to develop its own information, education and communication (IEC) materials, and the print media took the initiative to focus on gender-related news and articles.

The programme's work with government officials resulted in some improvements to government health programmes and services. The local government-formulated plans to hire male community health workers in rural areas for reproductive and child health programmes, and the District TB department promoted schemes to involve male volunteers. The District IEC department increased its promotion of non-surgical vasectomy, and the local government took the initiative to ban sex-selective abortions. The district hospital arranged regular health check-up camps in urban areas with the support of ICDS, and ICDS workers began to reach more people with gender-related messages, including the need to involve men in reproductive health.

Attitudinal and behaviour changes were also seen in the programme's participating communities. Participants in the core group meetings acknowledged the unfairness of gender bias in child-rearing, and some people pledged to make changes. Disapproval of female infanticide was also publicly discussed in the groups. As one project participant commented, 'If this practice [female infanticide] continues, there will be no wives for our sons to marry' (anonymous female participant in focus group discussion, 17 June 2005). Men discussed how they had started to help with household chores; some began to consider vasectomies and condoms as real family planning options, while others became involved in reproductive discussions with their wives. The case study below provides an example of how the programme impacted families, and the challenges that were experienced.

> *The family already had five children, and the woman was expecting their sixth. She was emaciated and quite weak, most likely anaemic. Given her poor health, it was not possible for her to undergo sterilisation after delivery. ESAF staff talked to the family about their situation. The woman's husband did not want to have a vasectomy done, but began to understand the need to take responsibility when the staff explained why his wife could not undergo an operation. He finally agreed to go with ESAF staff to the district hospital. There, the staff found that there was not a single doctor who was trained to perform a vasectomy. The only doctor in the area who was qualified was already retired. The staff then found the doctor, talked to him, and arranged for him to conduct the vasectomy at the district hospital. Hence the attempt to increase the number of doctors trained to perform the operation.* (Case study developed based on interviews held with an anonymous family on 8 May 2005)

Vietnam programme

The context

Although gender inequality has less extreme consequences in Vietnam, and contraceptive use is much higher (around 79 per cent), the country still has one of the highest abortion rates in the world (United Nations 2009). While rates vary across studies, one report estimates that the average Vietnamese woman has 2.8 abortions during her lifetime (Mai 2003, as reported in United Nations Population Fund 2007, 23). Social pressure to produce a son, coupled with Vietnam's unofficial two-child policy, contributes to a high rate of abortions undertaken to select the sex of the child, despite laws prohibiting the practice. Strong gender stereotypes, which make birth control the sole burden of women but which grant them little power to negotiate contraceptive use, also play a major role in abortion rates. The intra-uterine device (IUD) is by far the most socially accepted and widely used contraceptive method, accounting for more than half of all contraception (United Nations 2009). However, those who use IUDs remain unprotected from sexually transmitted infections. Due to their widespread association with infidelity and prostitution, condom use remains pitifully low, at less than 10 per cent (United Nations 2009). Women who experience problems with IUDs or hormonal methods are left with few reliable contraceptive options. Furthermore, society's negative view of abortion (in spite of its common occurrence) means that many abortions still take place in secret and illegally, and the prevalence of abortion-related complications remains high.

The Vietnamese Government has attempted to promote gender equality by funding and/or supporting a number of 'gender' programmes, not only by women-focused organisations or government ministries, but cross-sectorally.

Vietnam is however, in many ways, still a traditional society in which men are expected to be 'masculine' and women are expected to be 'feminine' – with each stereotype defined in largely negative terms. HealthBridge's baseline research on gender roles highlighted the widespread beliefs that overt sexuality forms a man's character, while participating in sexual and reproductive health initiatives, particularly those for women, is emasculating.

The programme

HealthBridge's programme in Vietnam was implemented at both the national and provincial levels in collaboration with a number of government, academic, and civil society partners. The project was implemented in 17 communes/wards in three districts of Bac Ninh province, and in 12 wards in Hanoi. Like India, its components included research, mass media campaigns, capacity building, and networking. The project began with baseline qualitative and quantitative research, on gender roles in the family, and reproductive health. In addition to contributing to a better understanding of *perceptions* of gender equality in Vietnam, the research also served another, more important, purpose: it exposed these stereotypes to study participants who were, for the most part, only vaguely aware of the extent to which stereotypes governed their behaviour around sexual and reproductive health. This 'feeding back' enabled the project team to develop messages and interventions collaboratively. By countering the most negative stereotypes, these were appropriate to the immediate needs of the study group. IEC materials, TV-spots, radio programmes, and dramas were combined with targeted training programmes to raise awareness of – and to change public attitudes about – the gender stereotypes that impact most negatively on women's sexual and reproductive health. In particular, project activities were designed specifically to encourage male involvement and couple-based decisions about sexual and reproductive health. For example, billboards were produced with messages such as 'He is very manly, he always cares for his family'. Radio broadcasts encouraged men to actively share in family planning and to use condoms, and promoted couple communication about reproductive health for a better relationship. A leaflet was disseminated that encouraged men to use male-focused contraceptive methods and to engage in partner-based decision-making about sexual and reproductive health. Drama scripts focused on the husband's role in family planning and in taking care of pregnant women, and on the need to change perceptions about son preference. Many of these activities built on the results of earlier projects in other provinces, during which the project team focused on modern contraception methods for both men and women and highlighted the importance of a positive role for men in family planning.

Capacity-building activities targeted mass organisations and health institutions that play an influential role in gender equality and reproductive health issues. The project team developed a train-the-trainers curriculum on gender equality and reproductive health, that focused on promoting men's roles and responsibilities in decisions about sexual and reproductive health. Targeted training workshops were conducted with the Bac Ninh Women's Union, at the provincial, district, and commune levels for communicators on gender equality issues. The main objectives of the training was to impart different approaches for promoting gender equality, and to encourage partners to promote positive social norms around gender roles, masculinity, stereotypes, and gender equality. A series of training sessions were also conducted with the Bac Ninh Farmer's Union, which promoted improved communication between spouses as a way to increase the involvement of men in reproductive health and family planning.

At the national level, the programme supported the National Committee for the Advancement of Women to strengthen its capacity to integrate gender issues into planning processes and implementation of action plans. Finally, increasing the capacity of journalists to address gender issues played an important role in increasing published, gender-sensitive articles that discussed the necessity of men's engagement in sexual and reproductive health.

Networking primarily involved sharing and exchanging information with other non-government organisation (NGO) networks about how to approach gender issues from a male perspective, rather than only from a female perspective. As a result of this networking, HealthBridge received multiple contacts from NGOs interested in incorporating this approach into their own programmes.

Successes

The Vietnam programme represented the first time that gender equality programming that specifically focused on engaging men in sexual and reproductive health had reached the provincial and commune levels. A post-project evaluation demonstrated that men living in the participating communes more regularly used contraception (rather than expecting their wives/girlfriends to do so), and participated more fully in their partner's pregnancies than they had previously. For example, prior to the project's implementation, no man or woman had asked about or purchased condoms at the local health station in the community of Suoi Hoa (Bac Ninh province). By the end of the four-year project, men in the community were not only asking about modern contraceptive methods, but also taking the initiative to purchase condoms. When asked about this change, men stated that their changed attitude and behaviour was due to the information and training provided by the project team.

In a similar manner, before 2004, men rarely participated in any aspect of their wife's/girlfriend's pregnancy (other than getting her pregnant!). They did not attend medical check-ups nor did they attend the delivery. Some men reported feeling shame or embarrassment during the baby's delivery and made a point of being 'elsewhere'. By 2008, however, many men in the three communities of Suoi Hoa, Que Vo, and Dai Xuan (Bac Ninh province) were observed taking their partners to health clinics, and attending their child's delivery. While such changes are reported for only three specific districts, they reflect the tide of changed perceptions that was initiated by the project across all participating communities.

More importantly, the project has contributed to significant changes that will improve women's sexual and reproductive health in the project communities. Respondents to the end-of-project evaluation reported that the abortion rate had declined, while 25 per cent of the surveyed families indicated that they would accept having only girl children. The condom use rate has increased by almost half. Young women now attend many more gynecological appointments than they had previously, and the rate of untreated gynecological disease has declined. Community-based clubs have been established for population and family planning. Domestic violence has reportedly declined, in some communities by a considerable amount. Although the attributable impact of the HealthBridge project is difficult to measure in the context of rapid social economic development, members of the participating communities noted that the project activities that specifically targeted men and addressed couples' decisions about sexual and reproductive health contributed not only to a better understanding of and desire for greater gender equality, but also to a change in practical behaviour, as shown by a project participant:

> After participating in gender equality training, I personally changed remarkably. I found that it is necessary and I have helped my wife with everything, including family planning. Especially, the perception of other people in my community improved, which helps me to change my behaviour. Before, I was ashamed if my friends knew that I helped my wife ... However, it is opposite nowadays: I would get people's criticism if I showed gender inequality. (Anonymous male participant of focus group discussion held during the final project evaluation, 4 March 2008)

Challenges and lessons learned

The design and implementation of this project was based on a number of challenges and lessons learned from earlier projects; it also evolved as new challenges were encountered, and lessons learned. Gender-stereotyped behaviour takes very different forms in different societies, depending on what people accept as normative. These stereotypes affect all areas of our lives, and, as was demonstrated in India and Vietnam, are often accepted without question, causing tremendous, albeit unintentional, harm. It may be assumed that the practices and attitudes are so deeply entrenched in the cultural traditions that there is little hope for change. However, some of the experiences in this project illustrate that often a small change in the system or information provided can result in large changes in practices and attitudes.

To challenge negative gender stereotypes in a way which brings about lasting change, it is critical to remember that men and women are equal and necessary contributors to such change, and ultimately to attaining gender equality. To gain the active involvement of men in sexual and reproductive health and family planning decision-making, men's necessary and positive contributions should be highlighted by providing culturally appropriate models of positive male behaviour and the positive consequences of engagement. At the same time, gender issues are sensitive, and HealthBridge recognised that even its local partners may have found it difficult to accept new concepts of gender equality. Many of the men in the project's target audience, and even the women, may have felt challenged and threatened by new approaches to looking at gender; in particular, the idea of discussing the ideas together may have been uncomfortable. HealthBridge attempted to lessen these problems by emphasising the positive aspects of change; that is, how both men *and* women would benefit from changes in men's involvement.

While addressing sexual and reproductive health can be a sensitive matter, it may not be as difficult as many believe. Research in Vietnam confirmed that many young people are eager to discuss the intimate details of their relations, but lacked the space in which to do so. The project team developed a manual that is now used by community workers to encourage the open discussion of sexual issues between husbands and wives. Despite cultural norms about men's sexual behaviour, many men are in fact willing and able to participate more fully in women's sexual and reproductive health if given a 'comfort zone' and opportunity to do so. That is, the main issue preventing men from assuming more responsibility for their and their partner's sexual and reproductive health may not be mainly cultural or personal, but rather the lack of an encouraging and enabling environment.

Similarly, low rates of condom use in some countries or communities may have less to do with culture than expected, and may thus be relatively easy to address. For instance, the usual source of condoms may be inappropriate (for example, wrong hours or location), or uncomfortable (men may feel embarrassed acquiring condoms from female health workers). Simply by establishing a 'condom bank' in a slum community in India, condoms became locally available at convenient times and locations, and were provided by a 'comfortable' community member, making their use far more likely *despite* existing attitudes. On the other hand, turning to our experience in Vietnam, it seems that availability of condoms is not a problem so much as the poor quality of condoms provided (free of charge) by the Vietnamese government to low-income communities. This poor quality actually hinders the promotion of condoms as a safe, male-oriented form of contraception. Since members of these communities cannot afford to purchase higher-quality condoms, they tend to avoid condom use, preferring instead to rely on (seemingly) more 'reliable' forms of birth control; unfortunately these methods are not always reliable, and abortion then becomes an acceptable method of birth control. Likewise, increased acceptance of vasectomies in India was hampered by the lack of physicians who had been trained to perform the procedure, rather than by a deep-rooted cultural reluctance towards vasectomies.

Flexibility and adaptability are critical to success in all aspects of development. This was particularly noted in India, where the entire design of the project was modified from a focus on advocacy to a focus on programme-oriented demand for services once the project team recognised that the concepts of gender equality and male involvement in sexual and reproductive health were completely new to the participating communities. In addition, the implementation of the project was modified, recognising that community training/information sessions held during the daytime resulted in only women participating. Subsequently, sessions were organised during other community events which had no overall health focus. This resulted in increased male participation.

It is important to be responsive to the expressed needs of the community. For instance, as mentioned above, project staff in India discovered that some parents were unable to send their children to school because they lacked a birth certificate. The project staff temporarily turned their attention from their main focus of gender inequality and sexual and reproductive health to address this need. As a result, children were supplied with birth certificates, and the community was more open and responsive to the project team. In the end, major changes were possible with respect to males accepting responsibility in family planning and hence in the sexual and reproductive health of their wives.

Finally, aspects of this programme would need to be modified if they were replicated. For example, to appeal to, and be equally relevant to, both urban and rural populations, aspects of the project – for example, methods of communication and the content and style of IEC materials – need to be target-specific. In rural areas, reading dramas over the loudspeaker is a traditional mode of communication and is an effective way to transmit information and raise awareness about sexual and reproductive health. In urban areas, this approach would be less appropriate and successful.

Concluding thoughts

The problem of gender inequality worldwide is manifold, and the reasons for it are embedded in culture, politics, economics, and even geography. Of critical importance in the quest for greater gender equality is the need to engage men in finding and implementing solutions. However, the majority of programmes aimed at greater gender equality address the most vulnerable only, the women. As men are more often in decision-making positions, involving them in the process of change, through positive messages and engagement, is critical to long-term and lasting impact.

Unfortunately, often men are not presented with appropriate role models for their treatment of women, or of themselves. While the negative role of men in gender dynamics is often lamented, messages aimed at encouraging men to play a positive role in their families, and particularly in the sexual and reproductive health of their spouse, are few in number; instead, gender-based programmes generally tend to portray men in a negative light, rather than making explicit what is desired or expected of them. Such negative messages may actually reinforce gender stereotypes by picturing men as abusive or disinterested sexual partners, rather than promoting greater equality by presenting positive role models for men to emulate. Engaging men and understanding the value of women are key components to improving gender equality and sexual and reproductive health, and family planning in particular.

HealthBridge has sought to address some of the root causes of gender inequality by addressing this gap, specifically by engaging men in the process of change, by promoting positive images of men's involvement in issues of women's sexual and reproductive health, and by highlighting the value of women to the household and society. A specific focus in the programme discussed here was to encourage men to take responsibility for contraception by using condoms or getting a vasectomy, and to understand the importance of their engagement in sexual and reproductive health decision-making with their partner. More equitable gender relations and efforts to involve men in the project led to increased participation of men in male contraceptive methods, as well as fostering an appreciation in them of the positive role they can play in the health of their family.

Although the project was successful in terms of increasing understanding of the importance of decision-making that involves both partners, and of men being engaged in women's sexual and reproductive health, changing gender-based perceptions and behaviour is a long-term process that must be addressed through a multitude of approaches. Cultural norms can change over time as perception and attitudes change; health systems can be altered to facilitate access to male contraceptive methods, and the burden of gender inequality on women can be lessened through shared decision-making.

Notes

1. The component on family planning was only implemented in Vietnam and India, while in Bangladesh the project team focused on violence against women. For more information on this project, please contact the authors.
2. HealthBridge undertook research estimating the economic value of the unpaid work regularly performed by women. The purpose was not to demand a wage or conclusively define the monetary value of such work, as it is impossible to put a price tag on caring for the family. Rather, we aimed to put in perspective the magnitude and value of the work women do without pay and, in doing so, gain women the respect they deserve and put an end to housewives being labelled as 'unproductive' members of society. For more information on this research, see Efroymson *et al.* (2010).

References

Ahmed, Saifuddin, Qingfeng Li, Li Liu, and Amy O. Tsui (2012) 'Maternal deaths averted by contraceptive use: an analysis of 172 countries', *Lancet* 380: 111–25

Barker, Gary, Christine Ricardo, and Marcos Nascimento (2007) *Engaging Men and Boys in Changing Gender-based Inequity in Health: Evidence from Programme Interventions*, Geneva: World Health Organization

Bawah, Ayaga Agula, Patricia Akweongo, Ruth Simmons, and James F. Phillips (1999) 'Women's fears and men's anxieties: the impact of family planning on gender relations in Northern Ghana', *Studies in Family Planning* 30(1): 54–66

Efroymson, Debra, Sian FitzGerald, and Lori Jones (eds.) (2006) 'Promoting Male Responsibility for Gender Equality: Summary Report of Research from Bangladesh, India and Vietnam', Dhaka: HealthBridge, www.healthbridge.ca/gender%20summary. pdf

Efroymson, Debra, Sian FitzGerald, and Lori Jones (eds.) (2010) 'Women, Work, and Money: Studying the Economic Value of Women's Unpaid Work and Using the Results for Advocacy', HealthBridge, www.healthbridge.ca

International Institute for Population Sciences (IIPS) and Macro International (2007) *National Family Health Survey (NFHS-3), 2005–06, India: Key Findings*, Mumbai: IIPS

Kaljee, Linda M., Mackenzie Green, Rosemary Riel, Porntip Lerdboon, Le Huu Tho, Le Thi Kim Thoa, and Truong Tan Minh (2007) 'Sexual stigma, sexual behaviors, and abstinence among Vietnamese adolescents: implications for risk and protective behaviors for HIV, STIs, and unwanted pregnancy', *Journal of the Association of Nurses in AIDS Care* 18(2): 48–59

Mai, T.T.P. (2003) 'Situation of abortion and factors associated in health clinics in Viet Nam', *Journal of Practical Medicine* 12(469): 23

Oppenheim Mason, Karen and Herbert L. Smith (2000) 'Husbands' versus wives' fertility goals and use of contraception: the influence of gender context in five Asian countries', *Demography* 37(30): 299–311

Roth, Joseph, Satya P. Krishnan, and Emily Bunch (2001) 'Barriers to condom use: results from a study in Mumbai (Bombay), India', *AIDS Education and Prevention* 13(1): 65–77

Sternberg, Peter and John Hubley (2004) 'Evaluating men's involvement as a strategy in sexual and reproductive health promotion', *Health Promotion International* 19(3): 389–96 United Nations (2009) 'World Contraceptive Use 2009', www.un.org/esa/population/publications/contraceptive2009/contraceptive2009.htm (last checked by the author August 2012)

United Nations Population Fund (UNFPA) (2007) *Research on Reproductive Health in Vietnam: A Review for the Period 2000–2005*, Hanoi: UNFPA

About the authors

Lisa MacDonald is a Project Manager at the HealthBridge Foundation of Canada Headquarters. Email: lmacdonald@healthbridge.ca

Lori Jones is Director, Special Projects at the HealthBridge Foundation of Canada Headquarters. Email: ljones@healthbridge.ca

Phaeba Thomas Regional Manager- South Asia at the HealthBridge Foundation, India. Email: pabraham@healthbridge.ca

Le Thi Thu Program Manager at the HealthBridge Foundation of Canada, Hanoi. Email: lethu@healthbridge.org.vn

Sian FitzGerald Executive Director at the HealthBridge Foundation of Canada Headquarters. Email: sfitzgerald@healthbridge.ca

Debra Efroymson Regional Director at the HealthBridge Foundation of Canada, Bangladesh. Email: debra@healthbridge.ca

CHAPTER 4

'Before the war, I was a man': men and masculinities in the Eastern Democratic Republic of Congo

Desiree Lwambo

Abstract

Humanitarian interventions that confuse 'gender issues' with 'women's issues' ignore the complex nature of gender and its potential as a tool for social change. This chapter reflects on this issue, in the context of an analysis of the relationship between sexual and gender-based violence and hegemonic masculinities in the conflict zone of North Kivu province in the Eastern Democratic Republic of Congo. It draws on a research study focusing on the discrepancies between dominant ideals of masculinity and the actual realities of men's lives. As men try to enact masculine ideals of breadwinner and family head, the current political and economic context puts them under increasing pressure. Respondents drew a direct connection between the resulting sense of failure and unhealthy outlets for asserting masculinity, lack of productivity, and violence. They were critical of the fact that most programmes dealing with sexual and gender-based violence focus exclusively on supporting women. I argue here that such interventions do not recognise the interdependent and interactive nature of gender. Their antagonising effect is evidenced by the high level of men's resistance to programmes and campaigns promoting gender equality. The chapter further highlights the role of 'hegemonic masculinity' in creating a general climate of violence and conflict, pointing up the need for holistic approaches that empower men to make non-violent life choices.

Key words: gender; masculinity; research; Africa; development; sexual violence

Introduction

Since 1993, the Democratic Republic of Congo (DRC) has seen a series of armed conflicts and wars that weakened the economy and destabilised the country. The DRC is frequently described as a 'failing state', marked by corruption, lack of functioningand adequate social services, and impunity. In the East, armed rebel groups and government troops continue to battle over

http://dx.doi.org/10.3362/9781780448664.004

territory, access to resources, and political recognition. Local communities are disrupted by frequent land conflicts. Political entrepreneurs tend to seize economic opportunities by manipulating ethnic tensions and mobilising armed groups. Especially in rural areas, the population faces a high level of insecurity, marking people's lives with experiences of displacement, extortion, and abduction, as well as sexual and gender-based violence.

Under a United Nations (UN) mandate, a peacekeeping force was deployed in the country in 2000. In spite of different peace agreements, violent conflicts continue. Meanwhile, funding for humanitarian interventions in DRC has benefited from an average of US$1.5 billion annually. However, donors are rarely attentive to the accelerators of peace and conflict, and their strategies are compartmentalised, particularly with regard to work on sexual and gender-based violence.

Both men and women in Eastern DRC are affected by this violence, though women and children are far more vulnerable to it than men. While 'rape as a weapon of war' has become a trademark element of reports on the DRC, the issue is far more complex and embedded into a broader context of unequal gender relations and general violence. Recent research has shown that rape permeates all levels of society and that perpetrators are frequently found among the civilian population (Dolan 2010). In addition to rape, women and children are subjected to other forms of sexual and gender-based violence, such as sexual slavery, domestic violence, economic poverty, and structural discrimination (e.g. poor access to education and political participation).

Humanitarian programmes and 'gendered' responses

Against the backdrop of the Millennium Development Goals, UN resolution 1325, and the Convention for the Elimination of All Forms of Discrimination Against Women (CEDAW), a multitude of humanitarian interventions in Eastern DRC have focused on the specific needs of women and girls in offering medical, psychosocial, legal, and economic support. The two major donor efforts, the DRC Pooled Fund and the Stabilisation and Recovery Funding Facility, account for over US$15 million and are accompanied by multi- and bilateral donor strategies and funding modalities targeting different issues related to sexual and gender-based violence.

While these programmes are packaged as 'gender-sensitive', they have sometimes been critiqued for pursuing a women-centred approach. Men (mainly military and local decision-makers) and male identity issues may be only marginally included in awareness campaigns and training sessions aiming to sensitise participants to gender issues. These trainings often fail to focus on men's needs, thereby missing the chance to tackle the complex nature of sexual and gender-based violence. For instance, both civilians and military have reported traumatic experiences of violent abuse (Johnson et al. 2010). Male survivors of violence have gender-specific needs for psychological care which are rarely addressed in sexual and gender-based violence programmes, and few of these offer men socioeconomic opportunities such as microcredit and training.

Strains on men to be family providers in fractured economic systems are known to lead to experiences of humiliation and vulnerability for men and that psychosocial stress is known to induce violent behaviour (Teasdale *et al.* 2006). Violence and aggression is often a sanctioned way of asserting masculinity. Male refugees can face a range of challenges which threaten their status as men, based on their inability to provide for, and protect, their wives and children (Turner 1999, 2–4).

Chief among the characteristics that reoccur across African masculinity research is the necessity of financial independence. This is reflected in the roles men are responsible for in the family. In their sweeping study on manhood in Sub-Saharan Africa, Gary Barker and Christine Ricardo state that: 'the chief mandate or social requirement for achieving manhood in Africa – for being a man – is some level of financial independence, employment or income, and subsequently starting a family' (2005, 55). These norms are maintained in rhetoric and socialisation regardless of the economic and social realities that pervade everyday life, often making such roles impossible to maintain. Men's sense of failure often results in unhealthy outlets for asserting masculinity. Women's increasing ability to exert economic influence and make choices based on their own needs can be seen as an additional threat to masculinity. Indeed, evaluations of livelihood programmes suggest that women's increased decision-making power can lead – at least in the short term – to an increase in violence by men (Ray and Heller 2009).

Of course, men may be entitled to sentiments of anger and frustration, but they are not entitled to violence. Treating violence against women as a 'natural' or 'understandable' effect of male disempowerment risks excusing it. As Helen Moffett argues, discussions that attempt to causally link rape to men's experiences of oppression

> *involve several pitfalls: first, they generate discourses that often begin to resemble a series of 'excuses'; second, in unproblematically detailing the degradation of masculine pride as the reason for the propensity to rape, such discussion offers no critique of patriarchal frameworks that shape such 'pride'; and third, it unwittingly lays the blame for sexual violence at the door of those who were discriminated against.* (2006, 134)

The research

The study on which this chapter is based sought to fill a gap in knowledge about how men in DRC actually experience masculinity, and perceive humanitarian and development programmes dealing with sexual and gender-based violence and gender equality. Studies of masculinity in DRC in the past have tended to confine themselves to the 'rape as a weapon of war' narrative, and several studies have sought to explain soldiers' violent behaviour against women in this light. However, while these studies are important contributions to knowledge about male identity in DRC, a sole focus on the military places sexual and gender-based violence 'outside' the broader society from where it arose in the first place. This study therefore explicitly focused on the views of civilian men. It also adopted a focus on the economic strains and stresses affecting their ability to provide, raised above. The study looked to identify different trends in masculinity based on men's occupation and social status.

Gender roles and relations are situated in specific geographies, temporalities, and ethnographies. In view of DRC's vast territory and its considerable diversity, with approximately 450 different ethnic groups, this study cannot be representative of the entire country. Neither can it be perfectly representative of the entire Eastern region, which also includes the provinces of South Kivu and Maniema as well as Ituri district in Province Orientale. Despite their geographical proximity and shared historical background, they have evolved differently in the current context. Variations in the degree of military presence and armed conflict, infrastructure, development, and geopolitical constellations create a diversity of layered contexts. Therefore, the study does not aim to identify general truths about masculinities in the region, but to map out some dominant trends.

Field research took place during two cycles between February and June 2010. The sample consisted of 231 men and women from urban, semi-urban, and rural settings in North Kivu, taking into account ethnic and class differences. Interviewees' professions included teachers, state employees, businessmen, farmers, blue-collar workers, market women, and women lawyers. Three semi-structured questionnaires were developed: one for male focus groups, one for female focus groups, and one for in-depth interviews with men. The different social environments do not represent comparative elements, but were chosen so that the existence (not the degree or the nature) of difference in perceptions of masculinity could be researched. Single male focus group participants were chosen for in-depth interviews. Participants were able to express themselves in French, Swahili and, in the case of Butembo, also in the local language Kinande. In order not to disrupt the interviewing process, no notes were taken, but digital recordings were made and later transcribed. During a second cycle, participants were given an opportunity to discuss results.[1]

In the next four sections, key findings from the research are explored. All quotations come from research respondents.

Idealised masculinities versus social realities

On first sight, most of the ideals that exist about men are positive. Men are supposed to be providers and household heads, they should behave in non-violent ways towards household and community members, be responsible, good negotiators and problem solvers. All participants – both male and female – knew these ideals, though not all were willing or able to put them into practice, as they are tied to a number of other conditions, such as physical aptitude, ability to procreate, access to economic resources, knowledge and skills, influence, and decision-making power. Other factors are a functioning and intact family background, and good social networks. Participants generally felt that a man's income determines his position in society, but money does not make a man; and that the benefits from his good fortune should be shared in order to have meaning. A 'real man' generously lends his support to family and friends.

This expectation placed on men can amount to extreme pressure, as a state employee noted:

> *Once you find yourself in a good social situation, you are faced with the problem of the extended family. All members of the extended family tend to come to you with their difficulties and you have to bring a solution. So a real man must look to satisfy everybody.* (Interview, Goma, 5 February 2010)

Many of these supposed prerequisites for being a 'real man' do not withstand economic and social stresses, and are easily lost under unfavourable conditions. Their absence can be experienced as weakness and a loss of male identity, resulting in crisis. Masculinity is a constant enactment of power; it is nothing a man simply *has* or *is*, but rather a way of being that he needs to perform and assert. Men are expected to take on a leadership role based on delivery of assets and performance of dominant behaviour.

Male privilege is connected to responsibility – a 'real man' *earns* his position of authority through non-violent leadership and the capacity to provide, as the following statements show:

> *Saying that the man is the head means that the man has responsibilities, and not that he dominates his wife. There should be parity at 70%.* (Focus group, Butembo, 24 March 2010)

> *Boss is not a title, but a responsibility. See, you can't call anyone boss without responsibility, there must be practice. Someone must be a mulume, which in Kinande means both 'man' and 'a person who works hard'. This term can also be applied to women if they take the position of worker and provider.* (Focus group, Butembo, 24 March 2010)

However, strength can turn into violent behaviour, sexual prowess into sexual aggression, and public performances of generosity into abandonment of the private sphere, of family and household.

While the previous statement suggests that women can access male privilege by assuming male responsibilities, we shall see later that discontinuities between gender and gendered tasks create a high potential for conflict that must be addressed.

Women co-create ideals of masculinity through the expectations they place on men. Even if the women interviewed for this study had their own income, they still adhered to the model that the man should be the main breadwinner. From market women to highly educated lawyers and activists, female respondents stated that they expect men to guide, protect, and support them. Their idea of empowerment is to demand respect, rights, and liberties *within* a patriarchal system. Just like men, the women interviewed for this study frequently stated that 'a real man is not bossed around by his wife' and that 'if the woman submits herself to her husband there will be harmony in the household'.

Perceptions of masculinity did not vary significantly from one ethnic environment to the next, though some differences could be noted depending on the social environment (e.g. urban or rural). Different and even conflicting ideals of masculinity co-exist, creating layered identities. For example, the majority of respondents of the Hunde ethnic group in the semi-urban environment of Sake cited productive, responsible, and faithful masculinity as ideal. Openly polygamous unions are no longer considered practical in the modern context.

> *In our customs a man was respected when he had a lot of goats, grains and women. Such a man was called a musholai. Someone who only had one wife was less respected. Today, on the contrary, a polygamist is less respected, because he won't be able to manage his children and his field. Today, polygamy indicates a lack of responsibility.* (Focus group, Sake, 20 February 2010)

Nonetheless, cultural attitudes according to which men are encouraged to have several sex partners and to spend on alcohol and meat consumption continue to impact male identity, leading to a conflict in values. This conflict also emerged when respondents identified honesty and impartiality as crucial characteristics of a 'real man'; while at the same time contradicting this idea and depicting honest men as naïve, ridiculed, and unable to progress in life.

Wealth is considered as the most important prerequisite of a 'real man' in all social environments, yet the definition of what wealth encompasses varies. In an urban environment, this includes status symbols such as cars, luxury housing, and costly leisure activities. In the rural context, where farmers have lost their livelihoods due to the war, even the small income of a blue-collar worker is seen to constitute wealth.

Farming has come to be a stigmatised profession for two reasons. One is that youth dream of different, more prestigious occupations that are accessible only through higher education, but also because they do not appreciate the long-term labour investments connected to farming. Youth are more likely to seek rapid access to status symbols, prestigious leisure activities, and consumption. The other reason is ongoing insecurity that has turned farming into a highly unstable sector, arguably even more so than mining.

Farmers feel that they are no longer able to fulfil their responsibilities, as armed men often occupy their fields, steal their livestock, and render roads too insecure for trade. Rural Congolese are frequently displaced, leaving them unable to care for their families. Yet even when they stay close to their own fields, they frequently remain unable to access them. As a farmer in Kiwanja explained,

> *There are armed men who live in the forest. They impose taxes on you for working in your own field. When you refuse, access to your field is barred for any member of your family.* (Focus group, Kiwanja, 2 March 2010)

War-related trauma also plays a role in reducing male productivity, as many farmers testify to feeling discouraged, exhausted, and even emasculated. A farmer in Kiwanja underlined this in an interview when he said: 'before the war, I was a man' (interview, Kiwanja, 2 March 2010). According to the respondents, a man can lose his masculinity. It is thought that he then becomes automatically reduced to the status of a woman. Masculinity is thus regarded as something precious that must be maintained through continuous performance in order to preserve male dominance. As farming has turned into an increasingly precarious occupation, it has come to be considered low-level work that bears the stigma of weakness. As a result, farming is increasingly feminised, with the majority of tasks in production, processing, and marketing reserved for women. A growing number of young, rural men today refuse to participate in any form of fieldwork.

Economic poverty and political instability thus polarise gender roles at the same time that they limit opportunities to perform them. The homestead on which a family can be created and raised remains symbolic of achieving manhood, viewed as the seat of male power and social coherence. Such norms remain in place despite economic circumstances that make the acquisition of a homestead difficult or unlikely for many. As the following statements indicate, male respondents frequently linked lack of income to lack of personal value and male self-esteem:

> *In life, if you have nothing you are without value.* (Focus group, Sake, 20 February 2010)

> *Without possessions, a man has no meaning.* (Interview, Goma, 6 February 2010)

> *Without money, everybody leaves you. When you are poor you are not respected by anybody; not even by your own spouse. Money means everything to man.* (Interview, Kiwanja, 2 March 2010)

Just as men's lives are marked by contradictions between social realities and idealised masculinities, Congolese women experience conflict between cultural expectations and their actual roles in society. Idealised femininity is defined as mothering and caring, as well as subordinate, dependent, and sexually available. Women struggle to adhere to these ideals while at the same time acting as breadwinners. A female market vendor in Goma explained:

> *On one side they say to girls, it is bad if they don't study; on the other side, when they study, the boys are afraid of them. If a woman brings home nothing, they criticise her. If she earns, her husband hits her. So what is one to do?* (Focus group, Goma, 2 February 2010)

This quotation sustains the aforementioned theories of a surge in domestic violence due to the changing economic role of women. Women's changing economic and educational status motivates many women to demand more rights within the household and within society, while men hold on to their claims of authority as exemplified by this statement from a young motorbike chauffeur in Sake:

> *Men and women cannot be equal. For example, when a woman has studied and works and both bring home the salary, it is difficult for the woman to respect the man. The tradition that places woman below us helps us … to stay strong. Men would be damned if women were equal. Women could leave men, and they would not serve us.* (Interview, Sake, 22 February 2012)

According to this man, gender equality threatens to annihilate manhood. The less women depend on men economically, the more men seek to preserve female subordination by reverting to the concept of 'tradition'. Men must 'stay strong' and women must stay subservient. Maintenance of gendered hierarchies – and thus, male privilege – is at the base of men's reluctance to engage in housework, childcare, or fieldwork.

With their own gender identity at stake, men do not regard an economically successful wife as an asset, but as a nuisance. The privileged, such as upper-class entrepreneurs in Butembo, commonly insist that their wives stay at home:

> *If the husband allows his wife to work, she rises up and becomes more advanced than the man. When a woman works she does not respect her husband anymore.* (Focus group, Butembo, 24 March 2010)

A prevailing narrative to discredit women's empowerment is to connect female entrepreneurship to prostitution. Men expressed concerns that their wives sleep with superiors and co-workers. Female merchants were outright accused of trading sexual favours for food and lodging during their travels.

As the above results show, the conflict-laden relation between idealised masculinities and actual realities noted in international gender research exists also in the Congolese context. The particularity here is that social change, and the consequences of war, overlap. In Congo, men have not only lost their ability to provide, but as victims of violence and in not being able to protect their families, men's physical strength and general dominance is challenged. A few men are in a process of reshaping or re-attributing their ideas of masculinity, but the majority cling to the ideal of male dominance that places pressure on both women and men. However, men's beliefs, attitudes, and practices around sex roles are part of their identity and therefore not easily disposed of.

Most men appear not to understand how a change in gender relations can benefit them, and meet social transformation with resistance. Yet in reality, change is already happening, and men experience extreme stresses as they seek to defend their privilege.

However, some respondents also understood this dynamic and pointed out the need to transform gender relations.

How to become a man – gender education and social environment

Masculinities in North Kivu are not homogenous; different social groups choose different points of orientation. Social class or profession seems to play a paramount role in the way men enact masculinity and view it. Other factors are availability of economic resources, education, and exposure to the world outside of the immediate community. For example, some rural boys are still initiated in the traditional sense, with the rites of passage as an important defining factor in their male identity. For boys growing up in urban centres, the influence of mass media or a university education can have an equally important impact. However, some general trends have emerged and are discussed here.

In contemporary gender research, gender is indeed not perceived as an innate quality, but as constructed in the process of conditioning. This process is commonly called 'doing gender' and describes the interaction between individuals in which gender is presented, performed, and perceived. Gender is thus not a personal quality that is constructed in everyday life. One does not automatically inherit one's gender but he or she will adapt by means of education and socialisation: 'virtually any activity can be assessed as to its womanly or manly nature .. ., to "do" gender .. . is to engage in behaviour at the risk of gender assessment' (West and Zimmerman 1987, 136).

The Congolese interviewed in this study stressed the impact of education on individual gender identities. Male or female behaviour is acquired from a very young age, for example through dress code, games, and activities. Children are thus conditioned for their future roles:

> *When you see a little boy who constructs a playhouse, we say that he will be a man. These are the games that are appropriate for boys. Games of carrying around babies on the back are appropriate for girls.* (Interview, Sake, 22 February 2010)

> *You learn how to be a good boss from observation. I learned how to be a man through the influence of my father. What he taught me is that the woman comes after me and that she cannot surpass this rule.* (Focus group, Goma, 2 February 2010)

Considering the importance of early childhood conditioning in the raising of men, the war-induced lack of steady family structures is particularly worrying. Boys often grow up in fractured or dysfunctional families due to the impact of war, urbanisation, and/ or poverty. Younger and middle-aged male respondents were critical of their experiences growing up in Eastern DRC. They reported that they often grew up without positive male role models, as the lion's share of rearing and educating children is placed on women's shoulders, with fathers frequently absent, distant, or violent.

Respondents depicted the social environment (extended family, neighbours, and the surrounding community) as an extension of the immediate household, where a boy can observe and learn from the examples of others. A crucial factor in 'becoming men' is the traditional setting where boys passively participate in the family and village councils, the *barza*. Older men believe that youth should consult the *barza* as a framework for education, local culture, and non-violent conflict resolution. Rural respondents pointed towards the importance of this setting, though they also noted that young men are losing interest in this form of education.

From a standpoint of gender equality, the *barza* is a mixed blessing. On the one hand, it offers a means for male youth to stay in touch with their cultural roots, internalise social values, and receive guidance in forming their identity. On the other hand, the ideas of masculinity and femininity promoted in the *barza* are often dichotomous and hierarchical. Indeed, exclusion and subordination of women are central themes in the *barza* setting, and play an equally important role during circumcision and initiation rites.

Social change undermines hierarchies within communities. Young men expressed tensions over the sacrifices inherent in either foregoing education for rural work, which will likely result in an inability to gain employment, or going to university, which disconnects them further from the way of life their parents lead. Young men are also affected by internal displacement. War and insecurity wash them into the safer urban centres, where they often remain but have little access to the labour market or to familiar structures.

Hierarchical traditions expect youth to be subordinate as long as they have no family of their own. As an unmarried youth in Butembo explained,

> *You can be boss some place, but not in your family. The others, who are married, will not respect you and your business. A bachelor is not part of the family counsel.* (Focus group, Butembo, 25 March 2010)

A bachelor can make financial contributions to family members in need only in his father's name, and he cannot speak for himself unless he seeks the support of other youth. It appears that parents do not understand that the consequences of a rapidly changing environment, as well as the war experience, make youth mature faster. Outside the home, boys in urban centres gain recognition for fulfilling new masculine ideals influenced by mass media, and may be excellent rappers, break-dancers, or athletes. Others may not be married, but hold several degrees and already run their own small business. Yet in the framework of their family structures they have no voice of their own.

The values elders try to communicate are often of little real meaning to young men trying to cope with the expectations placed on them. Farming does not pay well any more, and is not a respected profession, and young men seek other strategies to provide the income they need for recognition and respect. They are often willing to sacrifice values such as honesty or hard work for material gain. As a male student in Kiwanja admitted, 'having work is the most important thing for man. Even if a man behaves badly in order to get rich' (focus group, Kiwanja, 2 March 2010).

Formal education is seen as consolidating male power because it provides skills, knowledge, and opportunities. Likewise, girls' participation in academic education is perceived as a threat to existing gender norms, as educated women are frequently accused of being 'wanton', 'bossy' and 'hard to manage'. While education can be empowering to girls, the education system in DRC often places them at a disadvantage due to the widespread sexual abuse of girl students, a phenomenon that the Congolese nicknamed STGs – 'sexually transmitted grades'. With regard to gender education, proliferation of STGs conditions young people to believe that women must make themselves sexually available to their superiors in order to succeed. Similarly, the value of formal education for boys has frequently come into question.

As the following quotations show, some Congolese men believe that modern education can have a negative impact on their sons:

> *With what we earn from our fields, we paid the school fees for those same boys who now say that they are afraid of fieldwork. Education makes them corrupted* [the term that was used here in Swahili was *'kuaribisha'*, which literally translates into 'damaged']. *Your own children steal from you these days.* (Focus group, Beni, 26 March 2010)

> *Boys who have gone to university become egotists; they want what they don't have. Look at those leaders: they are all intellectuals, but they are all corrupt.* (Focus group, Butembo, 24 March 2010)

Masculinity and violence

In Eastern DRC, the most visible – and harmful – version of masculinity is the militarised variety. Nonetheless, the military experience was perceived by men in the research as disempowering, as it involves harsh living conditions, erratic income, and pressure to commit acts of violence. Combatants are able to achieve some economic and social gains that are inaccessible to many, but their supposed 'power' comes at a price. Joining a military group is also connected to social sanctions: 'I have never seen a family that respects a soldier, they will say of him that he has become a bandit' (interview, Goma, 4 February 2010). Students in Beni stated that the military was 'only for the desperate', meaning men from resource-poor backgrounds who lack education and social networks. Respondents also were aware that once men have become associated with the military, reintegration is a daunting task, as ex-combatants are stigmatised and often live with trauma. Not surprisingly, the young Congolese interviewed for this study would prefer to neither join the national army, nor a rebel group.

However, the distinctions between civilian and military cultures can no longer be so clearly defined in the context of a region that has experienced nearly two decades of ongoing warfare and is home to numerous armed groups. Combatants often operate in their home region, and many civilians are either ex-combatants or family members of combatants. Militarisation shapes not just the masculinity of soldiers, but also of civilian men in the regions torn apart by warfare. Forced migration, violence, and trauma all challenge notions of manhood. This is why it is difficult to draw the line between 'military violence' and 'civilian violence'.

This holds especially true for sexual and gender-based violence. Rape is intricately linked to war and conflict, both as a weapon of war and as an effect of social disruption that persists among civilians well after conflict has been terminated. In Eastern DRC, sexual coercion is in part normalised, and views of male sexuality as aggressive and forceful are used to justify rape. Even though it is focused exclusively on the military, Baaz and Sterns' groundbreaking study 'Why Do Soldiers Rape?' exposes the profound sense of entitlement to sex among Congolese men (2009, 506). This attitude is not created within the military, but is embedded into the broader context of society.

While traditional hierarchies have been transformed and now co-exist with other structures, the idea that power is connected to sexual prowess has been preserved. As one female lawyer in Butembo explained: 'according to tradition, a chief must have several women. But now everyone who is some kind of boss thinks he needs several women' (focus groups, Butembo, 24 March 2010). In addition, views regarding women's bodies as a tradable commodity encourage men to demand sex for services, goods and favours, and discourage them from valuing consent from a female partner.

Sexual violence is not isolated, but co-exists with other forms of gender-based violence. Female respondents reported domestic violence as a general rule. They related this to women lacking economic assets, their resulting low social status, as well as to male dominance. Violence needs to be seen in this broad context and also as emerging from the dynamics of violence among men, including social and economic inequality, impunity from prosecution, and the need to preserve privilege.

Respondents named the state as the primary source of violence in DRC, and identified it as a major obstacle to creating a society based on mutual respect. Due to corruption and impunity, state institutions are seen to be at the root of sexual exploitation, exploitation of labour, inter-ethnic tensions and, very prominently, land grabbing and cattle theft. In many cases, agents of the state not only enable, but also enact violent masculinities themselves, ranging from arbitrary taxation, to rape and extortion through armed forces or police. The common narrative is that these crimes are committed by the wealthy and influential against the resource-poor and under-privileged, as ministers of religion in Sake expressed:

> Those who rule do not accept advice and do as they see fit. Those who have capital believe that they are more elevated than those that do not have means. From the governor of the province to the principal of the school, no one respects the opinion of others ... Only those that have money obtain justice.

> It's the public authorities that are the most violent. You see, this is why most police chiefs prefer being posted to the hills of the interior. There, they are free

> *to impose a whole goat as a fine for nothing. Another characteristic of public violence is the proliferation of tax, even taxes that do not exist. And in conflict over land only those that have money get justice.* (Focus group, Sake, 18 February 2010)

State employees interviewed for this study depicted themselves as both victims and perpetrators in a system that is built on corruption and exaction. A state official in Goma compared his employer to an irresponsible father who does not care for his children, indirectly forcing them to become thieves. Though it is true that erratic payment of salaries promotes corruption, including bribery and extortion, this has also become a lifestyle for many.

Humanitarian and development interventions as seen by men

A range of different interventions was discussed in the research, including gender sensitisation, training on women's rights, community development focusing on livelihoods, work to support the survivors of sexual and gender-based violence, and programmes offered by churches to focus on men and violent masculinities.

Gender sensitisation and women's rights training

The research could not confirm that efforts to sensitise men to gender equality have the desired impact on changing their attitudes towards women. Most efforts appear to be one-sided and impractical, from the viewpoint of Congolese men:

> *You hear a lot about women and the rights of women, but about men, there is very little about men.* (Interview, Goma, 4 February 2010)

> *Men are always accused. We have never seen an NGO [non-government organisation] that does work on men.* (Focus group, Goma, 5 February 2010)

> *Everything is said as if men were condemned; this is why some will even turn off their radios.* (Focus group, Kiwanja, 3 March 2010)

Sensitisation programmes fail to recognise men's specific interests and needs, offering little information on alternative ways of affirming male identity. Men feel put on the defendant's bench, as most sensitisations are based on the assumption that men are the perpetrators, not the victims, of violence. While it is true that a great majority of individuals suffering from sexual and gender-based violence are female, a single focus on this group renders the equality aspect of programmes obsolete.

An increase in knowledge about women's rights does not automatically lead to a change in attitudes and behaviours among the population. Men will believe and do what appears to secure them with their share of the hegemonic dividend. For example, NGO sensitisations on HIV/AIDS promote abstinence, faithfulness, and/or protection. This is bound to conflict with dominant ideals of masculinity in DRC, where men are informally entitled to multiple sex partners – commonly called *second bureau, third bureau,* and so on.[2] Where sexual prowess signifies male strength, it may actually gain importance when men experience disempowerment in other areas of their lives. Suggestions to limit male sexual activity or pleasure may then be perceived as a threat to male identity and met with rejection. So how can men be convinced to abandon the quest for male dominance?

Comprehensive gender training would address these very difficult issues, together with others, including the issue of men's sexual violence against men, and women's role in preventing future sexual and gender-based violence by socialising coming generations. It would focus on children's education at the household level, a domain that is mainly reserved for women.

Community development and livelihoods

It seems that the best way to talk about gender equality with men is to integrate it into a broader discourse of community development. The great majority of respondents praised NGOs that provide practical, hands-on information, for example on community hygiene, nutrition, income-generating activities, and savings. A married respondent pointed out that his priority was being able to provide and care for his family, because this in itself would make him 'a good man'. If humanitarian interventions focus on meeting men's needs to perform as providers, then men are more likely to lend an open ear to concerns around sexual and gender-based violence and gender equality.

However, male respondents strongly criticised interventions aimed at women's socioeconomic empowerment that offer training and microcredit exclusively to women, often without the consent of their male family members. In view of the previously discussed results, promoting women's economic activities without combating men's unemployment or even responding to their feelings of disempowerment is a recipe for male resistance against 'gender-sensitive programmes'.

The research suggests that microcredit should be made available to both men and women, and economic programme components should be integrated with awareness campaigns and gender training in order to associate economic progress with gender equality. In order to respond to men's practical needs, gender training should be multi-dimensional, integrating gender issues with life skills.

Support to women survivors of violence

As discussed at the start of the chapter, humanitarian and development programmes tend to work with women survivors of violence. Men in our research stressed that they, too, were victims of wartime and other forms of violence, and needed protection, as well as psychosocial and medical help. While it cannot be denied that men are less vulnerable to sexual violence than women, they are also affected by the overall climate of violence and impunity in DRC. Some men are also in need of support as survivors of sexual violence, even though they are in a minority.

NGO workers were also accused of hypocrisy around sexual concerns: 'during the day you sensitise people on HIV/AIDS, but in the evening you are looking for prostitutes because you have money' (focus group, Sake, 20 February 2010). This statement was mirrored by an NGO worker in Kiwanja, who confirmed that 'humanitarians enjoy a high esteem in the community and there you can have a lot of girlfriends' (focus group, Kiwanja, 4 March 2010).

More generally, humanitarian and development interventions on the part of NGOs are seen as problematic. The strong presence of international donors and NGOs in parts of Eastern DRC has created an economic disequilibrium, where NGO workers are among the few that have access to wealth and prestige. As a result, most university graduates thrive to find employment in the humanitarian sector. Nonetheless, respondents believed that NGO workers – and also clerics – are part of the general context of corruption, favouritism, and sexual exploitation. As a bible student in Butembo explained, 'NGOs can have bad influence because some youth give up all they are doing just to have a place in an NGO. Yet to get there, you need to either pay [a bribe] or sleep with somebody' (focus group, Butembo, 23 March 2010).

A farmer in Sake stated:

> *often, NGO aid does not reach the population because those that distribute it are corrupted and they give only to their families and friends. Or the pastor receives something and he gives it only to the members of his parish.* (Focus group, Sake, 20 February 2010)

Against this backdrop of negative discourse on NGOs, human rights and women's rights, and gender equality, are concepts at risk of being perceived by the population as foreign import of little value, or even destructive to local societies, as evidenced by the words of a Kiwanja nurse: 'the Europeans have their traditions and we have ours. They want to destroy our traditions' (focus group interview, Kiwanja, 4 March 2010).

Work with men on violent masculinities

The importance of a focus on prevention of future violence – including multi-dimensional training and sensitisation that is specifically tailored to men's needs – was evidenced by the work of certain churches, discussed in our research. Churches are part of civil society, and many clerics and pastors are also activists. Church-based programmes are of particular pertinence to the rural context, as men here are more active in church. In the urban setting of Goma, respondents frequently claimed that going to church was a 'woman's thing'. Yet even in an urban setting, the social services offered by churches can have a far-reaching impact on men's attitudes and behaviours.

Some churches have created special divisions that deal with men and family issues. They communicate Christian ideals of how to be good men, such as respectful and non-violent behaviour towards others. They organise seminar series that deal with different issues and allow men to communicate in a safe setting. Issues range from family finances to sexuality, allowing participants to broaden their horizon in an integrated way, without a singular focus on topics related to gender. In Butembo, the Mouvement des Jeunes pour Christ (Youth Movement for Christ) has responded to the growing number of young bachelors, a group particularly at risk of failed masculinities, by creating a radio series on getting married on a low budget. The series includes hands-on information on how to start a pig-raising business, save and invest, identify a future spouse, negotiate the bride price with parents, and keep celebration costs down. This training understands the priorities of Congolese youth and their need to experience success and self-worth.

Respondents pointed out that mass events and radio messages alone are not sufficient to induce behaviour change. They suggested that sensitisation should take place in a *barza*-style setting, to allow them to use this intimate setting to weigh different options and discuss issues with other men whom they know and trust. Where a message needs to reach a wider public, male activists could be sent door-to-door, giving men a chance to communicate directly. Finally, respondents stressed the importance of good examples, as people in Eastern DRC are likely to imitate those individuals that are the most successful with their life strategies. If advocates for gender equality actually live by the standards that they communicate, then they are more likely to influence their peers.

Conclusions

As this chapter has illustrated, the hegemonic model of masculinity has negative effects on both sexes. It places extreme pressure on men, and has a high potential for social disruption. Men's relations with women and other men are often marked by stress and hostility. Intergenerational conflicts and erosion of values are an omnipresent discourse in people's narratives about their lives. The cultural shifts that result from changing gender norms and roles lead to resistance from men that can erupt into violent backlash. Therefore, focusing on women alone cannot solve the root causes of sexual and gender-based violence.

The study bears testimony to a wide array of positive forms of masculinity that impact Congolese men's understanding of themselves. Congolese men and women are integrated into, and influenced by, social networks that form their identity and providethem with a framework of knowledge, beliefs, values, rights, and obligations. Different social groups choose different points of orientation. However, general discourse on gender issues and the main problems highlighted here were very similar across different ethnic settings and social environments.

While numerous male advocates for gender equality have been encountered in Eastern DRC, significant opposition remains. The advantages men gain from inequalities, including material benefits and power, may lead them to defend male supremacy on the grounds of culture, biology, or religion. Yet the more anti-equality perspectives are challenged, the more importance they seem to gain. Anti-equality perspectives can also adapt rapidly to changing conditions – they may seem to disappear on one level, just to resurface in another area of society.

An important issue that emerged from the study was the lack of good governance and the fact of a failing state as a major stumbling block to peace building. Congolese citizens today possess poor civic education, and do not see themselves as agents of politico-economic change. As a result, they focus on survival tactics such as fraud, traffic of influence, and bribery, which in turn creates new conflicts. In addition, armed groups have *carte blanche* to terrorise the population, as both the government and the international community fail to provide grassroots communities with security. Against this backdrop of social inequality, many men dismiss gender equality as a low priority issue or reject it entirely.

This study did not intend to show how Congolese men 'really behave' or what may be the 'true reasons' behind violent acts. Nor did it try to justify male violence. Rather, it attempted to explain how everyday realities unsettle dominant narratives about Congolese men. It further highlighted the interdependent and interactive nature of gender, showing that the whole is more than the sum of its parts, as gender equality can only be reached by consensus, not through competition or antagonism. As respondents have pointed out, humanitarian interventions in Eastern DRC often fail to value positive masculinities and support men in their desire to enact them. Therefore, men regard most interventions towards gender equality as illegitimate and irrelevant.

Programmes to combat sexual and gender-based violence should focus on the broader context of gender relations and social inequality with a holistic perspective. Interventions should focus on both victims and perpetrators, and aim at transcending hegemonic masculinity. Men need to understand the advantages of gender equality for their own lives. If men believe that hegemonic masculinity is their best choice, then interventions aimed at transcending violence and transforming relationships should present men with different options and with ways to pursue these options. This should include training on non-violent ways of conflict transformation and communication, as well as enabling men to engage in partnerships with women that are built on respect instead of hierarchy and power.

Given the weight of gender roles, transformation needs to be a conscious process that can only be guided, but not pushed or pre-determined. Any intervention aimed at increasing gender equality within Congolese communities should engage communities in long-term, proactive dialogue. In co-operation with local leaders, communities should be supported to (re)shape their own, positive models of gender equality for their current context through participatory action research and community debates. In order to capacitate communities for implementation, they should be provided with civic education, and supported in efforts to lobby state authorities to create an environment of good governance and security.

Notes

1. The database of notes and transcripts was then coded using a software tool for computer-assisted qualitative data analysis. Deductive codes were developed and assigned to the data according to four key topics (discussed in the following section). The emerging matrices allowed for cross-case analysis by theme.
2. The French Secret service was divided into a first and second bureau from the 1880s to the 1940s. But the term describing an extra-marital affair was made famous by Congolese singer Lokombe in his 2007 song 'Deuxieme Bureau Nganda'. A lot of people say Franco Luambo Makiadi, another singer, also has something to do with making the term famous but he died much earlier. I find it quite fitting in a context where many have a primary occupation and other, unofficial business on the side.

References

Baaz, Maria Eriksson and Maria Stern (2009) 'Why do soldiers rape? Gender, violence and sexuality in the DRC armed forces', *International Studies Quarterly* 53(4): 495–518

Barker, Gary and Christine Ricardo (2005) 'Young Men and the Construction of Masculinity in Sub-Saharan Africa: Implications for HIV/AIDS, Conflict, and Violence', World Bank Social Development Papers: Conflict Prevention & Reconstruction, Paper No. 26, Washington, DC: World Bank

Dolan, Chris (2010) 'War is Not yet Over – Community Perceptions of Sexual Violence and its Underpinnings in Eastern DRC', London: International Alert

Johnson, Kirsten, Jennifer Scott, Bigy Rughita, Michael Kisielewski, Jana Astor, Ricardo Ong and Lynn Lawry (2010) 'Association of sexual violence and human rights violations with physical and mental health in territories of the Eastern Democratic Republic of the Congo', *Journal of the American Medical Association* 304(5): 553–63

Moffett, Helen (2006) '"These women, they force us to rape them": rape as narrative of social control in post-Apartheid South Africa', *Journal of Southern African Studies* 32(1): 129–44

Ray, Sam and Lauren Heller (2009) *Peril or Protection: The Link Between Livelihoods and Gender-based Violence in Displacement Settings*, New York: Women's Refugee Commission

Teasdale, Brent, Eric Silver, and John Monahan (2006) 'Gender, threat/control-override delusions and violence', *Law and Human Behavior* 30(6): 649–58

Turner, Simon (1999) 'Angry Young Men in Camps: Gender, Age and Class Relations Among Burundian Refugees in Tanzania', Working Paper No. 9,

Geneva: UNHCR, PDES West, Candace and Don H. Zimmerman (1987) 'Doing gender', *Gender & Society* 1987(1): 125–51

About the author

Desiree Lwambo is Senior Gender Advisor to HEAL, a Congolese NGO with a focus on sexual and gender-based violence that is based in Goma, DRC. She is deployed through the EED/Civil Peace Service, a programme which supports civil society institutions in post-conflict regions. Email: zwanck@gmail.com.

CHAPTER 5

Sympathetic advocates: male parliamentarians sharing responsibility for gender equality

Sonia Palmieri

Abstract

Gender mainstreaming, as a strategy that aims to achieve gender equality across institutions, does not work without the assistance of men. There has been a strategic shift in emphasis over the past decade from women's issues to those concerning gender equality. Underpinning this shift is a change in focus from women exclusively, to one on both men and women in working towards mutually beneficial social and economic development. The institution of parliament is no exception. Changing social values and the increasing gender sensitivity of younger men have resulted in stronger partnerships between men and women parliamentarians on gender equality. Using qualitative data from the Inter-Parliamentary Union and the International Knowledge Network of Women in Politics (iKNOW Politics), this paper presents some of the strategies that have encouraged men to come on board the gender equality project. Strategies uncovered include men's support for the legislative initiatives of women as well as men's co-sponsorship of gender equality legislation; the appointment of men as chairs or members of gender equality bodies of the parliament (that is, bodies designed to mainstream gender equality concerns in the work of the parliament); and inviting men to participate in public activities and outreach, such as public consultations and celebratory activities for International Women's Day.

Key words: gender equality; parliament; male parliamentarians

Introduction

> *Among men parliamentarians, even if with some of our colleagues it starts with sympathetic support, it's turning into a belief in these issues, more than just being sympathetic. It's a belief that this is how it should be.* (Male parliamentarian, Jordan, 2009)

It is almost 20 years since the United Nations (UN) established gender mainstreaming as the global strategy for promoting gender equality through what

http://dx.doi.org/10.3362/9781780448664.005

became known as the Beijing Platform for Action. Following the Fourth World Conference on Women in Beijing and the launch of this Platform, the concept of gender equality, understood as 'equal rights, responsibilities and opportunities of women and men and girls and boys' (UN 2001, 1), became one of the cornerstone development objectives of the UN and, by association, its member states.

The importance of men to both the project of gender equality and the strategy of gender mainstreaming cannot be overstated. A major consequence of the discourse shift from 'women's issues' to 'gender equality' was that men became implicated not only in the cause of gender inequality, but also in providing for its solution. Moreover, there is now an understanding that gender equality aims not simply to improve the lives of women and girls, but to ensure that policies do not adversely affect men and boys. 'Gender equality implies that the interests, needs and priorities of both women and men are taken into consideration, recognising the diversity of different groups of women and men' (UN 2001, 1). It is, in this sense, a societal objective.

More importantly, however, the inclusion of men in the project of gender equality is essential because, as R.W. Connell writes, 'any reform agenda requires resources ... and men ... control most of the resources required to implement women's claims for justice' (2003, 3). The achievement of gender equality, therefore, has certain pre-requisites. In the first instance, it requires cultural and social change; that is, men's and boys' acceptance of the importance and benefit of a gender-equal society. For R.W. Connell, this is more likely to occur when '[men] can see positive benefits for themselves and the people in their lives" (*ibid.*, 4). Second, and perhaps contingent on the first, achieving gender equality requires institutional change.

While the role of governments in addressing gender equality has been a focus for gender mainstreaming, less considered is the role of parliament. Political scientists involved in the field of gender and development have researched and written on the issues of women in formal politics and government, the aim of achieving gender parity in decision-making bodies at all levels of the state, and the challenges inherent in mainstreaming a gender perspective across the work of government (e.g. Goetz 1995). Parliaments are essential in holding governments to account on all policy areas, and as the Inter-Parliamentary Union (IPU) has suggested, are well-placed to play a lead role in the promotion of gender equality, not only by holding themselves up as role models for other institutions by ensuring that women are adequately represented, and that their rules, practices, and processes are gender-sensitive, but also by initiating and passing legislation that ensures gender equality across all policy spheres (Ballington 2008). In legislating on issues such as marriage, employment practices, health, and education, parliaments are active participants in the construct of gender relations.

However, the gender and development literature has not to date tended to focus on the role of men in parliament in addressing gender equality, despite the fact that there are good reasons to do so. R.W. Connell has argued,

> *Though ... gender policies mainly address women, in virtually every policy area ... [that] affects women, it also affects men. 'Mainstream' policies (e.g. in economic affairs, security) are often substantially about men without acknowledging the fact, and may also have important effects on gender relations.* (2003, 24)

Analysing the role of men in parliament from a gender perspective, and focusing in particular on their contribution to promoting gender equality, is therefore an important research priority. It gives rise to a number of questions. What are parliaments doing to ensure men play a role in promoting gender equality? How have women encouraged sympathetic men to support change for gender equality? What are some of the challenges and the successes? What else is required to ensure that the promotion of gender equality is not kept solely in the hands of women?

This chapter sets out to address these questions. First, it outlines the institutional context in which men and women members of parliament (MPs) work, by looking at some of the academic research on gendered institutions. This serves to reiterate the argument that parliamentarians work very much within the confines of institutional rules and norms that have been historically shaped by men. For parliament, as an institution, to more readily accept responsibility for the promotion of gender equality, change must therefore be accepted, endorsed, and advocated by the men who continue to make up the majority of parliamentarians in most countries.

This chapter examines and discusses qualitative data compiled from two sources: first, primary research conducted by the IPU between 2009 and 2011 in a project involving the author (Palmieri 2011)[1]; and second, an e-discussion organised by the International Knowledge Network of Women in Politics (iKNOW Politics) in 2009.[2] The quotations included in this chapter come from these two sources. I outline some of the positive examples of men parliamentarians taking action on gender equality, either on their own, or in alliance with women. The intention here is to promote and highlight positive examples of men's gender equality advocacy, so that others may follow suit. Strategies uncovered include men's support for the legislative initiatives of women and men's co-sponsorship of gender equality legislation; the appointment of men as chairs or members of gender equality bodies of the parliament (that is, bodies designed to mainstream gender equality concerns in the work of the parliament); and the involvement of men in public activities and outreach, such as public consultations and celebratory activities for International Women's Day.

Parliament as a gendered institution

In the literature on women and politics, there has been an increasing acceptance of the argument that parliaments, as institutions, are not gender-neutral bodies, but rather are embedded with cultural 'assumptions, practices, norms, belief systems', that have historically equated the norm with the masculine (Duerst-Lahti and Kelly 1995, 19).

Men have had the opportunity to shape the norms, assumptions, rules, and practices that today constitute the institution of parliament, because men have historically dominated the political sphere.

Power imbalances between men and women, or gender inequality, within this masculinised organisation are therefore perpetuated. Gendered processes

> ... *operate on many institutional levels, from the open and explicit to more subtle forms that are submerged in organisational decisions, even those that appear to have nothing to do with gender. They include the way men's influence is embedded in rules and procedures, in formal job definitions and in functional roles.* (Wacjman 1998, 41)

In parliament, examples of 'open and explicit' processes which favour male participation in parliament could be the late-night sitting hours that benefit the working pattern of men, who traditionally do not have to attend to family responsibilities after work. They could be the common appointment of men to defence and security, or budgetary portfolio positions, and to senior positions including ministers, and committee chairs. 'More subtle' processes could be playing out in the language and behaviour accepted in parliamentary discourse, which might typically be described as adversarial.

This inequality is often intangible, and has therefore been traditionally disregarded. Indeed, Azza Karam and Joni Lovenduski have argued that such 'institutional masculinity' has been so entrenched as to be 'taken for granted' (2005, 188). Thus, for parliaments to genuinely assume their responsibility to advocate and make change in favour of gender equality, the very institution requires significant change – that must, as suggested earlier, be endorsed by the men who continue to dominate the institution.

The call for change in parliaments

While there continues to be some resistance, there are external and internal factors that have been influential in promoting positive change. Changing social values, including the increasing acceptance of women's place in the public sphere and the changing nature of other workplaces as a result of women's increased participation have, over time, had a strong impact on parliaments. Specifically, the emergence of family-friendly or flexible employment policies and practices have had a real impact: marking, as R.W. Connell has written, 'the recognition by employers and governments of the importance of the work/home relationship' (2003, 15). This, in turn, has changed the attitudes of younger male parliamentarians now entering the institution.

Changing social values

While societies may differ across the globe, social values have tended to evolve universally. An important indicator of this change is the general acceptance of women's place in the public sphere, something unheard of at the beginning of the 20th century. Whatever the reason for this change – and there are many, including the role of feminist movements, the use of affirmative action measures including reserved seats and candidate quotas, globalisation, and the changing structure of state economies – women's participation in politics has been a positive and welcome outcome.

Parliamentarians surveyed by the IPU referred to changing social values as a primary reason for men's increased involvement in raising gender equality issues. Some noted that the electorate no longer tolerated women's absence from politics. Indeed, in some parliaments, it was seen as 'politically correct not to oppose gender initiatives' (female parliamentarian, Chile).

> I think that, in principle, men are more careful now. I think they are as chauvinistic as always, but there is something: in public, they are careful. They choose words well. If they tell a joke with a double entendre, they look around to see if there's a woman nearby. (Female parliamentarian, Argentina)

> Even though my party is conservative, when we talk about ... sexual discrimination, male MPs are reluctant to voice their opposition. This is because of female voters ... Male MPs tend to agree with these decisions, even though they don't really want to ... A good example was the anti-trafficking bill. Deep inside, many male MPs would not agree with the bill, but if they say no, then that means that they are FOR prostitution, so they had no choice but to say yes, and voted for the bill. (Female parliamentarian, Republic of Korea)

Tactics exist by which male parliamentarians can be 'persuaded' to give greater attention to gender equality issues. The media can also be used as a 'pressure tactic' on male parliamentarians; as a means by which the wider electorate could be alerted to men's reluctance to support gender equality initiatives:

> We tell them, if you don't approve this, we will tell the media that these congressmen, these members of commissions, don't want to approve the bills and are against women and against children ... We look for pressure tactics – healthy ones, of course – to achieve this goal. (Female parliamentarian, Peru)

Some MPs also referred to specific strategies employed by civil society groups to ensure that men reflected and endorsed these changing social values.

> Of course, there are men that you can hardly ever change, but they are the minority, and they are not courageous enough to speak out because they will

be the odd ones out. But we have 'enrolled' the others, as I call it. We have enrolled them as gender-sensitive men; they are now part of the whole gender framework. The civil society movement put a lot of pressure on them and is also pushing all parties to raise the bar within their ranks. (Female parliamentarian, Namibia)

We had a feminist group who was advocating in society for equal pay and for women to be appointed as heads of boards. The group nominated parliamentarians who they felt were the best in terms of advocating for women's rights. They nominated two guys and one of them is in our party. So there is a real awareness that if we want to progress we have to work together [with men]. (Female parliamentarian, Netherlands)

Young men and work–life balance

Another factor has been the increasing participation of younger men in parliament. The data suggest that younger men are less likely to hold traditional views of women's participation in the public sphere. In addition, they tend to accept their own responsibilities more when it comes to raising children and assisting with domestic chores, and support women's right to work outside this domestic sphere and not to carry sole responsibility for child care.

Younger men ... are much more responsive to gender issues. For example, in my own party, there are a few state chairmen who support the 30 per cent quota. While you have to make sure that the rest of the membership will agree with them, at least these [young men] *are willing to state that they understand that having more women can actually help the party's image. Having men on board does mean that they can help in persuading other men too.* (Female parliamentarian, Malaysia)

Among men you sometimes hear, informally, that women [because of their personal choice on how to combine their professional and private life] *are not taking politics seriously enough when they 'leave parliament early to attend to school meetings, etc.'. The younger parliamentarians – men as well – however, are more open to such choices. It is felt that the* [traditional] *parliamentary lifestyle has its limitations nowadays. There is a life outside politics. The cleavage between young men and women is narrower than the one across generations.* (Female parliamentarian, Belgium)

I do fear that a lot of men are less understanding of their wives' hectic schedules ... [but] *I do see some changes when it comes to the younger generation. I can assume that some men 'stand by their woman' so to say, but more so with the new generation than the older one.* (Female parliamentarian, Belgium)

Men's involvement in gender equality legislation

Simply by virtue of their greater numbers in parliament, women have had to command the support of men when initiating and passing gender equality legislation. This was well articulated by a woman MP in Viet Nam:

> *I expect to see more MPs participate more on gender issues in the National Assembly. In the parliament, when we address issues relating to the elderly, we receive support from men, but if we call for their active participation on gender issues, it does not come so easily. When a gender issue is [only] addressed by women it gives the impression of not being strong enough. We need men to be involved to make a stronger impact.* (Female parliamentarian, Viet Nam)

The IPU research uncovered a number of strategies to encourage men to step up as gender equality advocates. As men MPs noted themselves, they are often supportive of legislative initiatives made by women.

> *Being a new member of parliament, when opportunities arise, I never fail to participate and marshal agreements in favour of gender issues. Equality in education and employment opportunities are my favourite subjects on which I have expressed views.* (Male parliamentarian, India)

> *I do not only participate in the debate on [gender] issues but I also lobby the relevant ministers.* (Male parliamentarian, Mauritania)

> *I participated in the general debate relating to and affecting women's issues and strongly advocated for 33 per cent representation for women.* (Male parliamentarian, India)

However, encouraging men to do more than support women who challenge gender inequality and actually lead on this agenda can be difficult. Emphasising the wider social benefits of gender equality and avoiding the discourse of 'women's issues' has proven a useful approach. In Rwanda, the Forum of Women Parliamentarians (FFRP) deliberately couched the debate on gender-based violence in terms of it being a social (rather than a specifically women's) problem that impeded development. As one female MP noted during the debate on the legislation:

> *I would like to ask my fellow MPs not to take this law as if it is a women's thing, even though in many cases women are the ones suffering from gender-based violence. But this law will protect the whole Rwandan society.*

In this way, the FFRP was able to secure male co-sponsorship of the bill, an effective strategy that contributed to its ultimate passage.

The combination of male support and technical expertise was essential in drafting a bill related to abortion in Uruguay. The Special Commission on Gender and Equality (CEGE) of the Uruguayan Parliament asked that the bills be sent to the Commission on Public Health and Social Assistance (CSPAS), a committee composed of men who had previously been doctors, and who were more sympathetic to the decriminalisation of abortion.

Having the new measure drafted by CSPAS rather than CEGE was strategic for two reasons: first, since most of the CSPAS members were members of the scientific community, the bill would carry more weight and have greater legitimacy in the eyes of other members of Parliament and the public than if it were approved by a commission consisting entirely of women, many of whom identified themselves as feminists; and second, decriminalisation of abortion is an issue that divided the women who were members of the CEGE. Putting CSPAS in charge of drafting the new reproductive health bill, therefore avoided polarising positions within the commission and symbolised the unity of women politicians. (Niki Johnson, University of the Republic Uruguay, cited in iKNOW Politics 2009, 15)

According to Gisela Garzo´n of the Inter-American Development Bank, men's support for quota legislation in Peru was secured because the legislation was considered 'non-partisan' (cited in iKNOW Politics 2009, 12). Putting politics aside also appears to have been a key strategy in Mexico, where, as political scientist Niki Johnson describes, women MPs lobbied men 'in other parties':

The women legislators worked to persuade their male colleagues, not in their own parties, but in the other parties, on the grounds that it would be more difficult for the men to ignore or deny a request from women outside their own parties. (cited in iKNOW Politics 2009, 13)

When consensus across parties is required, as was the case in passing a bill related to sexual offences in Kenya, direct consultation with the strongest opponents appears to have been a successful strategy:

... members of the Kenyan Women's Parliamentary Caucus continued discussions in the House, identifying opposition and meeting with these members directly ... On the day the bill was presented, it was seconded by Hon Mutula Kilonzo, who in his remarks cited the detrimental effects of sexual violence, to a hushed audience. He was followed by another male MP who also gave facts and figures collated mainly by the women's civil society groups. Although there was opposition during the debates, eventually, the bill passed. (Nyambura Ngugi, UNIFEM, cited in iKNOW Politics 2009, 13)

It is also the case, however, that men have assumed the responsibility to introduce or co-sponsor gender equality legislation.

We are the authors of the bill on shared custody and the bill requiring notaries to establish conditions for the transfer of ownership of assets by one of the spouses. (Male parliamentarian, Colombia)

Male legislators mainly limit themselves to accompanying, with their signature, the introduction of draft legislation. There are notable exceptions, however, such as the introduction of the bill on same-sex marriage by a male Socialist deputy, accompanied by male and female deputies from different parties. (Female parliamentarian, Argentina)

In the Lower House I can think of a young male colleague who is working towards the realisation of an increase in women's pensions; for widows and single women. In the past he was active within the unions, and he advanced these ideas. Now he fights for the same issues in the Lower House. Yes, the expertise of men on these matters increases, as well as the 'openness of mind'. (Female parliamentarian, Belgium)

Taking responsibility as gender equality champions

It is widely agreed that male champions are critical to involving men in the advancement of women in politics. Appointing men as a chair, or encouraging men to participate in parliamentary gender equality bodies, may seem counter-intuitive, but has proven a successful means by which to give men responsibility for the gender equality agenda and to create male champions. A man has chaired the Belgian Commission on Gender Equality, and the Sub-Committee on Gender of the Vietnamese National Assembly's Committee on Social Affairs. In Sweden, a former Equality Ombudsman was a man. Stockholm University political scientist Drude Dahlerup has argued that this Ombudsman was very 'visible and influential, not only because he was good, but also ... because he was a man" (cited in iKNOW 2009, 14).

This point was also made by participants involved in the IPU research:

The standing committee on gender is chaired by men. We did that purposely to give them the responsibility. It is just like a public accounts committee being chaired by the opposition; so that there is transparency. (Female parliamentarian, Namibia)

Men need not necessarily be given the top leadership positions in gender equality bodies; they can also be active participants. In Spain, it is noteworthy that the participation of men on the Gender Equality Committee is a result of the allocation of committee memberships according to the respective size of each parliamentary group. Men on this committee are members of the smaller parties that have no women in their parliamentary group but which are still entitled to membership of the committee. As one woman MP from Spain explained:

The Committee is basically female. In big groups there are women and men, and ... women almost always defend the proposals. But in the parliamentary groups where there are no women, the spokespersons are men who take part willingly, effectively and wonderfully. (Female parliamentarian, Spain)

I have identified some men to collaborate with us in addressing these issues ... In the Social Affairs Committee's activities I invite men to attend so that we can seek their support and opinions. I also invite ministers to attend committee meetings for their perspectives and feedback. For the first few meetings, men were quiet. But after a few meetings, they began to give their opinions, for example on the law for the adoption of children, the law on legal normative documents, and the law on public servants. (Female parliamentarian, Viet Nam)

They told us, 'we will vote for the four women to be on the Women's Committee because for the [last] 30 years [it has been] run by men'. We have let three men join this committee, so there are now seven members. We review everything with the government. Everything that has to do with women or education, health and social work, we can put any rules, any problems, we can call the minister and discuss with them and negotiate with them. (Female parliamentarian, Kuwait)

The inclusion of men in these bodies is not always easy, as demonstrated by the case of Peru. Here, the male parliamentarians who served on the gender equality commission in two legislative sessions attracted some commentary from colleagues. As one representative put it,

If they see a man sitting there, people start to tease, [but] I think we need to get past that. Men must be invited to participate and listen, because they can help develop proposals and offer good ideas ... Unfortunately, prejudice is an obstacle to development in Peru ... We should improve the Rules of Congress and require that there be men and women on all the commissions. It would be a way of inviting men to serve on the Women's Commission. If we have a gender percentage in Congress, why not on the commissions? (Female parliamentarian, Peru)

Including men in gender equality activities

Women have also invited men to participate in public activities and outreach, including public consultations or hearings or celebratory activities for International Women's Day. The idea is that men will learn from this first-hand experience and from direct discussion with those facing discrimination. Men's subsequent support has been almost always assured. These are the 'learning opportunities' that provide men in leadership the knowledge necessary to address gender inequality.

Every International Women's Day and National Women's Days, we have activities according to themes we have chosen. For example, when we chose the theme of domestic violence we invited all the men to prepare themselves, like for a debate, and participate in these events. And all of them participated. [With men who are more reluctant to participate], our strategy is to take them outside [the parliament] ... in the past, we brought three men who were not very gender-sensitive to the Philippines for a study tour. When they went back to Timor Leste, they were very strong in speaking out about gender issues!

Sometimes [men] *feel they don't know about gender issues. They must have* [more information] *about gender issues.* (Female parliamentarian, Timor Leste)

We visited the areas where women were trafficked in trucks, and it was very painful for the male colleagues to experience it at first hand. I arranged meetings with those women and they were prepared. They actually told the MPs first hand why they were doing it and so on. It was very painful and I think it made the men more passionate. I learned from that and I saw that it was a very good strategy for people to visualise, to have that direct contact and interaction with people. I think that changed so much and the impact that it had on men, specifically in our house; it was tremendous. (Female parliamentarian, Namibia)

The way forward: making systematic change

It is clear that there are men parliamentarians willing to endorse gender equality, and fight for it. More systematic institutional change is required, however, if gender equality is to become a reality rather than an aspiration. For this to occur, the very foundations on which parliaments are built must be reconsidered.

In the first instance, parliaments need to review their modes of operation and culture. This can be done as a 'self-assessment' exercise – driven by MPs themselves – or as an externally driven, 'gender audit' process in which stakeholders also have some input. In either case, the following questions could be raised:

- Are there sufficient women in parliament, and what positions do they hold? Is there a need for affirmative action measures (such as quotas) to increase the number of women? Is there provision for men and women to share leadership positions, particularly those relating to gender equality responsibilities?
- Has the parliament passed laws to support gender equality?
- Does the parliament have a gender equality policy? Does the strategic plan include references to gender equality? Who is included in the process of writing these high-level plans?
- How is gender equality mainstreamed in the work of the parliament, in its debates and committee work?
- Does the parliament need to review the way in which committees oversee gender mainstreaming? Should it be through a dedicated gender equality committee, for example, or should all parliamentary committees share responsibility for ensuring gender equality principles are upheld?
- Is the culture of parliament gender-sensitive? Are there adequate workplace policies to enable MPs to balance work and family life, such as parental leave?

There are examples of good practice. In the Nordic countries, women have successfully worked with men to make parliamentary timetables, places of meeting, child-care provisions, and working hours and travel arrangements more suitable to men and women (iKNOW Politics 2009, 3). Diana Espinosa, Coordinator of the More Women, More Politics Campaign in Colombia, argues that the objective is to show that changes to the session timetable is a mechanism 'not only for balancing women's family life, but also that of men' (cited in iKNOW Politics 2009, 11).

On the basis of these reviews, parliaments need to find ways in which to address any gaps that are uncovered. They need to make decisions to change their institutional infrastructure and culture. Arguments in favour of this change might be premised on an eventual positive outcome for society as a whole, or in terms of democratic development.

Conclusion

Among parliamentarians of both sexes, it is increasingly accepted that men need to participate in parliamentary activities aimed at gender equality. This acceptance comes as a result of changing social attitudes: voters understand that women can no longer be excluded from the political sphere, and political elites understand that ignoring women's and gender issues can result in political backlash.

Men are therefore increasingly coming on board. Men participate in gender equality debates and advocate gender equality outcomes. They are co-sponsoring legislative initiatives with women to ensure non-discrimination – and some are even sponsoring such initiatives themselves. They have been appointed to chair or participate in their parliaments' gender equality bodies. In some parliaments, changes are being considered to the rules of the parliament to require male and female membership of all parliamentary committees – including those on gender equality – to ensure a gender perspective on all issues addressed by parliament.

A successful initiative in encouraging men's participation has been the inclusion of men in public outreach activities, to raise awareness of gender equality issues. Men have participated in celebratory activities for International Women's Day, have joined delegations to the annual UN Commission on the Status of Women, and have been included on field visits to sites of obvious and manifest discrimination.

While the efforts of a few men are commendable, parliaments must ensure gender equality is addressed comprehensively. This requires institutional change that is accepted, endorsed, and advocated by men. A first step is an analysis of current parliamentary arrangements, and a strategic plan to address any 'uncovered gaps'. This could include changes to internal rules, changes to the oversight responsibilities of parliamentary committees on gender equality, or increased transparency in the process by which promotions to positions of parliamentary leadership are decided. Entrenching gender equality principles is increasingly mandated by legislation, and states are thereby obligated to ensure that men and women promote and achieve gender equality together.

Notes

1. In 2008, the IPU, in partnership with the UN Development Programme in the Arab States and International IDEA in Latin America, initiated a collaborative project to examine the gender sensitivity of parliaments. Research was conducted through questionnaires and face-to-face interviews with men and women parliamentarians from around the world. National case studies were commissioned from gender and parliament experts in 17 countries: Argentina, Australia, Belgium, Bolivia, Burkina Faso, Cambodia, Costa Rica, Jordan, Malaysia, Mexico, Peru, Rwanda, South Africa, Spain, Sweden, Tunisia, and Viet Nam.
2. The International Knowledge Network of Women in Politics (www.iKNOW-Politics.org) is an online network, jointly supported by the five partner organisations, that aims to increase the participation and effectiveness of women in political life by utilising a technology-enabled forum to provide access to critical resources and expertise, stimulate dialogue, create knowledge, and share experiences among women in politics. Between 16 and 31 March 2009, iKNOW Politics organised an e-discussion on the theme 'women and men working together to address social issues by fostering cooperation between men and women in politics'. The discussion included 43 comments from members and experts worldwide (16 in English, 25 in Spanish and two in French). Contributors came from 17 countries: Argentina, Azerbaijan, Belgium, Bolivia, Canada, Colombia, Egypt, Fiji, Kenya, Kosovo, Mexico, Norway, Tunisia, Sweden, Peru, USA, and Uruguay.

References

Ballington, Julie (2008) *Equality in Politics: A Survey of Women and Men in Politics,* Geneva: Inter-Parliamentary Union

Connell, R.W. (2003) 'The Role of Men and Boys in Achieving Gender Equality', paper prepared for the United Nations Expert Group Meeting in Brasilia, 21–24 October

Duerst-Lahti, Georgia and Rita Mae Kelly (eds.) (1995) *Gender Power, Leadership and Governance,* Ann Arbor: University of Michigan Press

Goetz, Anne Marie (1995) 'The Politics of Integrating Gender to State Development Processes: Trends, Opportunities and Constraints in Bangladesh, Chile, Jamaica, Mali, Morocco and Uganda', Occasional Paper 2, United Nations Research Institute for Social Development, United Nations Development Programme, http://genderandsecurity.researchhub.ssrc.org/the-politics-of-integrating-gender-to-state-development-processes-trends-opportunities-and-constraints-in-bangladesh-chile-jamaica-mali-morocco-and-uganda/attachment

International Knowledge Network of Women in Politics (iKNOW Politics) (2009) 'Working with Men to Promote Women in Politics', http://

iknowpolitics.org/en/2009/05/summary-e-discussion-working-men-promote-women-politics-march-16-312009

Karam, Azza and Joni Lovenduski (eds.) (2005) *Women in Parliament. Beyond Numbers*, revised edition, Stockholm: International IDEA

Palmieri, Sonia (2011) *Creating Gender Sensitive Parliaments: A Global Review of Good Practice*, Geneva: Inter-Parliamentary Union

United Nations (2001) 'Gender Mainstreaming: Strategy for Promoting Gender Equality', Office of the Special Advisor on Gender Issues and Advancement of Women, www.un.org/womenwatch/osagi/pdf/factsheet1.pdf

Wacjman, Judy (1998) *Managing Like a Man: Women and Men in Corporate Management*, Sydney: Allen and Unwin

About the author

Sonia Palmieri is an Honorary Senior Research Fellow in the School of Politics and International Studies, University of Queensland, and the Manager of the Pacific Women's Parliamentary Partnerships Project at the Australian Parliament. Email: Sonia.Palmieri.Reps@aph.gov.au

CHAPTER 6

'Because I am a man, I should be gentle to my wife and my children': positive masculinity to stop gender-based violence in a coastal district in Vietnam

Tu-Anh Hoang, Trang Thu Quach and Tam Thanh Tran

Abstract

Despite the efforts of the government to promote gender equality in Vietnam, gender-based violence is still a critical issue. This chapter explores a pilot project, the Responsible Men Club, developed and implemented in a coastal district in Vietnam from 2010 to 2012 to work with men to stop violence against their wives. Focusing on masculinity and promoting gender equality in a culturally relevant way significantly improves acceptance of the programme by men themselves and their communities, and enhances its impact. We argue that empowerment, a process often used for women, is also important for men. To construct and encourage a positive, non-violent version of masculinity, men need relevant knowledge, skills, mentoring, and peer support. It is a challenge for gender-based violence programmes to work on increasing public awareness of the issue of violence against women, and reduce society's tolerance of it, without increasing stigmatisation of and objections to men in general, and to perpetrator men in particular.

Key words: masculinity; gender-based violence; perpetrator; Vietnam

Introduction

There are several initiatives in Vietnam currently working with men and boys to change their attitude toward women and gender equality through promoting new values of manhood and masculinities. This chapter focuses on the Responsible Men Club, which was developed and implemented in 2010–2012 as a pilot programme in a coastal district in Vietnam. The aim of the Responsible Men Club was to work with men to stop violence against their wives, enabling them to develop positive ideas about what it is to be a man and about masculinities in their society, and empowering them to adopt these

http://dx.doi.org/10.3362/9781780448664.006

new values in their thoughts and practices. Programmes like this, which work with men and boys, and focus on challenging their ideas about masculinity, show that they can successfully change men's attitudes toward issues including sexual relationships, reproductive decision-making, HIV-prevention, and gender-based violence (Schueller *et al.* 2005).

The Responsible Men Club was instigated by the Center for Creative Initiatives in Health and Population (CCIHP), which aimed to work with perpetrator men (that is, men who perpetrate violence against women in interpersonal relationships) in Cualo, a town in the north-central coastal district of Vietnam. CCIHP is a non-government organisation (NGO) based in Hanoi, Vietnam. Since its establishment in 1999, the organisation has been active in the country and in the region in research, intervention, and advocacy on gender-based violence, sexual and reproductive rights, and civil society participation. The Responsible Men Club was a collaboration between CCIHP and Cualo People's Committee (CPC), an administrative body at district level. We chose CPC as our partner, reasoning that other local partner organisations would then be motivated to be involved in a way which would not have been possible had we chosen the Women's Union, which is known for a woman-centred approach.[1] The Responsible Men Club was funded by the Ford Foundation. In its start-up phase, the programme was supported by input and training from RESPECT, a UK-based membership association for domestic violence prevention programmes and integrated support services.[2]

This chapter briefly surveys the work of the Responsible Men Club. It starts by violence against women in Vietnam, focusing in particular on violence in intimate relationships. It explores the ideas about masculinities and empowerment behind the programme. We then share our findings about the impact of the programme: on men's ideas about what it means to be a man in their social and economic context, and on the incidence of violence perpetrated by them on their wives and female partners.

The context: violence against women in Vietnam

In 2006, the Vietnamese government passed the Law on Gender Equality, which promotes gender equality in all areas of life and details the responsibilities of organisations, institutions, families, and individuals in ensuring the health, economic, and social status of girls and women in Vietnam. In 2007, the Law on Domestic Violence Prevention and Control was passed, which provides explicit protection from violence within the family to its members, covering a wide range of acts of domestic violence. Other forms of violence, such as sexual abuse and sexual harassment, including rape, are addressed in the Penal Code and other criminal laws. Reducing gender-based violence is one of the key objectives in Vietnam's 2011–2020 National Strategy on Gender Equality (The Prime Minister 2010, 4).

Despite these efforts, research shows that violence against women is still prevalent in Vietnam. In the National Study on Domestic Violence Against Women, more than half (58 per cent) of women who have been married reported having experienced at least one of three types of violence (physical, sexual, and emotional) in their lives. Twenty-seven per cent of women report having experienced violence in the past 12 months (General Statistics Office 2010, 21). The National Study on Domestic Violence Against Women also showed that about 50 per cent of married women who have violent husbands remained silent about this, and nearly 90 per cent of them did not seek assistance from formal services or authorities (General Statistics Office 2010, 91).

Vietnam is similar to many other countries in the region and internationally, in that there is a high level of acceptance of violence and male privilege. Many violent acts caused by a husband to his wife are considered acceptable by both women and men. Research suggests that while gender equity and the ideology of women's liberation are promoted by government, they have not yet been adopted at the household level, where the status of women can be summarised as 'limited equality' (*bình đẳng có giói hạn*) (Santillan *et al.* 2002, 256). The Multiple Indicator Cluster Survey Vietnam 2011 indicates that 35.8 per cent of women aged 15–49 accept violent treatment from their husbands in various situations (General Statistics Office 2012, 18).

Violence against women, masculinity and empowerment: the theory

The Responsible Men Club pilot programme used theories of masculinity in combination with empowerment approaches. Men are under very high pressure to perform in the conventional masculine roles expected of them (Martin 1995). The pressure for conformity is high, obliging men – whether they like it or not – to put on a 'mask' of dominant masculinity (Edwards and Jones 2009). Yet this can be challenged. However, men and boys are not passive victims of the roles that society gives them. They are active in shaping and challenging powerful ideas about masculine norms (Courtenay 1999). Gender roles and unequal power relations place men in a superior position in relation to women – which is why violence against women remains widely socially condoned. However, individual men can use their agency to challenge this, and adopt a different mode of masculinity.

The Club used theories of masculinity in combination with empowerment approaches, which have been widely adopted in the field of gender and development to support women to challenge inequality and violence. Empowerment has been defined as 'all those processes where [women] take control and ownership of their lives' (Strandberg 2001, 4). Three core elements of empowerment are awareness of gender power structures; agency and sense of agency; and self-esteem and self-confidence (*ibid.*). In the rest of the article, the Club's aims and activities (based on review of the Club manual and observations of facilitator training and Club sessions) will be discussed in relation to these three elements.

The programme and our research

The Responsible Men Club programme involved 36 perpetrator men, who participated in three Clubs. Each man joining the Club had to go through an extensive process of introduction to the Club – referred to as 'in-take'. In-take involved both workshop sessions, and interviews. In each Club, the men went through 14 sessions, which discussed gender norms and values, family conflicts, violence, anger management, sexual relationships, and fatherhood. The materials used by the Responsible Men Clubs are adapted from those developed by RESPECT. In addition to Club sessions, the Club members also participated in events to mark special occasions including Family Day, Women's Day, Valentine Day, and New Year, when they were joined by their wives.

The pilot programme was implemented in three out of seven communes in the district. These communes were selected based on the level of willingness, enthusiasm, and commitment of the commune leaders to working with the men. A pilot Club was set up in one commune, and ran from May 2010 to March 2011. With lessons learned from this, two more pilots were established in two other communes, which ran from May 2011 to March 2012.

Our research, which was undertaken while the pilot programme was running, included in-depth interviews (conducted before and after involvement with the programme), mid-term interviews (during the programme), and pre- and post-questionnaire interviews with 36 perpetrator men. The in-depth interviews used extensive checklist (that is, closed) and open questions, aiming to collect information about the couple relationship, children, form and frequency of violence, and context of violence. Each interview was conducted in 60–90 minutes. The mid-term interviews were in-depth interviews conducted with four Club members to get insight into men's interaction in the Club sessions and activities. All participants also took part in the pre- and post-Club surveys which covered not only the histories of particular individuals mentioned above, but their knowledge, attitude, and practices regarding gender equity, sexuality, and violence. The survey questionnaire was developed to specifically cover themes that were discussed in the Club sessions.

To ensure the participation of men and reduce the risk for women, comprehensive information was recorded about all the men involved in the Clubs. This recorded the status of the relationship between the man and his wife including any ex-wife, children, and his history. The men ranged in age from their thirties to their fifties. All of them had been behaving violently to their wives for three to more than 20 years. Data were collected on each man's violent behaviour (both forms of violence and frequency), the impact of violence on the woman or women involved, and on children, and risky behaviour of different kinds, such as drinking, gambling, drug abuse, and extra-marital relationships. Information collected from each man also included his motivation to participate in the programme, the time he had available to give to it, and his level of openness in communicating with his wife. Men were selected only when they showed some level of enthusiasm for participating in the programme. The men were also asked to write a consent letter for participation in the programme. In this letter, men had to promise not to drink for 12 hours before the Club sessions and not to miss the sessions, and not to prevent the programme staff from communicating with their female partners, and vice versa (CCIHP 2010).

'I am just at home so I feel depressed' – raising awareness of gender power structures and gender roles

The Club encouraged men to deconstruct and reconstruct their ideas about masculinity, relations between women and men, and relations between men. While empowerment is often an approach used with women, researchers into masculinity suggest that empowerment is an issue for men also. In Vietnam as well as many other patriarchal societies, men are viewed and consider themselves the 'strong gender'. Yet when perpetrator men were asked about the causes and contexts of their violence to women, it was very common for them to mention 'drinking' and 'being poor'. The national data do suggest a link between these factors and violence (General Statistics Office 2010, 69). However, in-depth interviews found that it was not the poverty and the alcohol in themselves which caused violence. Instead, it was the tension caused by the sense of poverty causing them to be weaker and less manly than the other men that caused men to drink, and to be violent.

One man in the Responsible Men Club summed the dynamics up as follows:

> To be honest with you, I made violence also because of the economic situation. I was sick, so I could not go for work. I had to be at home so I felt depressed. Looking out in the society, they [men] went for work and I had to be at home. I felt depressed and once you are depressed you easily make violence in the family ... As a man I like to be the pillar in the house. I do not like to be dependent on my wife ... As a husband, I should never be dependent [on my wife]. The saying, 'Man is a pillar in the house', means that a man should be able to make money to support his wife and children. (Interview, October 2010)

Examples like this of the tensions that play out in couples were collected and used to help men understand their violence in context, and to challenge men about their notion of 'being men' and 'strong'. Using men's own narratives in discussions in the Club was crucial in enabling them to identify and deconstruct dominant masculinity. Having been born in Vietnam's patriarchal society, men had not usually questioned their privileged position in society and the family. They took for granted the idea of the man as the pillar of his family, seeing men in just one way as 'strong, going out and earning money to support the family'. They had no consciousness that it could be resisted as it was so 'natural'.

Men were also asked to think about similar pressures on their wives to perform their social roles perfectly. Men were asked to list things that they expected from their wives, and their feelings if their wife did not meet these expectations. They were also asked to think about how their wives would feel about meeting their husbands' expectations, and being compared to other women (CCIHP 2012). Men then started to recognise that their wives actually shared a lot in common with them in terms of social pressures and tensions around gender roles. Role-plays, in which men played the roles of wives, were often used in sessions focusing on this.

For some men, playing the role of being a wife was very hard, as it was new for them to think about their wives' feelings. Men often said women should know how their husbands feel, and what their husband think so they could satisfy them better. However, there were no parallel expectations that men should know women's feelings. One man summed up the comments of others in a Club session, that it was impossible to know how women felt and portray this in a role-play session: 'How can we play this? How can we know her feeling?' (personal observation, workshop session, October 2010). Sometimes, men simply stopped and laughed as they could not continue: 'I cannot know what she would think and do next'. Through the exercise they recognised that mutual understanding was essential in marriage.

This attempt to challenge men's ideas about gender roles and masculine identities seemed to be successful. In the evaluation after men had done the programme, the average score about gender attitudes of men in the Clubs was 9.1 (out of maximum score of 10) in comparison with 6.16 in the pre-survey.

'In couple relationships, the most important thing is emotion': feeling a sense of agency

A useful definition of agency is 'the ability to define one's goals and act upon them (Kabeer 2000, 4). As mentioned above, men are under social pressure to act in a particular way, conforming to social expectations rather than their own wishes. Notes in counselling sessions with perpetrator men in the areas showed that often lengthy conversations aiming to help men see what they really wanted from their relationships (Cua Lo Counseling Center 2009). With this in mind, the second focus in the Responsible Men Clubs was to help the men understand more about themselves – in particular, their own feelings and values.

Attitudes to marital relationships

These were often covered heavily by the ideas they associated with the men they were expected to be, making it hard for men to know what they really wanted. Only after deeper discussions could men see that behind their wish for power over their wife and their children lay a wish for love and intimacy. One man said:

> *In a couple relationship, the most important thing is emotion. This means when I am back home, my wife smiles and welcomes me. She treats me gently. When we go for sleep, we have intimacy so we can hold each other. If we do not have this intimacy, we do not have emotion, we sleep as the dried tree.* (Interview, October 2010)

The idea that family life should be full of love and positive emotion was obviously at odds with the idea of violence within the family. No man in the Club was proud of his violence or images of it, in the form of bruises on the face of his wife. One man brought photos to a Men and Family Event at the Club, presenting his image of a smiling and happy family as his victory.

> *I brought here three important photos about my family. One is the photo of my wife and I side by side, big smiles and happy. The second photo is of my two children. The third photo has the four of us. I am very proud of my family – a happy family with good children.* (Field trip report, Men and Family Event, March 2012)

Violence is based on an abuse of power. Men wanted to be respected by their wives and children. In the initial discussion, men said that they had power in the family. Their wife and children listened to them, and did according to their wishes and orders. To deconstruct this notion of power and how it is exercised, the men in the Clubs went through reflection exercises about their experiences of being punished, beaten, or threaten in their childhood. They were asked about what they thought of people that had been violent to them. The common answers included 'scared', 'afraid', and 'hatred'. One man talked about his feeling about an older man who controlled him in childhood. He stated:

> *I had to follow his request but I hated him. I tried to find an opportunity to rebel.* (Observation note, 2010)

After exploring their own memories of violence, men were then asked to put themselves in the position of their wives, and to think about how they feel after being beaten, forced to do something, or insulted. Feeling how it was to be 'in the woman's chair', men then recognised that the power that they gained from violence was not 'real power' and was not sustainable since it was imposed. Men recognised that though they could force their wives and children to follow their orders, they could not control their wives' and children's feelings. Thus, the power that they gained was not 'true power'. Underlying the ideas of harmony in the family lay positive notions of power exercised in a responsible way.

Sexual violence and sexuality were also discussed in the Club. Sexual violence is believed to be very under-reported in Vietnam. The national survey estimates that around 10 per cent of women have suffered it (General Statistics

Office 2010, 56). However, sexual violence is often not specifically mentioned in education and communication programmes on violence. Women often do not report sexual violence, and if they do report it, the local authorities are challenged to respond effectively to these cases (Consultant of Investment in Health Promotion 2008).

Sex plays an important role in constructing and reconstructing gender relations (Vance 1995). A specific session was designed in the Club programme to work with men about sexuality and sexual violence (CCIHP 2012). Men were very excited with this session. Many of them shared the challenges in their sexual relationships. Men very much valued the intimacy and pleasure of sexual relationships. They also admitted that they had never considered that sex was complicated, thinking of it simply as a biological need. They stated they just acted from their side and did not pay attention to the women's needs and feelings (observation note, 2010).

Changing men's perception of their own sexuality and that of women was still more difficult. While the changes in gender attitudes in general improved significantly, as shown above, the post-survey result on sexuality perception showed an average score of 14.2 (out of 20). This score was 9 in the pre-survey. The slower change in perception on sexuality could be due to the fact that sex was still a sensitive issue in Vietnam while gender equity had been in public discussion and on the government agenda for a long time.

Overall, men seemed to value what they learned in the Club about marital relationships. They said they learned more from thinking about issues from their wives' point of view, and they wanted to be continued in the programme to learn more about improving the relationship with their wives. Though all men in the Clubs were fishermen, the attendance rate was quite high. Only 8.3 per cent of them attended fewer than 10 out of 14 sessions. One man said:

> *I do not feel shameful. If I think this brings benefit to my family, this helps my wife and my children then I will do whatever I think I should do. I don't care what other people think about me.* (Interview, October 2010)

Fatherhood and the impact of violence on children

In addition to 'husbandhood', fatherhood was also an important aspect to work with men. Children in Vietnam are acknowledged by the authorities to be very much affected by violence against women in the family (General Statistics Office 2010, 78), but they are almost completely voiceless and have no presence in most interventions on domestic violence. In Vietnam, motherhood is a familiar issue in public and family discourses, but there is little parallel discussion about fatherhood.

To increase their awareness of fatherhood and its importance, men were asked to collect objects from home which reflected their love towards their children. Their children were also secretly invited to write letters to their father.[3] In the exchange session, men had the opportunity to present the objects that showed their love and care to their children. For that they could be proud of being a good father. In the Men and Family Event, men read and listened to the letters from their children, learning what the children expected from them. One daughter wrote to her father:

> *I want my father first to be a true father, a husband in the family, and a good grandfather who can sacrifice for his children.* (Letter, March 2012)

A son wrote to his father:

> *You [Dad] are the pillar at home. You are very responsible, work hard, take care of us – your children and always encourage us to study ... What I like about you is your puncture and cleanness. However, what I do not like about you is that you smoke and drink too much. Drinking is not good for your health. I love you very much and I want you to know.* (Letter, March 2012)

These letters had a strong impact on the men; several men cried in this session. One man reflected on how this changed his opinion on using violence:

> *I often drink and feel that I am wrong ... I used to use violence to educate my children but now I know that we should not use the rod as a way of educating them.* (Field trip report, March 2012)

'Time-out' – the 'new men's' technique

Based on thinking about themselves, the different points of view of their wives and children, and about power, men started thinking about change. They learned that women – and even children – wanted to be respected just like men, and thus respect was the foundation of love and intimacy. They also learned that self-control and good communication were very important. The Club programme provided the men with concrete techniques and skills that they could use to master their feeling and behaviours. These men learned to express their disagreement and anger in non-violent and smart ways: one session was actually called 'Express your anger in a smart way' (CCIHP 2012).

From the very first Club session, men learned 'time-out' techniques to help them recognise the changes in their feelings and bodies which predicted the violence so they could avoid violence before it happened. Though this was a simple technique, all the men in the Clubs felt very much released as it helped them control themselves. They even saw this as a 'magic wand' to stop violence. Men seemed very interested and appreciated the 'time-out' technique. The technique later was also presented and promoted in local and national newspapers and on radio and television. In an interview, one participant was asked what was meant by a 'responsible man'. He answered:

> *Because I am a man, when I am at home I should be gentle with my wife and my children. When my wife is in a hot temper, I should keep silent. For example, when she gets angry, I should be silent and go somewhere else. When she has calmed down, I will come back home and talk to her.*

However, it was also emphasised in the programme that the time-out technique was only a temporary solution. It helped men stop violent behaviour in a short time but did not ensure the impact in the long term as it did not change the relationship. Thus, parallel with the deconstruction processes as described above, men learned how to have effective communication with their wife and their children. They learned to make 'I' rather than 'You' statements, so they could express their feelings in a non-violent and respectful manner. They also learned the importance of telling their wives about their love for them. One man stated:

> *I should talk to her* [about my thoughts]. *For example: if she is back from work and she is tired, I will talk to her gently: so you are tired now, please leave this for me I will do it. Or if I am tired, I also have to tell her: I am tired, so please help me do this. And I have to say it gently. It is because family work is equal. No one has to take all responsibilities. We should share so we can be happier and the family is better.* (Interview, September 2011)

This is very important: expressing love in concrete words and gestures such as kissing, hugging, and even holding hands is not common practice in Vietnam's culture. During a field trip, one of the authors of this chapter was having dinner on the beach and had a very interesting conversation with a woman who was the restaurant's owner:

> *Woman: It is good that you are from the city. You and your husband can hold hands on street. Here we do not do it.*
> *Author: But do you like it? Do you want to do it?*
> *Woman: Yes, it is very nice, it is very romantic. Of course, we also want to be like that but here we do not do.*
> *Author: Why you do not do here?*
> *Woman: It is embarrassing* [ngây]. *If we do it, everybody will look at us.* (Field-notes, 2010)

Men were requested to practise what they had learned at home with their wives, and to share experiences in the group. In addition, different occasions were organised in the programme to help men strengthen these skills. In these occasions, the couples would join in games that test their understanding of each other and their collaboration. On the Women's Day, men were asked to prepare a small gift which should cost less than 50,000VND (about US$2.5) for their wives, together with the words that they wanted to tell their wife. These events created a new men's culture in expressing love and intimacy.

The post-survey evaluation suggests that these techniques to reduce violence showed that 66.7 per cent of the men reported having peaceful and comfortable discussions with their wife the last time there was tension or conflict. This number was 31.3 per cent in the pre-survey. Most notably, after participating in the Club, almost 70 per cent of the men in the Clubs said they had not behaved violently. The remaining 30 per cent reported one episode of violence during the six months prior to the post-survey, in comparison with two to six times or more in the pre-survey.[4]

'She is proud of me' – self-esteem and self-confidence of the new men's image and power

Though it was clear throughout the programme that violence was not natural or good, but was in fact a violation of women's rights and the law, the programme emphasis was not on blaming men individually, but on analysing violence from a structural and cultural perspective. Thus, men did not see their participation in the programme as a 'punishment', but a process of learning and improving. One man commented:

> *People here still think that this* [participating in the Club] *is a kind of punishment for people who are not good. However, as participating in the Club, I understand that this is for us to be given instruction and guidance to live better. I find this is very useful. I like to go to the Club to learn. Mr. Y said that there are seven sessions more. I already put them in my schedule.* (Interview, man in Club, October 2010)

Furthermore, the programme created opportunities for men to see the benefit of being a 'responsible man'. One thing that men were often concerned with was that if they did not use violence any more, or if they tried to be equal with their wife, their family would be 'disordered', and their wife would take power over them. However, they had different experiences in the programme. They saw how their changes brought positive changes in their wives' attitudes and in their relationship. One participant stated:

> *I think that we should not differentiate women and men. In general, people should be equal. Men have rights and women have same rights as men. Men also have rights as women such as doing housework and going to the market. Man can always do these things. We should not leave all this for women to be in charge … Since I have been involved in this, I go to the market more. I change. When my wife is tired, I go to the market. And our relationship changes too.* (Interview, September 2011)

Another reported:

> *Since I am involved in the Club, we feel more love in our relationship. We do not quarrel each other as much as before.* (Interview, September 2011)

In a Couple Session where the men handed gifts that they had to prepare by themselves, with words to their wife, some wives cried with happiness. In this session, men held a competition to make the best gift for their wives. The man who won first prize in the contest said:

> *I was very happy and excited when I and my wife got the prize. It was very simple but made our children respect us. They can see that we are a proper*

couple, we know how to talk to each other ... I have not seen the documentary film yet. I was fishing that day. My children are very proud of me as I am on the television. This is the first time that I make my children really proud of me and I do not have to use any violence. (Interview, October 2010)

As mentioned above, social attitudes towards male violence towards women are complex and contradictory. While the statistics suggest that society is tolerant to male violence (General Statistics Office 2010, 69), violence is not overtly seen as good behaviour, or openly encouraged. Thus, when men publicly stopped violence, they saw a positive change in the attitudes of other people in the community about them. One man pointed out:

This [new non-violent behaviour] *is beneficial for me. If we had a quarrel, the neighbours would make negative comments as we were already* [at a mature age] *but still talked badly, and shouted at each other. So now they make* [different] *comments, that is a benefit for me.* (Interview, October 2010)

A final element of the programme was different public campaigns to change wider society's view of masculinity too. Though using different words, there was a consistent message throughout these campaigns, which emphasised the new ideas about masculinities promoted at the Club, which mean responsibility and caring. The messages were developed based on the traditional men's values of being strong, but a twist was given to them. The following are examples of slogans that were promoted in public campaigns in the programme:

Give love and share responsibilities.
Father teaches son fishing and living without violence.
We are sharing, we are doing housework.
Strong for love and sharing.

Conclusions and recommendations

Though the Responsible Men Club was implemented as a relatively small-scale pilot programme, the initial results showed that building men's ideas of an alternative, non-violent and caring masculinity was important for preventing future gender-based violence in men's relationships with their wives.

This process, however, was not just about transferring knowledge. Recognising the pressures that men are under from economic and social factors in society, and the need for them to understand these and deconstruct their impact on men's culturally rooted notions of 'being a man' and the power that men have in society and the family were all crucial. Discussions of husbandhood, fatherhood, and sexuality should be included in the discussions about the wider concept of being a man. Men also need concrete skills and techniques that can help them to effectively perform their role within marriage and the family, ensuring they are able to participate in decisions and articulate their wishes in non-dominating, non-violent ways. Men needed support to remove their 'masks', and gain confidence to present themselves as 'new men', not only in their family, but also in public. All these processes could be seen as a process of empowerment for men. Discussions about sexuality are important not only to help to address sexual violence, but to contribute to positive changes in the concept of the 'new man' in general.

Women and children play important roles in helping men to gain legitimate self-confidence and self-esteem from exercising power and agency responsibly, respectfully, and non-violently. Thus, separated supporting activities for the wives of these men should be also organised, so they can become supportive partners in this transformation process in gender relations. Society, also, still tolerates husband to wife violence to some extent, men that cause violence are stigmatised because of the violence and behaviours such as drinking, gambling, or irresponsibility. This social tolerance is often the main reason that prevents men from participating in intervention for them intended to end their violence. Thus, it is very important to work to challenge wider social acceptance of violence as well as working with men in ways which raise their awareness that they will find their reputation higher in their community if they are non-violent. Programmes working with men should be accompanied by public education programmes to change the social perceptions of 'being a man' and all causes of violence, from individual behaviour to the issue of social structures and ideology.

After the funding for the Responsible Men Club ends, the district and commune people's committee plan to continue to run the programme with the facilitators trained in the programme and using the manual developed in the programme. The model and the manual were disseminated at the National Conference on Domestic Violence in 2012, a major event in Vietnam, and got a very good response from the audience. Following the conference, the Ministry of Culture, Sport and Tourism (MOCST), which is responsible for domestic violence prevention and control programming in Vietnam, brought different national and provincial delegates for a study visit at the programme site and recommended that the Responsible Men Club model be implemented in other provinces.

Acknowledgements

The research team would like to thank the local authority and people in Cualo for their support in the research. Special thanks is to the 36 men for their willingness to participate in the programme and share their stories. We are grateful to the Ford Foundation for financial support for the research. Last but not least, we would like to thank Dr. Caroline Sweetman, editor of *Gender & Development*, for encouraging us to submit the paper and giving her kindness and support in editing the paper.

Notes

1. By having the People's Committee at the co-ordinator role, the programme has advantage in getting the involvement of all other local mass-organisations and sectors in the programmes including the Women's Union

and other organisations working with men such as the Youth Union, Farmer Union, Veteran Association, and education and health sectors. Involvement of the People's Committee also means a high level of commitment by the local authority. Thus gender-based violence prevention was integrated into the Communist Party resolution even before the Domestic Violence Prevention Law was passed.

2. During the programme planning phase, CCIHP searched for technical resources on working with men from a gender perspective, and found the website of RESPECT, a UK-based organisation, which became a resource agency during the start-up phase of the project. Two trainers were invited from RESPECT to Vietnam for a master training session. In the training curriculum that CCIHP used later, it adapted some materials from RESPECT, integrating these with training materials developed by CCIHP trainers based on the Vietnamese context. For more information on RESPECT, see www.respect.uk.net.

3. To protect the safety of the children, the children were not physically present in the meeting. Their letters were numbered and the men randomly chose the letter and read out loud to the group.

4. Men's own reports of violence were depended on in our research and this could potentially mean under-reporting, particularly in the post-programme stage when men realise that violence is socially unacceptable and the programme does not condone or tolerate it. In this research, men's self-reports were also certified by interviews with their wife, Club facilitators, and local people in the supporting system.

References

Center for Creative Initiatives in Health and Population (CCIHP) (2010) 'Introduction of "Responsible Club Model"', project document, Hanoi: Center for Creative Initiatives in Health and Population

Center for Creative Initiatives in Health and Population (CCIHP) (2012) *'I Am Responsible Man': Manual on Facilitation of Men Group to Prevent Violence*, Hanoi: Center for Creative Initiatives in Health and Population

Consultant of Investment in Health Promotion (2008) 'Invervention on Sexual Violence: Lessons Learned', PPT presentation in project dissemination workshop, Consultant of Investment in Health Promotion, Hanoi

Courtenay, Will H. (2000) 'Constructions of masculinity and their influence on men's well-being: a theory of gender and health', *Social Science & Medicine* 50(10): 1385–401

Cua Lo Counseling Center (2009) 'Annual Report', Nghe An, Vietnam: Cualo Counseling Center

Edwards, Keith E. and Susan R. Jones (2009) '"Putting my man face on": a grounded theory of college men's gender identity development', *Journal of College Student Development* 50(2): 210–28

General Statistics Office (2010) *'Keeping Silence is Dying': Results from the National Study on Domestic Violence Against Women in Vietnam Nam*, Hanoi: General Statistics Office

General Statistics Office (2012) *Multiple Indicator Cluster Survey Vietnam 2011: Key Findings*, Hanoi: General Statistics Office

Kabeer, Naila (2000) 'Resources, Agency, Achievement: Reflections on the Measurement of Women's Empowerment', paper presented at 'Power, Resources and Culture in a Gender Perspective: Towards a Dialogue Between Gender Research and Development Practice', Uppsala, 26–27 October

Martin, Carol Lynn (1995) 'Stereotypes about children with traditional and nontraditional gender roles', *Sex Roles* 33(11–12): 727–51

Santillan, Diana, Sidney Schuler, Hoang Tu Anh, Hung Minh Tran, and Thanh Mai Bui Thi (2002) 'Limited equality: contradictory ideas about gender and the implications for reproductive health in rural Vietnam', *Journal of Health Management* 4(2): 251–67

Schueller, Jane, William Finger, and Gary Barker (2005) *Boys and Changing Gender Roles: Emerging Program Approaches Hold Promise in Changing Gender Norms and Behaviours among Boys and Men*, YouthNet: Youth Lens on Reproductive Health and HIV, Vol. 16, Research Triangle Park, NC: Family Health International

Strandberg, Nina (2001) 'Conceptualising Empowerment as a Transformative Strategy for Poverty Eradication and the Implications for Measuring Progress', paper prepared for the expert group meeting on 'Empowerment of women throughout the life cycle as a transformative strategy for poverty eradication' of the United Nations Division for the Advancement of Women, New Delhi, 26–29 November

The Prime Minister (2010) 'Decision Approving the 2011–2020 National Strategy for Gender Equality', Public Law Objective 6, No. 2351/QD-TTg, Hanoi

Vance, Carole S. (1995) 'Social construction theory and sexuality', in M. Berger, B. Wallis, and S. Watson (eds.) *Constructing Masculinity*, New York: Routledge

About the author

Tu-Anh Hoang Centre for Creative Initiatives in Health and Population. Email: tuanh@ccihp.org

Trang Thu Quach Centre for Creative Initiatives in Health and Population. Email: qttrang@ccihp.org

Tam Thanh Tran Centre for Creative Initiatives in Health and Population. Email: tranthanhtam2610@gmail.com

CHAPTER 7

Domestic violence prevention through the Constructing Violence-free Masculinities programme: an experience from Peru

Rhoda Mitchell

Abstract

This paper examines work undertaken with male perpetrators of violence in the Construction of Violence-free Masculinities, a project run by the Centro Mujer Teresa de Jesús, a Women's Centre located in a poor peri-urban district of Lima, Perú, in conjunction with Oxfam-Quebec. Centre staff faced the challenge of how to work with men who are violent towards their intimate partners. They use a community education approach, to challenge powerful stereotypes about gender roles, to question men's assumed dominance over women, and support men to construct new forms of masculinity, without violence. Ultimately, the programme seeks to modify and change the beliefs, values, attitudes, and behaviours of men who are aggressors.

Key words: masculinity; intimate partner violence; violence against women; domestic violence; men's groups

Introduction

> *She provoked me, we have disagreements about decisions that I make, she tells me I'm a fool and compares me with others. It irritates me, makes me feel like I've failed as a man and that makes me feel ashamed, that angers me, she knows how I get but likes to provoke me and that's why it is her fault that I shout and hit her!* (Centro Mujer Teresa de Jesus (CMTJ) Men's Programme participant, cited in Reyes Mori and Palacios Trujillo 2010, 53)

This chapter examines the case study of a project working with a men's group called Constructing Violence-free Masculinities, which is part of Oxfam-Quebec's 'Mieux agir, Mieux influencer' (MAMI) volunteer co-operation programme.[1] Constructing Violence-free Masculinities is run by a women's centre in urban Peru that responds to the need for the eradication of violence against women by working with violent men. The men's group has been running for three consecutive years, from 2009 to 2011, and is part of a wider project which CMTJ runs in conjunction with Oxfam-Quebec.

http://dx.doi.org/10.3362/9781780448664.007

This chapter discusses the intervention project with men, Constructing Violence-free Masculinities, and draws on conversations with CMTJ psychologists Angel Palacios Trujillo and Jose Reyes Mori, who developed the programme, and also facilitated the men's group processes. It also draws on insights and learning from conversations with the programme participants, by the author, in my capacity as Gender Advisor for Oxfam-Quebec in Peru, accompanying and monitoring the CMTJ projects from the period of 2009-2012.

The context: gender relations and violence in Peru

Peru, a country of 29 million, is a country which is still in the recovery phase in the wake of its internal conflict of the 1980s and 1990s, between the government and the Shining Path guerrilla movement. This conflict cost many men and women their lives, and affected and displaced innumerable others. Violence became a commonplace and everyday occurrence, and this 'naturalisation' of violence is an ongoing issue (Boesten 2012; Comisión de la Verdad y Reconciliación 2003).

Peru is currently experiencing an economic boom, but that boom has had varying effects on various different parts of the population (Instituto Nacional de Estadística e Informática (INEI) 2012; UN Development Programme 2010). The great levels of inequality between men and women are visible in both urban and rural sectors, and can be seen in economic, social, and political interactions. While there have been advances in respect of women's rights in recent years, the subordination of women continues to be seen and perpetuated in the private and public spheres. This subordination and unequal distribution of power between men and women is a major causal factor of domestic violence. The traditional gender norms and roles, while in the process of changing, still are perpetuating violence; 38.4 per cent of women who have ever lived with an intimate partner, have suffered physical or sexual violence, this number increases to 39.2 per cent in urban areas (INEI 2010, 314). More than two-thirds (67.9 per cent) of women who have ever had an intimate partner, manifest that their partner has exerted control over them at some point (*ibid.*, 310).

Peru has one of the highest levels of feminicide in Latin America, with ten women dying at the hands of their partners or ex-partners each month. Feminicide is understood as the murder of women as a result of gender discrimination. 'Feminicide connotes not only the murder of women by men because they are women but also indicates state responsibility for these murders whether through the commission of the actual killing, toleration of the perpetrators' acts of violence, or omission of state responsibility to ensure the safety of its female citizens' (Guatemala Human Rights CommissionGHRC 2010, 1). Marcela Lagarde (in Monarrez Fragoso 2002) states that femicide is genocide against women and occurs when the historical conditions generate social practices that allow attacks on the integrity, health, freedoms, and lives of women. In 2010, there were 130 victims of feminicide and 49 other deaths which were believed to be cases (Observatorio de la Criminalidad del Ministerio Público 2010, 3).

The work of Centro Mujer Teresa de Jesus (CMJT)

The CMJT is a grassroots non-government organisation (NGO), located in the district of San Juan de Lurigancho (SJL), a peri-urban community that forms part of Lima. It is the most populous district in Latin America with a population of over one million people, over 60 per cent of whom are under the age of 25 (Davis 2006, 144). It is a relatively young district, whose major growth in the last 20 years is the result of internal migration due to displacement caused by political conflict. Many people in SJL came to escape violence in their communities, and represent many different cultures from the various regions of Peru. Much of the population of SJL has limited access to resources, job opportunities, and basic services (Puente Yaranga 2002). According to the Ministry of Women and Development, the district of SJL also has one of the highest rates of domestic violence in Peru. It is estimated that the levels of physical and sexual violence in intimate partner relationships is 60 per cent (Ministerio de la Mujer y Desarrollo Social 2004, 44), with nine out of ten of the perpetrators being male (*ibid.*, 46).

In a study of masculinities and conjugal violence in the poor areas of Lima and Cuzco (Ramos Padilla 2006), it was found that in the social context in which they grow up, Peruvian boys learn at an early age that the father is privileged and the women are subordinate, and that the father can and does use violence to impose his will. Men repress feelings that show vulnerability, and if they openly show such feelings they are laughed at and humiliated by their peers. Expressions of aggression and violence are actively encouraged and often celebrated. In this way boys, are socialised to have the dominant role. As young men, they learn that their masculinity depends on their authority over women.

The context and origins of the men's programme

From its beginnings in 2004, the CJMT has been dedicated to working with women who have experience of, or are currently living with, domestic violence. The Constructing Violence-free Masculinities programme was founded by an understanding of men not only as part of the problem of male violence against women outlined above, but also as part of the solution (Tripathy 2010).

Overall, the CJMT's programmes have focused on promoting women's sense of identity and economic empowerment, through providing specific skill sets and support in creation of small businesses and co-operatives. The approach used has been one of empowering women so that they can make choices over their own lives. The results of the programme which the CJMT has aimed for are the empowerment of women: in their personal development, their development of leadership skills, and their 'economic empowerment' – many of them have formed small businesses, and become economically independent (for more information, see http://cmtj.blogspot.com).

Women involved in the CJMT's programmes have often reported an increase in domestic violence as an outcome of their participation. Women have typically reported that their husbands object to their wives' absences from home, and feel threatened by their wives' new sense of self-esteem, seeing changes in the power dynamics in the relationship. The culturally defined role of men as sole providers for the family can be perceived by both men and women to be undermined. This, combined with the *machismo* (that is, culturally approved roles and ways of behaving that men adopt, including stereotypical masculine roles of aggression, misogyny, hyper-sexuality, domination, and control, including the subordination of women) that often goes unquestioned, has led to increased frequency in, and severity of, violence against women in the home (Mitchell 2008).

At first, programme staff at the CJMT assumed that the appropriate approach to the problem involved supporting an affected woman to separate from her intimate partner. This approach was modelled on standard practice for mainstream domestic violence intervention programmes. An approach to domestic violence which involves women separating from their intimate partners who abused them is based on an assumption that it is essential to separate because the man could not and would not change (Connell 2001). In the Peruvian context, at government level, as well as in the majority of NGOs working in the field, domestic violence is understood in a punitive context, centred in the justice system, of reporting and denouncing domestic violence to the authorities.

Although many women do choose to leave their abusive partners, one consequence of this is the break-up of the family unit. When women involved in CMTJ programmes made this choice, this was met by resistance from the community. The Centre became known as a space that separated couples and broke up the family unit. As a result, CMTJ programmes were boycotted by people whom they aimed to serve. In addition, leaving your partner is obviously not possible for all women, as many are unable to make ends meet economically on their own. In the poor community in which the CMTJ is located, families often struggle economically with lack of access to employment and the jobs that are available often pay very little and require long working hours, which for many women, especially those with children, limit their ability to support themselves and their children financially. In many cases when women enter the workforce and begin to gain economic independence from their partners they reported that the levels of violence often increased.

The women from the community who participated in the CMTJ programmes were demanding other alternatives. Many of the women involved in CMTJ's programmes said that when they reported domestic violence, they were not saying that they wanted to separate from their partner. They were saying that they did not want their partner to be violent towards them, and they saw a distinction there. This intuition is very prevalent among women in Peruvian society, especially where there is a strong cultural importance to the family, as a whole. The following response characterises the kind of request the programme staff received from many women:

> I've changed, I've improved as a person, I love my partner, I don't want to live in a violent situation anymore, but neither do I want to separate from my partner. Can you please help my partner?

The legal process is fundamentally important in the fight against domestic violence. Government and NGO policies are focused on working with women – both in prevention and intervention. But the CMTJ programme staff recognised that there is a lack of programmes, both intervention and prevention-oriented, that work with men in addition to women. Men must be integrated into these programmes, both as *part of the problem but also to become part of the solution*. Staff of the CMTJ felt they needed to respond to the intuition of women that their men were capable of change, and the right of women to have an emotional life, and a healthy, harmonious life without violence; programme staff took the step towards a more comprehensive approach. Just as CMTJ programmes had helped open up spaces for women to grow, to change, to become empowered, and to question existing gender norms, it should not be assumed that men could not have similar journeys.

The programme and its methodology

The Constructing Violence-free Masculinities programme was developed and run over three years, from 2009 to 2011. The programme was developed by Angel Palacios Trujillo and Jose Reyes Mori to enable the CMTJ to respond to women's realities. It presents a model for decreasing domestic violence through actively engaging men by challenging their deeply held gender norms and conceptions of masculinity which are seen as a causal factor of violence against women. The aim of the programme was to contribute to stopping men's physical violence against women, and reducing their psychological violence. The process used to do this includes raising men's awareness of the social and cultural conditions and constructs that reinforce violent behaviour, challenging participants to take responsibility for their violent acts, and supporting participants to examine ways of being a man which do not involve violence – in other words, thinking about new forms of masculinity.

The Constructing Violence-free Masculinities programme was devised with two objectives. The first objective of the intervention with men was to recognise the social construction of masculinity. The second goal of the programme is that men, who are violent towards their intimate partners, assume responsibility for their violence and reflect on their violent behaviour. The final goal of this programme was for participants to end their violence.

The programme method took an educational and therapeutic approach to working with men who are violent towards their partners. The programme was based on the notion that programmes supporting women's empowerment and leadership had led to changes for the women involved because spaces and opportunities for personal development and growth had been provided. Women had spaces in which they could grow in a supported environment. But these same spaces for personal, critical self-reflection had not been provided to men. Many women affected by domestic violence were not saying, 'You hit me, and therefore you are wretched and never going to change', but, rather, believed that change was possible. This insight led programme staff to propose opening spaces for men to reflect on their own experiences and create change.

All of the participants in the Constructing Violence-free Masculinities programme were migrants who had come to Lima from other areas of Peru. While they come from different cultures in the coastal, highland, and jungle areas of Peru, violence against women is known and seen as normal and natural by all. A typical comment from a participant is, 'In my community, you are taught as a young boy that you have to beat your woman very strongly, but usually just once, and you will see that she will not cause you any more trouble'. This speaker saw violence as a cultural element; something that was taught as a value, and which was crucial to convey to your children and to others. The different worldviews represented among the programme participants, and the various ways in which they thought of violence as natural, was an ongoing challenge for the programme. Despite their differences, men needed to reach consensus about ending violence.

Participation, referral, and scheduling

In the first year, the strategy that the Constructing Violence-free Masculinities programme used to get the participants to come to the programme was through formal invitations from government agencies. The police, the judiciary, and health-care professionals all showed interest in the programme, but in practice, made no referrals. This shows the disconnect between government agencies and NGO programmes like our own. In the end, throughout the three years of the programme, the vast majority of the participants were referred by their wives and female partners who had passed through the women's empowerment and leadership programmes offered by the centre. The disadvantage of this method of getting men involved in the programme was of course that it required a certain level of empowerment for the women to challenge their partners, who had been violent toward them, to participate in this process. These referrals from women who had actively participated in the programmes at the centre were the most effective means of recruiting male participants, and ensuring that they stayed the course.

However, it was important for all concerned to recognise that it was not the woman's responsibility to 'change' her partner. Many of the men were reluctant to say that their spouse had caused them to come along, because they saw it as not socially acceptable for a woman to tell a man to do something. The facilitators took this into account, aiming to support men to recognise

the positive role of their spouses, yet without undermining the man's participation in the group.

Participants met for four hours on Sunday mornings. The fact that the
programme was run at that time and on that day meant that men had to be
willing to sacrifice time that they would otherwise be spending in leisure. It
was obviously important for the scheduling of the group sessions to coincide
with available time when men are not occupied in work, but this did mean
that those men who wanted to spend time with their families were not able
to. However, in a resource-poor environment where time is at a premium, this
is not an easily solved problem.

Horizontal working to establish mutual support

An important aspect of the Constructing Violence-free Masculinities programme was that it involved a 'horizontal' relationship between facilitators
and participants – that is, one of equality, recognising that everyone present
had been affected by violence, and all were in the process of reconstructing
their masculinities and questioning their violent acts and attitudes. This
approach is in line with writing on masculinity, gender, and development
which asserts that through the deconstructing of the assumptions and cultural
and social norms that define masculinities, men can take part in processes of
change and empowerment (Cornwall 1997).

Working in groups

The Constructing Violence-free Masculinities programme approach was to use
techniques from popular education, in a group format. In a low-resource community, working in a group format is a more economical option. In addition,
approaches based on a one-on-one basis normally require interventions of a
longer duration than that based on a group dynamic.

Over the three years, the programme involved convening one men's group
each year to meet and work together. Each year group had between 10 and
20 regular participants. Participants who completed the group process then
received additional training as group leaders and workshop facilitators. In the
first two years, the groups ran and worked together for three months, but in
the third year the period was extended for six months in the hope of achieving a greater impact.

Mutual support groups were vital in the programme methodology because
the men come together in a group to discuss their violent behaviour and recognise that they are not alone: they are a part of a wider society where this
violence exists and in some ways is seen as normal. Finding that they are
not alone and working together in solidarity helps to de-pathologise men's
violence, in a mutually supportive environment. In other words, it helps to
remove the stigma of the violent individual being 'sick', and promotes participation, reflection, and learning.

The mutual learning includes the process of men recognising themselves in each other. Listening to another person's story says something to people about their own history, their own culture, and their own community. The ability to empathise is something that the men struggle with, but it is really critical. In the construction of gender norms, the ideas of feeling what another person is feeling is fundamentally important in order to be able to measure the impact of their actions on their partner and children. When they act in violent ways, how does a wife or child feel? When they hear the stories of other men's violence, men also begin to see their own behaviour in a new light, empathising with the women and children who are experiencing violence at the hands of other members of the group. This process of mutual support and learning is therapeutic; men in the group begin to feel a sense of positive power through their collective work. This is an efficient way of creating change in people. The group environment also allows them to learn the ability to be empathetic. Learning from each other, they begin to promote change individually, and challenge the others in the group.

In the process of reflecting on learning and thinking of new ways in which they can express themselves as men without violence, individual men would have found it difficult to do so alone – it would have meant that they have to go against the flow. The participants have reported that they feel great societal pressures, from friends, family, and the media, to continue to demonstrate their hegemonic masculinity and use violence and control of their intimate partners. They state that they are sometimes chastised for choosing different, more egalitarian forms of interacting with their partners (personal communication, 4 August 2012). As part of the group in this programme, they participated in a new kind of community which is supportive and continues to challenge patterns of behaviour.

Look, judge, act

CMTJ developed a three-step process of reflection in the Constructing Violence-free Masculinities programme, to get men to think about themselves and their actions in context. Men first *looked* at their reality, and examined how they built their masculinity, the social constructions of their masculinity. Even though they were all members of the same society and community, the way in which each man was brought up – that is, socialised – had actually varied considerably. In the group sessions, men examined the influences on them from their families, religious practice, school, and from the wider community, thinking of themselves as part of, and not separate from, the context in which they live. They were encouraged to take a long hard look at themselves, asking themselves, 'Who am I as a man?'

A fundamental aspect of this process of self-examination was challenging myths related to gender norms which each individual may use to explain and justify his violence. One of the most common myths described and defended by the participants was that their violent action was a response to a provocation by their partner: 'She provoked me'.[2] The belief was that if someone acted in a certain way that was contrary to the way a man thought she should, or acted in a way he believed to be threatening, then as a man, he must react with violence in order to put the woman in her place and defend his honour as a man. This process of challenging myths focuses on rebuilding ways of thinking, feeling, and acting.

Many of these myths are based in social mandates – to be strong, to avoid showing emotion, to exert control over your spouse, and so on. The researcher Michael Kaufman (1994/1999, 1999) has referred to the constant pressure and fear of not being thought a real man as a key factor that drives male behaviour. The groups in the Constructing Violence-free Masculinities programme were encouraged to question social mandates, as well as the question of who drives them. An example is the use of male power over women which is an ongoing issue in wider society, often reinforced by the media. The idea of women's bodies as sexual objects was discussed and analysed in the programme.

The second, 'judge', stage of the group work required participants to reflect critically on what they are doing in their lives. It meant they became aware of their violence, and the impact that it had; becoming self-critical, and developing critical thinking about their actions. This stage involved a process of reflection about the life men wanted. Questions were asked: When I use violence who wins and who loses? Who challenges me? What is my life plan? What kind of masculinity do I want for myself? What kind of man do I want to be for my children and for my family?

Group members were then encouraged to take action, in the final 'act' stage of the group work. The first step was to articulate what they would like to do: 'I am committed to .. . ' No one proposes what is the right way, or the solution to the problems, it is a choice based on the experience of each person individually. This process involves a confrontation between the public and private spheres.

Complementary individual therapy

In addition to group work, the participants had the choice of individual therapy sessions with a psychologist, which were intended as complementary to the programme, ensuring that other issues and mental health concerns can be addressed in a therapeutic setting. About 70 per cent of the participants took advantage of this service, many of them working on mental health issues, and drug and alcohol consumption; that is, concerns that affect their violent behaviour, while not being the root cause of it. This also allowed for the facilitators to build rapport with the participants, promoting a rich group experience.

Accompaniment

Another important component of the Constructing Violence-free Masculinities programme was the accompaniment of participants and their families outside the group setting. A men's group needs to be run in the recognition that men are integrated into the larger context of which they are a part: family, community, and wider society. It is the wider context that needs change, not just the individual, but that process of challenging gender relations starts from the man himself.

The programme also included a component of accompaniment of the family, both the women and children which allows for a more integrated intervention. This involves a community worker visiting the family, which allows for concerns expressed by the family to be addressed, and also ensures they do not feel isolated from the process. This family involvement also helps to make men accountable for their behaviour, and make the home environment safer for the women and children. The information gained via contact with the families also allows the programme to be adapted to the needs of participants, based on a holistic view of their surroundings, and individual experiences.

Assessing achievements, and challenges for the future

The experience of three years has validated the decision to respond to the women who called for alternatives, to the communities who gave their input, and to the need to create programmes aimed at engaging men in the process. In the families of the participants in the programme, all of them had stopped the physical and sexual violence previously meted out to their intimate partners. The process that accompanies the group, the follow-up with the families, showed that this was the case – both the self-reporting from the participants and the interviews with their families. Less positively, psychological violence had decreased but not completely stopped. This requires attention in the longer term. While this programme has been running for the last three years, there needs to be further research and follow-up done to measure the long-term effects of the programme on the participants and their families as well as the impact on the community. This requires an analysis and response in terms of what ongoing support is needed for the sustainability of the results. One of the greatest challenges is the sustainability of the programme and its results.

The groups have created spaces for sharing. The programme has been able to create spaces that can challenge how masculinity has been constructed and raised the possibility of building new masculinities, pointing to a new way of what it means to be a man, of relating to one's partner, of being a parent, of showing affection and emotion. One of the men stated: 'Isn't it curious that we can share openly and cry in this group without having to be drinking [alcohol]?' Alcoholism itself has been identified as a problem, and strategies developed – 'I've learnt that I can have fun without the need to drink', and put that into practice at home. In the process of the programme, men have made friends and experienced new ways of interacting among groups of men. They have become facilitators, leaders, and spokespeople. In fact, the majority of the men who pass through the process become very driven about spreading the message that being a man does not have to mean being violent. Many share their life stories in events with different community groups and engage other men in the process. This process of personal development and growth, and men's need to share the learning, creates change from the personal to the community level.

Many of the women whose partners have participated in the programme have stated that they have seen changes in many aspects of their husbands' attitudes and behaviour. The beginnings of changes in the power dynamics within their relationships are apparent in that the changes in the distribution of domestic work and care of the children that had previously been the responsibility of the woman became more equitable, shared responsibilities. The women also reported changes in the consideration of their opinions and greater participation in the decision-making processes within the household. The male participants began to see the possibilities of their partners in taking different roles, they reasoned that these new power dynamics did not make them 'less of a man', but instead led to a healthier, happier family life.

Gender equality is not only a matter of importance to women; it is important to men also, because it affects the relationships of power between men and women. As a result of its work with men, CMTJ has been recognised for its innovative approach to domestic violence in the context of the empowerment of women and gender equality work. There has been interest both from government agencies and NGOs in its methods and results. The public prosecutor's office has begun to refer cases of men who have been charged with domestic violence and to follow up on their participation and progress. The CMTJ has also become part of an inter-agency collaboration: a network of organisations successfully advocated for the creation and implementation of a Municipal Plan for No Violence Towards Women, Children and Adolescents in San Juan de Lurigancho,[3] making it the first district in Peru to have such a plan. It is important for this wider collaboration to take place: while this programme represents an important step in developing approaches to address domestic violence that include men, it is only part of the process. It requires dissemination and longer-term programmes that not only allow men to challenge their violent behaviour and critically reflect on their masculinities, but to become change agents for the long term. The issues of domestic violence and violence against women require greater, more integrated approaches that work at numerous levels, to create lasting change.

Notes

1. This programme is made possible through the financial support of the Government of Canada, acting through the Canadian International Development Agency (CIDA).
2. The central government, Ministry for Women and Vulnerable Populations, has developed a pilot programme for men (Centro de atención institucional frente a la violencia familiar) who have been through the justice system accused and sentenced for domestic violence. The participants are mandated by court order to attend, but the results and impact of this programme are in the initial stages.
3. This idea is discussed further in Reyes Mori and Palacios Trujillo (2010).

References

Boesten, Jelke (2012) 'The state and violence against women in Peru: intersecting inequalities and patriarchal rule', *Social Politics* 19(3): 361–82

Comisión de la Verdad y Reconciliación (CVR) (2003) *Informe Final*, Lima: CVR

Connell, R.W. (2001) 'On men and violence', written for the United Nations INTRAW Virtual Seminar Series on Men's Roles and Responsibilities in Ending Gender-based Violence, www.un-instraw.org/en/index.html

Cornwall, Andrea (1997) 'Men, masculinity and "gender in development"', *Gender and Development* 5(2): 8–13

Davis, Mike (2006) *Planet of the Slums*, London: Verso

Guatemala Human Rights Commission (2010) 'Guatemala Human Rights Commission/ USA Fact Sheet, Femicide and Feminicide,' Washington DC: Guatemala Human Rights Commission/USA

Instituto Nacional de Estadística e Informática (INEI) (2010) 'Encuesta Demográfica y de Salud Familiar – ENDES. Informe Principal, Violencia contra las mujeres, niñas y niños', Lima: INEI

Instituto Nacional de Estadística e Informática (INEI) (2012) 'Informe Técnico: Compor-tamiento de la Economía Peruana en el Primer Trimestre de 2012', Lima: INEI, www. ghrc-usa.org

Kaufman, Michael (1994/1999) 'Men, Feminism and Men's Contradictory Experiences of Power', Chapter 8 in H. Brod and M. Kaufman (eds.) *Theorizing Masculinity*, Thousand Oaks, CA: Sage

Kaufman, Michael (1999) *Las siete P's de la violencia de los hombres*, Toronto: Emakunde/Instituto Vasco de la Mujer

Ministerio de la Mujer y Desarrollo Social (2004) 'Violencia familiar y sexual en mujeres y varones de 15 a 59 años: Estudio realizado en distritos de San Juan de Lurigancho, Puno y Tarapoto', www.mimdes.gob.pe/pncvfs/index.htm

Mitchell, Rhoda (2008) 'A Case Study: Empowering Women and Including Men', Calgary, Canada: University of Calgary

Monarrez Fragoso, Julia (2002) 'Feminicidio sexual serial en Ciudad Juárez: 1993-2001', *En Debate Feminista* 25(April): 279–305

Observatorio de la Criminalidad del Ministerio Público (2010) 'El Registro de Feminicidio del Ministerio Público', November/December, Lima: Observatorio de la Criminalidad del Ministerio Público

Puente Yaranga (2002) 'Rompiendo las cadenas: Violencia Familiar en el Asentamiento humano Sauce Alto-San Juan de Lurigancho. II Encuentro Metropolitano de Jóvenes Investigadores Sociales', Lima: UNMSM

Ramos Padilla, Miguel (2006) 'Masculinidades y violencia conyugal: Experiencias de vida de hombres en sectores populares de Lima y Cusco', Lima: Universidad Peruana Cayetano Heredia

Reyes Mori, Jose and Ángel Palacios Trujillo (2010) 'Una experiencia de trabajo con varones que ejercen violencia familiar en el distrito de San Juan de Lurigancho: Construyendo Masculinidades sin violencia, cambiando maneras de pensar, sentir y actuar', Lima: Centro Mujer Teresa de Jesú s

Tripathy, Jyotirmaya (2010) 'How gendered is gender and development: culture, masculinity, and gender difference', *Development in Practice* 20(1): 113–21

UN Development Programme (UNDP) (2010) *Assessment of Development Results Peru: Evaluation of UNDP Contribution*, New York: UNDP

About the author

Rhoda Mitchell is a Gender Specialist in Oxfam-Québec, working in Peru. Email: MitchellR@oxfam.qc.ca

CHAPTER 8

'One Man Can': shifts in fatherhood beliefs and parenting practices following a gender-transformative programme in Eastern Cape, South Africa

Wessel van den Berg, Lynn Hendricks, Abigail Hatcher, Dean Peacock, Patrick Godana and Shari Dworkin

Abstract

'One Man Can' (OMC) is a rights-based gender equality and health programme implemented by Sonke Gender Justice in South Africa. It has been featured as an example of best practice by the World Health Organization, UNAIDS, and the UN Population Fund, and translated into nearly a dozen languages and implemented all across Africa. South Africa has strong gender and HIV-related policies, but the highest documented level of men's violence against women in the world, and the largest number of people living with HIV. In this context, OMC seeks to improve men's relationships with their partners, children, and families, reduce the spread and impact of HIV and AIDS, and reduce violence against women, men, and children. To understand whether and how OMC workshops brought about changes in men's attitudes and practices related to parenting, an academic–non-government organisation partnership was carried out with the University of California at San Francisco, the University of Cape Town, and Sonke. The workshops appear to have contributed powerfully to improved parenting and more involved and responsible fathering. This chapter shares our findings in more detail and discusses the promises and challenges of gender-transformative work with men, underscoring the implications of this work for the health and well-being of women, children, and men.

Key words: fatherhood; masculinities; gender equality; care; children; 'One Man Can'

Introduction

South Africa has the highest rates of gender-based violence of any country in the world and by far the largest number of people living with HIV and AIDS of any country. These two public health epidemics are inextricably linked; both

http://dx.doi.org/10.3362/9781780448664.008

are driven in significant ways by gender inequalities and by gender norms that equate manhood with dominance, aggression, sexual conquest, and the pursuit of multiple partners. These norms about manhood, combined with corresponding norms about womanhood that emphasise women's submission to men, make it difficult for women to negotiate condom use or to say no to sex. Masculinity, in other words, is deeply implicated in the spread and impact of HIV and AIDS, and in the pervasive domestic and sexual violence that scars South Africa's post-1994 democratic dispensation. Increasingly, organisations such as Sonke Gender Justice are making the case that men and masculinities are implicated in the successful resolution of both of these health and human rights problems.

A growing body of research indicates that the lives of men, women, and children can be improved by transforming masculine norms to be more equitable, expressive, and respectful (Barker *et al.* 2010). Such programmes have been deemed promising in the evidence-base and several have been found to have a positive impact on gender equality in relationships and on health outcomes (Barker *et al.* 2010; Jewkes *et al.* 2008; Kalichman *et al.* 2009).

Fatherhood is a key part of male identity and needs to be addressed in work which tries to transform masculine norms (Richter 2006). Research shows that fathering is socially patterned, and in the context of South Africa, this means it is intricately linked to histories of apartheid, unemployment, poverty, migration, racism, family structure, and masculinities (Ramphele and Richter 2006). Many men's sense of themselves as fathers rests on a sense of being able to provide materially for their children (Morrell and Richter 2006), but it is often difficult for men to live up to this traditional role (Montgomery *et al.* 2006).

In the study discussed in this chapter we explored how participation in one gender-transformative programme known as 'One Man Can' shifted men's beliefs and practices associated with masculinity, fatherhood, and parenting. Far from revealing a static notion of all men as distant, uncaring, or uninvolved parents, the literature in South Africa shows that masculinities are in flux, allowing for the positive roles that men play as fathers and caregivers (Richter and Morrell 2006).

Sonke Gender Justice Network and its approach to gender transformation and women's rights

Sonke Gender Justice Network is a South African non-government organisation (NGO) that was established in 2006 in order to support men and boys to take action to promote gender equality and prevent both violence against women, and HIV and AIDS. Sonke's vision is a world in which men, women, and children can enjoy equitable, healthy, and happy relationships that contribute to the development of just and democratic societies. Sonke uses a broad mix of social change strategies, reaching nearly 25,000 men each year through workshops and community dialogues, nearly ten million listeners a week via community radio shows, and millions more as a result of media coverage of high-profile advocacy work to effect change in government policies and practice.

While Sonke is best recognised for its work to transform harmful norms of masculinity and its efforts to mobilise men for gender justice, it deliberately rejects the term 'men's organisation' because this can easily be misconstrued to mean that Sonke advances men's rights – which it does not. Instead, Sonke defines itself as a feminist organisation working to achieve gender transformation, and using as one of its principal strategies the engagement, education, and mobilisation of men. Sonke's board of directors, staff, and volunteers are nearly 50 per cent women, and it works in close and ongoing partnership with many more traditional women-led women's rights organisations. Sonke's advocacy campaigns often deliberately profile men and women working together for gender justice. This demonstrates simultaneously that gender issues are also men's issues, and that men and women can and should work together to achieve a gender-equitable world.

Understandably, some women's rights groups remain uncertain – and in some cases sceptical – of the value of work with men for gender equality. This is often for two reasons: firstly ideological differences, and secondly concerns about competition for resources.

In terms of the first category of concerns, Sonke's analysis holds that this work carries more similarity with, than difference from, more conventionally women-led and women-focused approaches. Some feminist analysis, especially second-wave feminist thought, holds that men are so deeply invested in patriarchy, because of the unearned power and privilege it grants them, that they will therefore resist change, often violently. Not surprisingly, this analysis offers little hope that it is possible to work with men to bring about more equitable gender relations. While recognising the unfair advantages men gain from patriarchy, Sonke views patriarchal privileges as coming at a high cost for men (this dynamic is discussed in the theoretical literature by writers including Messner 1997 and Morrell *et al.* 2012). These costs to men range from compromised physical and mental health, and heightened risk for injury, to limited intimacy and superficial friendships. Recognising these costs, and the love and solidarity many men feel for women in their lives, can and does motivate men to work for gender transformation. Sonke holds that power and control are not the only currency in relationships, and that both women and men deserve greater joy, passion, and connection. Equitable, caring, and connected relationships between the sexes are more satisfying and more consistent with a commitment to human rights and democracy.

In terms of the second concern of competition for resources between women's rights organisations and organisations that work with men for gender equality, Sonke is well aware of the issues, which are real. Resources for gender transformation are far less than is needed for the work in general. In order to achieve the shared goals of gender transformation, Sonke maintains a dual strategy of firstly keeping feedback channels open by engaging in regular discussion with traditional women's rights organisations and representatives; and secondly striving to share access to resources. Sonke has brokered relationships between other women's rights organisations and Sonke donors, and developed joint work and proposals with women's rights partner organisations, securing grants that have sustained their work. Through a longstanding history of collaboration with women's rights organisations, Sonke has developed relationships of trust that have defused some of these tensions. Whenever they emerge, Sonke welcomes a dialogue.

The One Man Can Programme

The One Man Can Programme (OMC) was launched on International Day to End Violence Against Women, 25 November 2006 in South Africa, and then in Geneva on 6 December 2006, as part of the Office of the United Nations High Commissioner for Refugees's 16 Days of Activism to End Violence Against Women campaign. Recognising the importance of collaboration and the significant contribution made by many rights-based organisations across the world in developing OMC, the initiative was launched as a formal partnership with a wide range of South African and international organisations.

OMC was designed by men and women working together, and then reviewed by many different women's rights activists in South Africa. OMC activities are adapted based on the project goals, the specific groups of men focused on, and the specific community context. OMC is based on the premise that changing deeply held gender and sexuality-related beliefs and practices require comprehensive, multifaceted strategies. OMC works with men and boys of all ages and all walks of life, and is rooted firmly in the belief that all men can become advocates for gender equality and active participants in efforts to respond to HIV and AIDS. As such, the programme is implemented in urban, peri-urban, and rural areas, and with an enormously wide range of men and boys, including religious and traditional leaders; young and adult men in prisons and upon release; farm workers; miners; commercial fishermen; school children and their parents; policymakers and health service providers at national, provincial, and local level.

The OMC Fatherhood Project, which is the focus of this chapter, was developed and implemented in 2007-2009 in response to a request from UNICEF to increase men's involvement in meeting the needs of children affected by HIV and AIDS, including children who had lost one or both parents to AIDS in two rural communities, Nkandla in KwaZulu-Natal and Mhlontlo in the Eastern Cape. UNICEF's work in these regions had confirmed what a significant body of research already suggested would be the case: that men were not playing an adequately active role in supporting children made vulnerable by AIDS. Indeed, research by many authors indicated that women were carrying a disproportionate burden of caring for those affected by AIDS and that many children were falling through the cracks as a result.

In South Africa, social scientists and public health experts alike have rec-ognised fatherhood as an important driver in health and development for individuals, families, and communities. A seminal campaign, entitled The Fatherhood Project, was launched and implemented by the Human Sciences Research Council in 2005. It placed fatherhood on the agenda of civil society and policymakers alike, as an important area of opportunity, and of challenge. The project produced an anthology of important research outputs on father-hood, entitled *Baba: Men and Fatherhood in South Africa* (Richter and Morrell 2006), and a subsequent focus on young fathers was published soon thereafter entitled: *Teenage Tata: Young Fathers in South Africa* (Swartz and Bhana 2009). These two books have become important resources for information on father-hood in South Africa, and continue to influence the development of local programming that is focused on parenting. However, few gender-transforma-tive programmes have been implemented in the arena of masculinities and fatherhood.

The OMC Fatherhood project worked with black South African men aged 18 or over, living in communities chosen by Sonke because of the effect of high AIDS mortality and its effect on children left vulnerable by the deaths of one or both parents, and Sonke's related desire to promote greater involvement of fathers in the lives of these children. They were recruited into the OMC Fatherhood Project through Sonke's community partner organisations, which included organisations focusing on gender-based violence and HIV- and AIDS-related matters. The project had three primary objectives. Firstly, it aimed to increase men's involvement, not only in the lives of their own children, but also in ensuring that children in general, and orphans and vulnerable chil-dren in particular, had access to essential social services, such as child grants, attending school and having their psychosocial and educational needs met. Secondly, the project set out to develop men's capacity to be advocates and activists in efforts to eliminate violence against women and children, to pre-vent the spread of HIV and AIDS, and to promote health, care, and support for orphans and vulnerable children. Thirdly, it planned to give voice to vulner-able children, training and engaging them in using multi-media approaches (photography, writing, and video) to bring the realities of their daily lives to the attention of the leaders in their communities. The object of this was to catalyse social change.[1]

Researching the impact of One Man Can Programme's fatherhood workshops: study methods

In an external evaluation of the impact of participation in the OMC workshops on Fatherhood, participants were interviewed once during the six-month period following their participation in the programme. Interviews took place from February to September 2010. Our collaborators from the University of California at San Francisco hired interviewers external to Sonke, but who were familiar with the communities of interest. Interviews focused on topics related to masculinities, gender relations and rights, violence, gender and HIV risk, alcohol, parenting and fatherhood, and relationships. Interviewers were trained by the last author for three days in qualitative methods, ethical research practices, and techniques of probing during interviews. Researchers were already experienced at discussing sensitive topics such as gender, masculinities, relationships, HIV, and sexuality. Interviews were carried out in the local languages, were transcribed into the local language, and then into English by the researcher themselves. Participants were offered R100 (about US$12) as reimbursement for time and transportation associated with participation.[2] In analysing our research results, we drew on conventions in thematic analysis and principles of grounded theory within qualitative research methods.[3]

The impact of the programme

In the study, we found that men have strong and articulate feelings regarding fatherhood, parenting, and masculinity. Here, we will illustrate this point with some of the perceptions and beliefs held by participants. All the quotations used throughout this chapter come from the sources we have outlined in this section. The chapter then goes on to identify changes in beliefs that men attributed to participating in OMC. In the last section we will explore what concrete changes in fathering practices can be attributed to participation in OMC.

Perceptions and beliefs about parenting and fathers

To get a picture of how OMC shifted men's parenting beliefs and practices, we need to know about men's initial perceptions and beliefs about parenting and fatherhood. Many of these perceptions involved discussions of men's household authority and decision-making power, and the use of discipline. In particular, some men felt that children *are representations of the community standing of fathers*. This view was expressed in comments such as:

> *I try to instil this discipline in my children because I am a community leader and if they behave badly, then it would contradict my good standing and the responsibilities I hold in the community. My children become a reflection of me in the community.* (54-year-old, five children)

In part to protect their own reputations, and due to the belief that children are a reflection of fathers, many fathers assumed an *authoritarian role as the primary disciplinarian*. In addition, it seems that improvements in women's and children's rights in South African society have led to some men feeling disempowered in terms of their household authority, and some men viewed strict rules and discipline as a way to retain such authority:

> *If my child thinks he has got rights, then he should go and build his own home where he will practise his rights. Under my roof, he is my child and he will follow the rules of my home.* (51-year-old, two children)

Some men also rationalised their disciplinary role through *traditional cultural practices that encouraged corporal punishment and spanking*. For example, one man articulated his position by arguing that:

> *I think the government was supposed to appreciate that we are not raised like white people because in our culture we believe that spanking plays a crucial part in the development and growing up of an individual.* (62-year-old, three children)

Although most men generally perceived fathers as the disciplinarians within the home, when asked to describe the ideal man, participants expressed sentiments that a man is someone who can sacrifice and take care of his family 'responsibly'. Many men described the 'real man' as 'a man that *loves his family*' (41-year-old, one child), or as 'someone who has dignity and who teaches children the right things' (19-year-old, no children). In addition, most participants of the OMC programme expressed discontent with the behaviour of men in the community who were not considered 'ideal' men; such men were described as those who swear at their children, drink too much, shirk family responsibilities, do not respect their female partners or children, or do not keep up their homes.

Parental involvement and communication

When asked how often the participants saw their children, the responses were inflected with both cross-generational comparisons with men's own fathers, and contemporary experiences. For example, some fathers suggested that their ability to talk openly with their own children was distinct from their fathers' approach to parenting. Many men in the research were brought up in South Africa's so-called 'homeland regions', where Black South Africans were forced to live and from which adult men of working age were forced to travel to find work in ways that required that men were absent from their families for most of each year. For some participants, therefore, fathering their own children who actually lived with them was perceived as more problematic because of the absence of a role model. Some men described how they learned to become a 'real father' on their own. For example:

> *I am an old man but sometimes I do get the time to chat with them, which is something I did not do with my own father. My father was a stranger to me when I was growing up and I would see him only once in a long time ... So it is only now that I have become a 'real father'.* (73-year-old, seven grandchildren)

However, the realities of having to spend too much time working – sometimes away from home as migrants – are a challenge for fathers. Only a relatively small proportion of men felt that the amount of time they spent with their children was sufficient, as explained by one man: 'I spend a lot of time with my child. Recently I haven't been travelling frequently and therefore I have more time to be with my child' (23-year-old, one child). At the same time, several fathers felt that they spent an insufficient amount of time with children due to their unemployment, and family structure and relationship complexities. For example, several men reported themes such as:

> *I am not satisfied. I get to see her on a few occasions and on those occasions the visits are not long enough. The problem is that I am unemployed and therefore am not financially stable to do for my child the things that I wish I could do. I cannot afford to just call both her and her mother because money is scarce and when they get here I should also provide for them. However, I try my best under the circumstances ... I would like to stay with them and see my child growing. It is not nice to be an absent father from your child. I admire other peoples' children that are growing up with both their parents.* (41-year-old, one child)

Not only the quantity of time, but the quality of time with children was also a topic discussed by participants. Several fathers described finding quality time with children despite busy schedules. For example, one father explained how he found time with his children 'after their school hours and also in the mornings. My elder child usually wakes me up in the morning when she is preparing for school and we get to talk about a lot of things, including her schoolwork and also some school announcements'. Some fathers, however, reported that they did not think it possible to play a meaningful role in the lives of their children because of their limited financial means and because they did not have functional relationships with the mothers of their children:

> *I never spend any time with them. They all have different mothers and I have no relationship with any of the mothers. I do not have any connection with my children and the only thing that I do is to send money for them if I have it. I am fine with that arrangement. I am comfortable with them being far from me because it would have hurt both me and them to see each other during the time I was sick. I would have felt useless being unable to provide for them. They are ok growing up under their mothers because I am sure they are getting enough parental love and care.* (34-year-old, three children)

Changes in fatherhood beliefs and practices due to participation in One Man Can Programme

Most participants reported that OMC had influenced their way of thinking about masculinity and fatherhood, and ascribed these changes specifically to the project. For example, many men described how OMC shifted their parenting style from a financial 'providership' role to one of increased involvement, companionship, nurturing, and affection:

> *OMC changed a lot in the relationship I have with my child because the bond I developed became even stronger. It's not that I did not have a relationship with my child but I was more of a provider than a companion to her. My*

relationship with her is much stronger. OMC taught us to show the love and affection we have for our children instead of seeing ourselves as providers. I learnt that as a father I should be able to do my child's laundry, take her to school and back, and have time to be with her so that the child can be proud of me as a father. (33-year-old, one child)

In addition, several fathers described a shift towards being less violent and being more caring and protective. For example, one man explained his firm and initial reluctance towards children's rights legislation that prohibits corporal punishment but he then shifted his view after programme participation:

I understood children's and women's rights as a way of undermining men by the government. However since I became part of OMC, I changed my views and appreciated the reasons behind granting special rights to women and children. They are being abused in their homes and I think it is fair to protect them. (62-year-old, three children)

Other fathering practices influenced by One Man Can Programme

In addition to influencing men's beliefs about fatherhood, interviewees also revealed how OMC led to changes in four other fatherhood-related practices. First, several participants described how OMC assisted them in changing fatherhood-related practices away from being an absent father and towards being a *present, positive role model* in their children's lives. For example, one father underscored the influence that OMC had on his relationship with the mother of his child and his daughter:

OMC helped me in that regard because I was a person that used to like fun and drinking alcohol. I was always out there with the boys drinking. I didn't have time for my girlfriend and my daughter. She would come with my daughter to the tavern and beg me to at least give them attention. Sometimes she would go to my place and find me absent and she would sleep and wait for me. On my arrival, I would get into arguments with her. However after that workshop, I got to understand the importance of care and it has helped me. I am also enjoying it as well. OMC changed the way I live my life and the decisions that I make as a man. I have done away with some things that I used to do because they were not helping me. Being a better man is good because it means I can give my daughter all the attention she needs. (23-year-old, one child)

A second practice influenced by OMC, as reported by most fathers, was that of *improved communication with children*. Most fathers in our sample reported improved communication with their children about issues such as talking about considerate behaviour, gender equality, and health. These fathers also reported a better friendship with their children, and a greater interest in listening to their children. For example, a 25-year-old father of one reported that: 'I communicate better with both my child and the mother of the child. I also dedicate more time to my child'. Several fathers reported sharing OMC resources with their families and reading to their children: 'It changed a lot because that book sometimes I read it together with my children and give them lessons'. A few participants described how OMC prompted them to discuss HIV risks with their children:

> *I learnt some things from that programme, especially on the HIV and AIDS disease. I even teach them [my children] some of the lessons I learnt there. I teach them to know what is wrong and to be aware of ugawulayo [HIV]. I think they listen because as far as I know none of them is infected.* (60-year-old, four children)

Third, many fathers reported using fewer *corporal discipline strategies* with their children. OMC allowed for a better understanding of the effects of corporal punishment, and encouraged listening and talking between fathers and children. For example, one father described how OMC highlighted new and different ways of parenting that were less violent towards children, a critical change given the very clear association between children's exposure to harsh physical punishment and subsequent increased risk of perpetration of violence:

> *I was previously a very strict man and a disciplinarian. In being strict, I have to admit that I was also rough in a way, but those young men at Sonke taught us different ways of disciplining children.* (54-year-old, five children)

Lastly, some men described that the OMC programme helped them to recognise the role they could play in positively socialising the next generation of youth to be respectful, gender-equitable, and to share household responsibilities with parents and siblings. For example, several men explained themes such as:

> *OMC also empowered me to be able to teach the younger generation, especially the school-going age group, on how to relate in a respectful manner with their parents. I am able to teach children to be considerate with their parents so that if the parents say they do not have money, the children should be able to understand ... I really learnt a lot from OMC. I learnt to teach the younger people to share responsibilities with their parents and siblings. This is particularly so with the boys as we teach them that they should also help with household chores, rather than sit around and not do tasks because they think it is the girls' duty.* (52-year-old, six children)

Several other men described how they increased their own contribution to household work, taking on work traditionally seen as female (including cleaning, cooking, and care work), and encouraged their male children to share household tasks with their sisters and female partners.

Discussion and conclusions

The research we carried out in our academic–NGO partnership afforded us the opportunity to provide an in-depth examination of changes in men's parenting beliefs and practices in a gender-transformative programme. Our results indicate that the OMC programme has shifted men's attitudes about gender roles and power relations in the direction of gender equality, and improved numerous health outcomes, due to reduced alcohol use, safer sex, and reductions in male violence, against both women and men (Dworkin, Hatcher, Colvin and Peacock 2013). In the current study, results confirmed that men's beliefs and practices around fatherhood need to be seen in the context of changes – economic, political, and social – which affect gender relations, including legal and policy changes which support women's and children's rights. A particularly important aspect of South Africa's history of apartheid is fathers and grandfathers lacking much experience of active fatherhood, since many of them were themselves children in absent, abusive, or emotionally void households. Many participants described significant shifts in their own fatherhood beliefs and practices due to participation in OMC. Specifically, men described a transition from a disciplinarian and provider role towards one of increased involvement, companionship, nurturing, and affection towards children. In addition to describing improved communication and a better quality of relationships with children, men also recognised the positive role they can play in bringing up the next generation to be citizens who are healthy, and respectful of the equal rights of all, including women and girls. The programme appeared to be particularly promising in its ability to engage men on the sensitive topics of masculinities, gender equality, and family life, and to provide a safe space for critical reflections on these topics.

The research revealed that there were several important challenges experienced in this work. First, a few men described how other men ridiculed them for taking on more gender-equitable beliefs or practices in households and relationships. This highlights how gender-transformative programming in the future needs to recognise more centrally that masculinity is not solely defined in relation to femininity, but also in terms of how men practice masculinities in front of other men. Second, not all participants in OMC were able to transition to roles that included companionship, affection, or less discipline with their children. Indeed, while we saw many positive changes, these are challenging to make in the context of South Africa, where the legacy of the migrant labour system has created a narrow definition of fatherhood as a financial and authoritative role. Indeed, persistent poverty coupled with a primary definition of fathers as material providers has been found to exacerbate men's feelings of uselessness and/or absenteeism in family life (Ramphele and Richter 2006). Some of the men in our sample highlighted this to us. Third, it is worth noting that it was older men in our sample who disproportionately described shifts in masculinities, gender equality, and parenting practices. This may be due to the fact that older men who were not working were at home in a way that breadwinners could not be.

Our research shows that it is critical to bolster gender-transformative health and parenting programmes with young men who may be particularly resistant to change given that their masculine identities are an important resource through which to contest the marginalisation and disempowerment that many men in this context articulate and face (Morrell 2006; Morrell and Richter 2006). Such contextual realities not only underscore the importance of the current work, but highlight how gender-transformative programming should increasingly view fathers as a critical point of intervention to improve the health and well-being of children, families, and men themselves.

Acknowledgements

This research was supported by a grant from the National Institutes of Health, University of California, San Francisco, Gladstone Institute of Virology & Immunology Center for AIDS Research, P30-AI027763.

Notes

1. This study was part of a large OMC study that consisted of 90 qualitative, in-depth interviews with men who participated in OMC in three areas of South Africa: Limpopo, Eastern Cape, and Western Cape.
2. This and other aspects of the research protocol were approved by ethics boards at the University of California at San Francisco, USA and the University of Cape Town, South Africa.
3. To begin the coding process, two researchers extracted excerpts of the transcribed interviews that related to shifts in masculinities, fatherhood, and parenting. To establish a codebook, five interviews were randomly selected and independently evaluated using an open coding process employed during the initial phase of coding in qualitative research methods. After this round of coding, coders met to ensure full refinement of primary and secondary categories referred to as focused coding (following Lofland and Lofland 1995; Strauss and Corbin 1990). Lastly, we wrote analytical memos, to capture main themes and to lift multiple subcodes to a broader thematic analysis.

References

Barker, Gary, Christine Ricardo, Marcos Nascimento, Ana Maria Nascimento, and Carlos Santos (2010) 'Questioning gender norms with men to improve health outcomes: evidence of impact', *Global Public Health* 5(5): 539–53

Dworkin, Shari L., Abigail M. Hatcher, Chris Colvin and Dean Peacock (2013) Impact of a gender-transformative HIV and anti-violence program on gender ideologies and masculinities in two rural South African communities, *Men and Masculinities*, January 13, DOI:10.1177/1097184X12469878

Jewkes, Rachel, Mzikazi Nduna, Jonathan Levin, Nwabisa Jama, Kristin Dunkle, Adrian Puren, and Nata Duvvury (2008) 'Impact of stepping stones on incidence of HIV and HSV-2 and sexual behaviour in rural South Africa: cluster randomised controlled trial', *British Medical Journal* 337: a506

Kalichman, Seth, Leickness Simbayi, Allanise Cloete, Mario Clayford, Warda Arnolds, Mpumi Mxoli, Gino Smith, Charsey Cherry, Tammy Shefer, Mary Crawford, and Moira Kalichman (2009) 'Integrated gender-based violence and HIV risk reduction intervention for South African men: results of a quasi-experimental field trial', *Prevention Science* 10(3): 260–9

Lofland, John, and Lyn Lofland (1995) *Analyzing Social Settings: A Guide to Qualitative Observation and Analysis*, (Third Edition), Belmont, CA: Wadsworth

Messner, Michael (1997) *Politics of Masculinities: Men in Movements* (Volume 3), Newbury Park, CA: Sage

Montgomery, Catherine, Victoria Hosegood, Joanna Busza, and Ian Timaeus (2006) 'Men's involvement in the South African family: engendering change in the AIDS era', *Social Science & Medicine* 62(10): 2411–9

Morrell, Robert (2006) 'Fathers, fatherhood, and masculinity in South Africa', in Linda Richter and Robert Morrell (eds.) *Baba: Men and Fatherhood in South Africa*, Cape Town: HSRC Press

Morrell, Robert, Rachel Jewkes, and Graham Lindegger (2012) 'Hegemonic masculinity/masculinities in South Africa culture, power, and gender politics', *Men and Masculinities* 15(1): 11–30

Morrell, Robert, and Linda Richter (2006) 'Introduction', in Linda Richter and Robert Morrell (eds.) *Baba: Men and Fatherhood in South Africa*, Cape Town: HSRC Press

Ramphele, Mamphela, and Linda Richter (2006) 'Migrancy, family dissolution and fatherhood', in Linda Richter and Robert Morrell (eds.) *Baba: Men and Fatherhood in South Africa*, Cape Town: HSRC Press

Richter, Linda (2006) 'The importance of fathering for children', in Linda Richter and Robert Morrell (eds.) *Baba: Men and Fatherhood in South Africa*, Cape Town: HSRC Press

Richter, Linda, and Robert Morrell (eds.) (2006) *Baba: Men and Fatherhood in South Africa*, Cape Town: HSRC Press

Strauss, Anselm, and Juliet Corbin (1990) *Basics of Qualitative Research* (Volume 15), Newbury Park, CA: Sage

Swartz, Sharlene, and Arvin Bhana (2009) *Teenage Tata: Voices of Young Fathers in South Africa*, Cape Town: HSRC Press

About the authors

Wessel van den Berg is Children's Rights and Positive Parenting Unit Manager, Sonke GenderJustice Co-coordinator, MenCare Global Fatherhood Campaign. Email: wessel@genderjustice.org.za

Lynn Hendricks is Psychology Lecturer, Midrand Graduate Institute at Durbanville and an Adjunct Lecturer at the University of the Western Cape, both in South Africa. Email: lynn_southafrica@yahoo.com

Abigail Hatcher is Assistant Professor of Health Behavior, Gillings School of Global Public Health, University of North Carolina. Email: abbeyhatcher@gmail.com

Dean Peacock is co-founder and executive director of Sonke and co-founder and co-chair of the Global MenEngage Alliance. Email: dean@genderjustice.org.za

Patrick Godana is National One Man Can Manager at Sonke Gender Justice Network, South Africa. Email: Patrick@genderjustice.org.za

Shari Dworkin is Dean and Professor, School of Nursing and Health Studies at the University of Washington Bothell. Email: dworkins@uw.edu

CHAPTER 9

Whose turn to do the dishes? Transforming gender attitudes and behaviours among very young adolescents in Nepal

*Rebecka Lundgren, Miranda Beckman,
Surendra Prasad Chaurasiya, Bhawna Subhedi
and Brad Kerner*

Abstract

Men who use caring words instead of violence, and who are equal partners in nurturing their children and caring for their homes, are not formed overnight. Attitudes and behaviours that lead to gender equality are developed through a socialisation process beginning at birth. Early adolescence presents a window of opportunity to intervene before individuals solidify their ideas about gender roles and norms. The knowledge, attitudes, and skills acquired between the ages of 10 and 14 are particularly influential. Unfortunately, development research and programme initiatives addressing gender inequity have focused little on these issues. Save the Children's Choices curriculum consists of eight developmentally appropriate activities, supporting very young adolescents – that is, children aged 10–14 – to explore alternative views of masculinities and femininities. The hope is that this will lead to better sexual and reproductive health outcomes for participants and their communities in the future. This chapter focuses on Choices and its impact in Siraha district, Nepal. Research revealed changes in children's gendered attitudes and behaviour relating to discrimination, social image, control and dominance, violence, attitudes to girls' education, and acceptance of traditional gender norms, before and after participating in Choices.

Key words: Nepal; gender; very young adolescents; projective techniques; gender transformation

Gendered hopes and dreams

A Nepali proverb states: 'Educating a girl is like watering your neighbour's garden'. This refers to the fact that while a Nepalese girl contributes immensely to her family's welfare, she is not considered worthy of investment, because she is destined to marry and contribute to her husband's household. However,

http://dx.doi.org/10.3362/9781780448664.009

despite this view, which justifies natal families investing in the boys who will stay at home rather than the girls who will leave them, a rights-based approach to development asserts that every girl deserves equal opportunities in life. For a girl, equal rights include the opportunity to embrace her hopes and dreams, continue her education, live free from violence, and choose when to have her first child. For these rights to be realised, boys, as well as girls, need to be on board.

Gender norms and the importance of very young adolescence

Gender norms – as well as the social reproduction of these norms in institutions and cultural practices – are directly related to behaviour that affects health, and the ensuing quality of life (Greene and Barker 2011). Norms around sexual relationships, fertility control, the use of physical violence, and alcohol and drug use, are strongly influenced by gender norms which determine how men interact with their partners, families, and children (Interagency Gender Working Group 2011). In 2006, a global systematic review of factors shaping young people's sexual behaviour confirmed that gender stereotypes and different expectations about appropriate sexual behaviour for boys and girls influence sexual decision-making (Marston and King 2006). These same gendered expectations dictate the extent to which young girls can travel away from home, and the extent to which they are allowed to mix with boys (International Center for Research on Women (ICRW) 2010). Gender stereotypes also shape the way young people communicate. Girls are often encouraged to be docile and reserved, while boys are expected to dominate and use rough language. While girls may show their feelings, boys are often teased for revealing their emotions. Boys learn early that yielding power and authority over others brings them praise and recognition of their masculinity (ICRW 2010).

Changes in gender-related social norms, values, and practices can ultimately transform the way society values girls, and improve women's status. Over time, these changes should result in improved health and increased well-being for men and women. In order to influence these deep-rooted beliefs, however, development programmes seeking to promote gender equality and sexual and reproductive health must start early (Centre for Development and Population Activities 2010). Research shows that it is possible to challenge dominant roles of masculinity and femininity by modelling alternative options, and when norms become less rigid, the outcome is improved reproductive health, increased female educational attainment, and decreased interpersonal violence (Barker *et al.* 2007).

Increasingly, global practitioners recognise that early adolescence presents a unique window of opportunity to make a difference in the lives of boys and girls before their gender roles and norms are solidified. This chapter details the results of a gender transformative curriculum, Choices, designed and implemented by Save the Children. Choices sought to enable very young adolescents (VYAs) – that is, boys and girls aged 10–14 years old – to transform their thinking about gender norms – that is, social expectations of appropriate roles and behaviours for men (and boys) and women (and girls); and to recognise gendered differences and inequality. The Choices programme aimed to help VYAs by identifying simple actions to reduce this 'gender gap' so that girls and boys face the future on equal terms. Choices is one of the first interventions specifically designed to address inequitable gender norms for use with VYAs. The curriculum encourages these children to explore expressions of positive gender roles – at a time in their lives when they are forming the basis of their identities, roles, and responsibilities as individuals among their peers – within their households, and within their communities.

Choices was piloted in May 2010, in Siraha district in the Terai region of Nepal. Here, orthodox religious beliefs have resulted in a higher prevalence of practices, such as early marriage, early motherhood, and *dahej* (dowry), than in other regions of the country (Bista 2008). The people of Nepal have closely held beliefs and customs based primarily on Hindu and Buddhist traditions. Women and girls in Nepal face discrimination on multiple levels by virtue of their sex, caste, and ethnicity. Throughout their lives, many women are required to practise restrictions that perpetuate gender discrimination and inhibit their full participation in school, family life, and economic activities, and are vulnerable to various forms of psychological and physical violence.

The pilot intervention was evaluated by the Institute for Reproductive Health of Georgetown University, USA. The programme evaluation provides ample opportunities to learn more about the vulnerabilities, challenges, and opportunities faced by children aged between 10 and 14. While research on gender equality and disparity is growing, there is a dearth of information about these issues as they relate to young adolescents. The World Health Organisation has recognised this as a critical issue (Dixon-Mueller 2011). Learning about this group is urgently required to ensure that development programmes – in particular, those focusing on sexual and reproductive health – effectively address the specific needs of this age group.

This chapter draws on the results of the Choices pilot evaluation. Both qualitative and quantitative research methods suggest that participation in Choices led to more equitable gender attitudes and behaviour. Children reported that they felt and behaved differently after participating in Choices, with boys becoming more involved in household chores, for example, and advocating on behalf of their sisters.

Choices: a gender transformative curriculum

Baseline research conducted with VYA boys and girls while developing the Choices curriculum showed a persistent gender gap regarding the division of household work, access to education, freedom to play, and overall autonomy. The Choices curriculum uses an emotion-based approach to target the key emotions and feelings that lead to behavioural choices. It does this through activities that encourage behaviour based on an understanding and acceptance of gender equality. This results in girls, as well as boys, feeling respected, secure, and successful. Save the Children initially intended the curriculum to focus on boys; however, formative research conducted early on to identify boys' interests, beliefs, and values suggested that a relational approach – that is, involving both girls *and* boys – was more likely to be effective. The curriculum was designed to stimulate discussions between boys and girls, in which they can reflect on topics relating to power and gender, which are appropriate to their stage of development. Examples are hopes and dreams, actions that are fair and unfair, communication and respect.

The curriculum explored the following themes:

- Gender inequity and power; including the recognition that gender equity begins with small actions that earn respect from others.
- Boys can be respected even if they treat girls as equals.
- Social norms restrict boys from treating girls as equals.
- Boys and girls can express emotions and realise their hopes and dreams.
- Boys can empower girls to achieve their dreams.
- Girls can empower themselves to achieve their dreams.

Choices was piloted in 12 child clubs in the Bhawanipur and Pokharvinda Village Development Committees (VDCs) in the Siraha district of Nepal. Save the Children supports over 140 active child clubs in Siraha district in collaboration with local partner non-government organisations (NGOs). Child clubs are community based and governed and facilitated by children, with help from partner NGOs. Membership is open to all children in the community, both boys and girls and from all ethnic castes. Recruitment is done through children with a special emphasis on targeting marginalised children. The child clubs hold meetings every weekend of the year. Choices was implemented in weekly two-hour sessions during regular child club meetings, over a three-month period from May 2010 to July 2010. Implementation was overseen by a team of trained 18-20-year-old child club graduates from the community, one male and one female per club. A total of 309 children (48 per cent of whom were girls) participated in Choices. A further 294 children were used as a control group in our evaluation. They attend 12 child clubs in Chandraaudhayapur and Devipur VDCs. The control group was matched to the experimental group on a range of factors such as access to roads, language, schools, and socioeconomic characteristics.

Evaluation methods: shifting the balance of power from researcher to participant

The evaluation of Choices set out to measure whether participation in the programme resulted in a statistically significant change to boys' and girls' attitudes to gender issues, and whether this led in turn to a change in behaviour

Table 1. Outcomes measured in the evaluation

Attitudes	Behaviours
Girls and boys can imagine a life in which men and women have equal opportunities.	Girls and boys talk about their feelings and dreams with each other.
Girls and boys accept non-traditional gender roles.	Girls and boys promote gender equity in their lives.
Girls and boys value relationships based on equality, respect, and intimacy.	Boys take action to improve the lives of their sisters.
Girls and boys value the role of men caring for their family as well as providing financial support.	Girls and boys don't tease their peers for behaving in ways which are not consistent with traditional gender norms.
Girls and boys expect to make decisions jointly with their spouses.	

and practices. The evaluation used both quantitative and qualitative data. Outcomes measured in the evaluation are shown in Table 1.

Young people in the experimental group were interviewed before and after participating in Choices. Structured interviews were conducted with members of both groups at baseline and endline, the latter one month after completion of the final session of Choices. Qualitative information was collected at the end of the programme only, with a selection of participants. In-depth interviews were conducted with 36 children from both the control and experimental group, and 24 boys and girls from each group participated in Photovoice: a technique in which participants are provided with cameras to capture issues of importance to them. Maithili-speaking field researchers conducted individual interviews and group discussions with young people and their parents. In keeping with ethical standards for research involving minors, Child Club facilitators held introduction sessions for parents and guardians to gain consent for their children's participation. Informed assent was obtained from the children themselves. The research protocol and tools were approved by ethical review boards at Georgetown University and the Ministry of Health in Nepal.

The literature suggests that interviewer-led quantitative surveys and focus group discussions do not work well with VYA, who often have difficulty articulating their responses clearly, and may feel pressured to please the interviewer (Chong et al. 2006; Powers and Tiffany 2006). Most research methods advantage adults in terms of social and communication skills and knowledge; in light of this, the Choices evaluation developed participatory, visual, game-based methods which shifted the balance of power from researcher to participant (Dell Clark 2011). These more empowering methods include techniques designed to tap into underlying motivations by offering youth stimuli on to which they can project their feelings (Soley and Smith 2008). These methods, often called projective techniques, are especially useful when respondents have contradictory attitudes, are reluctant to discuss sensitive topics, or are unable to articulate responses. Because there are no right or wrong answers, participants are often more comfortable providing honest responses than when asked direct questions (Soley and Smith 2008). For example, showing photos to respondents (photo interviewing) may trigger submerged responses, sharpen memories, and keep them focused on the topic. The Photovoice technique, which entails providing cameras to study participants to take photographs on a given topic and then facilitating discussion of respondent-selected photos, has proven particularly effective in engaging youth and promoting dialogue (Hergenrather *et al.* 2009).

Both the structured and in-depth interviews with VYA and parents used a mixture of rigorously pre-tested techniques such as card games, pile sorts, case studies, drawings, and a chore-tracking calendar. In-depth interviews included projective techniques using photos to explore boys' and girls' hopes and dreams, and to measure gender roles and attitudes. The interviews also included a projective drawing activity, asking children to draw a boy or a girl who had not participated in the Choices curriculum holding something that they value. They were asked to write something the child might say and then to draw that same child after completing the Choices curriculum. This technique quickly identified children's perceptions of their changes in behaviour and practices. In addition, six focus group discussions were held with 54 randomly selected parents (28 control, 26 experimental) to determine whether the children discussed gender topics at home, or had incorporated any changes into their routines since participating in Choices. The results of the in-depth interviews and group discussions were coded and analysed manually by theme.

Quantitative data were collected using four methods: a card game, an exercise sorting photographs, a scenario game called Arun's Dilemma, and an activity collecting brothers' and sisters' time-use data. In the next section, more details are given of each of these methods and the results are discussed. In addition, scales were developed to measure statistically significant changes in attitudes to gender norms and roles. These were used during baseline and endline interviews with children in both the experimental and control groups. Most of the data were compiled into scales measuring discrimination, gender roles, and gender-equitable behaviours and practices.[1]

What was the effect of Choices participation?

Quantitative perspectives

1. Gender attitudes: card game. To explore gender attitudes, a deck of colour-coded cards was printed with gender value statements. In interviews with individual boys and girls, they were asked to read the statement on each card (while the interviewers also read the statement out loud to make sure they understood well) and place them into a container marked agree, disagree, or strongly disagree. Each of the statements was grouped into one of five scales:

discrimination, social image, violence, control/ dominance, and girls' education (Table 2).

Our findings show that the attitudes of boys and girls, as measured by each of the scales, were significantly more equitable after participating in Choices (see Table 3). For example, the mean score of participants expressing gender-equitable attitudes towards girls' education increased from 0.43 to 0.78 (scores ranged from 0 to 1, where values closer to 1 represent more gender-equitable outcomes than scores closer to 0). No significant differences were observed between the attitudes of youth in the control and experimental groups at baseline, and slight or no changes were observed in the control group over time.

Table 2. Gender attitudes scales

Scale name and description	Items included in scale
Discrimination scale: discrimination based on sex	• Daughters should be sent to school only if they are not needed to help at home. • A woman should not expect to inherit her father's property. • It's more important for boys to get an education than it is for girls. • Daughters should have just the same chance to work outside the home as sons. • Boys should have more free time than girls. • If a family can only afford for one child to go to school it should be the boy. • At home boys should always eat first.
Social image scale: perception of social image and expectations from men/women in society	• The more successful the boy is in his profession the more he deserves to get dowry. • Boys who help with chores are considered weak by their friends. • A boy who expresses his affection for his sister is weak.
Violence scale: attitudes toward gender-based violence	• It is okay for a man to hit his wife if she disagrees with him. • A woman should tolerate violence to keep the family together.
Control/dominance scale: social norms toward control and dominance over women within the family	• A girl who disagrees with her brother in public is impolite. • A good woman never questions her husband's opinions, even if she is not sure she agrees with them. • When I get married, I would rather my spouse be obedient than educated.
Girls' education scale	• Daughters should be sent to school only if they are not needed to help at home. • Giving dowry to a daughter is more/as important than investing in her education. • It's more important for boys to get an education than it is for girls. • If a family can only afford for one child to go to school it should be the boy.

Table 3. Gender attitudes – card game results

Scales	Baseline		Endline	
	Control (n = 294)	Experimental (n = 309)	Control (n = 294)	Experimental (n = 309)
1. Discrimination	0.388	0.421	0.475	0.823
2. Social image	0.401	0.426	0.419	0.786
3. Control/dominance	0.372	0.364	0.419	0.629
4. Violence	0.457	0.457	0.440	0.812
5. Girls' education	0.322	0.385	0.434	0.778

2. Gender roles: photo pile sort. Children were asked to review a deck of cards with photos of common household duties or roles traditionally categorised as either male or female. Participants sorted the cards into envelopes indicating whether they felt that this task could be performed by a male, female, or someone of either sex. Figure 1 shows that baseline measures for this scale were similar at baseline in the control and experimental groups, with a significant change in the experimental group only (from 0.33 to 0.82). Thus, boys and girls who participated in Choices were more likely to consider a broad range of household roles such as washing dishes or sweeping the floor as gender neutral, tasks that should be performed by both boys and girls.

3. Gender inequality: Arun's Dilemma. To further assess gender role attitudes, the evaluation used scenarios to elicit the children's opinions in response to a fictional character. Participants were presented with a story about Arun, who wanted to help his sister with her chores, but feared the reaction of his parents and friends. During baseline and endline interviews, children were asked to state whether they agreed or disagreed with gender role statements related to the story. Most agreed with the traditional gender norms when interviewed at baseline, in both control and experimental groups; but after Choices, the experimental group rejected the idea of such rigid, stereotypical gender norms, their score increasing significantly from 0.49 to 0.85 (Figures 2 and 3).

4. Gender-equitable behaviour: brother/sister time and task distribution. This activity, which measured gender inequality, was limited to sets of opposite-sex siblings (brothers and sisters) who were both participating in the child clubs. A total of 31 sibling pairs participated in this activity in the experimental group; in the control group, 31 pairs participated at baseline, and 33 at endline. Siblings were asked to indicate on a pie chart the frequency with which they performed household chores, assisted siblings with schoolwork, and expressed affection for their brother or sister in the past week, as well as how frequently their sibling had performed that same activity. Expressing affection was included as a goal of the intervention because the formative research results revealed that boys were motivated to change their behaviour by receiving appreciation from their sisters. Answers were converted into percentages

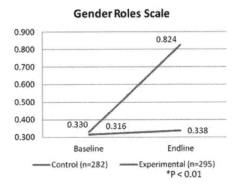

Figure 1. Change in acceptance of gender roles before and after Choices.

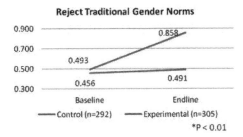

Figure 2. Changes in scale rejecting traditional gender norms.

and compiled into a scale. While the number of participants in this activity is too small to test statistical significance, there is an apparent shift toward more gender-equitable behaviour among boys who participated in Choices. Self-reported increases in gender-equitable behaviour (e.g. boys helping girls with their schoolwork) were corroborated by their siblings.

Qualitative perspectives

As stated earlier, three qualitative components captured the words of children and their parents on gender roles and attitudes: an in-depth interview using photo interviewing and projective drawing techniques; Photovoice; and focus group discussions with parents. A total of 76 randomly selected children participated: 36 participants each from the control and experimental group for the in-depth interview, and 48 for Photovoice. Equal numbers of boys and girls were selected. Three focus groups were conducted with parents in both the control and experimental groups, using similar activities to those employed in the in-depth interviews with young people.

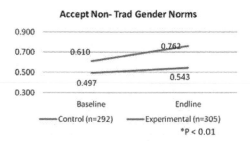

Figure 3. Changes in scale accepting non-traditional gender norms.

1. Photo interviewing: hopes and dreams.

> *After I learn to read and write I will be able to educate my family. I will also teach my sister and help her in her work.* (Boy, from experimental group, Focus Group Discussion, Siraha, August 2010)

This activity used photos of a wide variety of doors (some open, others closed, locked, simple, ornate, new or old and broken) to help children visualise their hopes and dreams for the future. Children were told to choose a door, imagine walking through it and were then asked to describe the future awaiting them on the other side. Girls and boys alike, from both control and experimental areas, dreamed of becoming doctors and teachers, earning respect and money, and supporting their family. Most also mentioned their hopes for a happy family and the ability to educate their children. Choices participants were optimistic about their futures; all, except one boy, expressed the belief that their dreams would come true, with hard work, discipline, attentive study, and support from their families. Control group members were less confident, and more fatalistic; out of 18 boys, seven reported that their dreams would not come true, and five others were unsure. The results of the girls in the control group were similar. Several boys stated that they were working toward equality in their village, and advocating for their sisters' education.

2. Photo interviewing: 'What I want in my spouse'. This activity measured VYAs' ideas of adult masculinity and femininity in a way that would be relevant to them. Participants examined photos depicting Nepali men and women performing different activities and responded to questions about what they desire in their future spouse. All children valued education, with girls also emphasising financial stability and a man's ability to express affection to both his spouse and children. 'We often see mothers playing with children, but to see a father play with his children is really important for me', commented a girl in the experimental group.

Boys from both groups stated that a girl roaming independently or freely was not desirable. Boys in the control group expressed greater disapproval of wives who perform non-traditional roles, such as working outside the home, than those in the experimental group. In contrast, boys in the experimental group valued a woman's financial contributions. Spousal traits that girls cited as undesirable included: alcohol use, domestic violence, fighting, being 'quarrelsome', irresponsible, lazy, and 'Eve-teasing' (sexual harassment), the latter cited only by girls in the experimental group.

3. *Photo interviewing:* gender roles.

> *If everyone's brother was like this, life would be better.* (Girl, experimental group, Focus Group Discussion, Siraha, August 2010)

> *The country will develop with girls' independence and change the living standard.* (Boy, experimental group, Focus Group Discussion, Siraha, August 2010)

This activity explored VYAs' attitudes towards gender roles, empathy towards girls, and awareness of gender inequity. VYAs were shown photographs of boys and girls in traditional and non-traditional gender roles, such as boys studying while girls washed dishes, or boys helping their siblings with female-associated chores. Subsequently, they were asked to share their opinions of the situation depicted in the photos and their feelings for each of the individuals pictured. Choices participants were much more likely to express acceptance of non-traditional gender roles and to value the role of men providing emotional support than were non-participants. VYAs in the experimental group were also more confident discussing their feelings and promoting gender equality. For example, Choices boys consistently mentioned that they were acting to improve the lives of their sisters, most notably assisting them with their work and advocating for their continued education. They also appeared less likely to tease their male peers when they engaged in tasks commonly associated with women, such as housework. It is important to note that although boys from the control group expressed discomfort with the idea of performing 'girls' work', they also felt empathy for girls, and discomfort with situations where boys received preferential treatment. Girls do not need the Choices curriculum to understand that their lives are difficult. For example, one girl looked at a photograph and commented, 'This girl must feel hurt and wish she had time to study'. Choices girls were more likely than their counterparts in the control group to state that their brothers should help them.

4. *Projective drawing: journey of change.*

> *People laugh at a man who cooks food in their home. But from the day we have taken Choices classes, our brothers have started helping us and we help them too. We will teach the same to our friends in our village as well.* (Girl after participation in Choices)

A projective drawing activity entitled 'Journey of Change' collected information on VYAs' perceptions of changes in their attitudes and practices after completing Choices. The 18 participants were instructed to fold a piece of paper in half and draw: (1) a boy or a girl holding something they value; (2) images in the background depicting their life situation; and (3) a comment they might make, before and after completing the curriculum. Children in the control group were asked to complete the same activity for the present moment only. Drawings from the control group included girls cooking food, cutting grass, sweeping the house, returning from school and washing dishes, and boys going to school, playing games, studying, and working in the house. Few girls drew photos of girls studying, and only one drew a girl playing a game.

Most girls who completed Choices sketched sickles to cut grass, brooms, and washing dishes in the 'before' sketch, and books and pens in the 'after' sketch. Boys drew farming, ploughing, smoking cigarettes, teasing girls, hanging out, herding animals and grass cutting 'before', and drew pictures of going to school in the 'after' sketches. Boys and girls alike wrote phrases encouraging school attendance and sibling co-operation. When discussing the sketches, girls stated that they were too focused on household chores prior to the Choices curriculum, and now give priority to their education and made an effort to express their love and thanks to their brothers. Choices seeks to encourage siblings to express affection because the formative research revealed that boys are motivated to act in gender-equitable ways when they receive positive feedback from their sisters. Boys stated that they now realise how important it is to advocate on behalf of their sisters and help them with their chores and schoolwork.

5. *Photovoice*. Previous research has shown that in order to change gender norms, it is necessary to show that alternative gender norms exist in the community. Photovoice was selected as a method of exploring young people's expectations of gender roles in their community. Forty-eight VYAs, from both control and experimental groups, were given disposable cameras, and instructed to take photos with the guiding question: 'What is life like for boys and girls in your community?' Children were taught how to use the cameras, but the guiding question was not qualified. After the photos were developed, two groups each of children in the control and experimental areas discussed their opinions of the situations depicted in their photographs. Facilitators guided the discussions, but the children selected the photos they wanted to talk about, directing the course of the conversation and eliciting the themes important to them.

The images of gendered behaviour captured by Choices participants differed markedly from those of the control group. Participants photographed community members acting in non-traditional roles, for example men and boys cooking, washing dishes, or helping women and girls with household chores. Most photos from the control group reflected difference-based gender stereotypes, with only a few photos depicting individuals challenging these stereotypes through adopting atypical roles.

The discussions that followed in the experimental and the control groups had similarities as well as differences. Almost all of the boys in both groups recognised that life for boys and girls is not equal in their community. In response to one photo, a Choices boy commented, 'I don't feel good about my culture and the roles assigned to boys and girls. He [the boy in the photo] should talk to his parents about his sister's education. [The boy] doesn't know about gender equality and relationships'. Participants discussed educational disparities, explaining that boys are sent to higher-quality private schools, while girls tend to be sent to the less-desirable government schools, and then only if they can manage school in addition to their household chores. Boys stated that men enjoy freedom and they can hang out or play cards in their leisure time, while girls must remain at home. Boys in both groups recognised their potential role as advocates for their sisters, and nearly all stated the need to work toward gender equality.

A difference noted between Choices participants and members of the control group is that most participants in Choices stated that girls in their community were unhappy and would be happier if they had more opportunities and freedom like their brothers. Both boys and girls said there should be no discrimination between sons and daughters and that parents should strive to provide equal opportunities for both. Girls participating in Choices said that women are capable of doing all things; earning money, working in the field, and cutting wood. They further stated that when men and boys wash clothes or prepare meals at home, they are ridiculed; but after participating in Choices, girls' brothers started helping them, and they encouraged their friends to do the same.

In the control group, by contrast, some boys stated that work should be assigned based on gender norms. Most boys felt it was beneficial for girls to be groomed to be good housewives, although a handful stated that girls may want to study, and might not be happy with their lives. Girls in the control group said there is discrimination between girls and boys in terms of the division of work, education, and mobility; but most also expressed acceptance of the status quo.

6. Focus group discussions with parents. Parents in control and experimental areas were selected, based on their availability and willingness to participate, for three single-sex and mixed-sex focus group discussions, using the method of photo interviewing described earlier. None of the parents participated in Choices directly, but parents of children in the experimental area had attended an orientation about Choices, and were aware of their children's participation. In the control area, parents were only aware that their children were in child clubs. Focus group discussions with parents were used to determine whether they perceived any changes in their children's attitudes and/or behaviour in relation to gender roles within the household. If parents were able to report such changes, they were asked how they had reacted to those changes, and what the impact of those changes were.

Parents in both groups recognised inequality in the photo of the boy studying while the girl did her chores. They disagreed with the division of gender roles portrayed in the photo, felt empathy for the girl, and stated that the boy would probably prefer that his sister also attend school. While discussing photos depicting brothers and sisters co-operating, parents whose children participated in Choices stated that although it was unusual to see brothers helping sisters, in the past three months (the duration of the curriculum) it had been occurring in their households, suggesting that participation in Choices did impact behaviour, and also mentioned increased 'harmony' in their home. Mothers in the control area commented that their sons did not help their sisters like this and they do not see this type of co-operation in their community. Participants were also shown photos of parents and children talking. Only parents of Choices participants reported that their sons talked to them about equality for their sisters.

Conclusions about the programme impact

The results of this evaluation suggest that participation in Choices led to more equitable gender attitudes and behaviour. Statistically significant changes were observed in the pre- and post-test scores of the experimental group, while no differences were seen in the control group. Qualitative data support this conclusion: VYAs reported that they felt and behaved differently after participating in Choices. Parents noted changes in their children, and siblings noted changes in each other. Participation in Choices appeared to broaden children's perception of gender roles, including the role of women as wage earners and men as nurturers. It also seemed to have helped them recognise that sexual harassment and teasing boys who step out of the 'gender box' is inappropriate. Choices boys started expressing love and thanks to their sisters by helping them with their household chores and school assignments. Choices girls began speaking out in peer discussions and felt empowered to talk to their parents about their future. Some talked with their parents about staying in school or delaying marriage. Girls also reported that their brothers advocated with their parents on their behalf.

While parents did not participate directly in Choices, the results of the parent focus groups suggest that the programme did encourage parent–child communication, and exposed parents to new ideas and ways of behaving through their children. Parents in the experimental group remarked that brothers and sisters were more co-operative, helping each other with household chores and studies.

However, despite these promising results, it is worthwhile noting that the study was limited geographically and applied over a short time period, so the results may not be generalisable to other contexts. Moreover, demonstrated gender-equitable forms of behaviour observed during the intervention may fade over time without adequate reinforcement.

Future directions: gender-equitable hopes and dreams

The results described here suggest that implementation of Choices at greater scale, along with complementary activities for parents, and interventions to address structural factors, could make a significant contribution to efforts to achieve greater equity between men and women in areas such as education, household decision-making, and sexual relationships. Choices effectively used the period of early adolescence, when children are rapidly changing, and receptive to influences which challenge their attitudes and beliefs, through the use of participatory and reflective approaches, to engage VYAs and help them develop more gender-equitable behaviours. Scaling up the curriculum through schools and engaging parents through complementary programming is part of a multi-prong approach to community-level mobilisation to advance gender equity that Save the Children is pursuing in Nepal and other countries around the world. Indeed, gender transformative programmes for VYAs, such as Choices, have the potential for widespread scale up through existing organisations such as child clubs, schools, and other faith-based organisations. In Nepal alone, for example, there are over 30,000 child clubs run by NGOs and multi-lateral and government organisations.

These findings suggest that even short-term interventions for children in the very young adolescent phase can, if well-planned, make a difference, and it is probable that a longer-term intervention could have sustainable impact. Challenging gender disparities and norms through reflection and action should not be restricted to older adolescents and adults; early adolescence is an opportune moment to lay the foundation for transformation of gender-equitable norms. Many programmes struggle to 're-form' gender norms among youth who have already reached puberty; our experience in Nepal suggests that efforts to 'form' pro-social, equitable gender norms at younger ages may be an easier route to gender equality. VYA programmes could also complement other gender equity initiatives, laying the foundation, for example, for sexual and reproductive health interventions for older youth. In addition, interventions such as Choices that engage emotions as levers of change can prepare the ground for gender-equal policies designed to elevate women's status.

Early adolescence, the developmental stage in which children begin to move from concrete to semi-abstract thinking, represents a real window of opportunity for sowing the seeds of gender equity. During this phase, children begin to understand the concept of fairness and equity. In fact, recent research on the brain suggests that VYA are naturally inclined to feel empathy for others (University of Chicago 2008). Therefore boys, for example, can begin to understand the sadness of girls who are unable to aspire to the same futures dreamed of by their brothers.

Some may ask, 'Is it fair to encourage girls to develop hopes and dreams which they are unlikely to achieve?' It is our belief that girls, as well as boys, have a fundamental right to dream big, and cherish their hopes. When boys realise that their sisters aspire to the same dreams they do, but see little hope of achieving them, they are taking an important step along the road to gender equality. Our hope is that this journey will help create healthier, happier, and more productive families and communities.

Acknowledgements

The views expressed in this publication do not necessarily reflect the views of the United States Agency for International Development or the United States Government.

Note

1. PASW Statistics18 software was used to develop scales to measure gender attitudes and roles. Scores ranged from 0 to 1, where values closer to 1 represent more gender-equitable outcomes than scores closer to 0. Items which expressed gender-inequitable norms were reverse coded, such as, 'If a family can only afford for one child to go to school it should be the boy'. Analysis yielded a Cronbach's alpha coefficient of greater than 0.60 for each scale, signifying good internal consistency or reliability of the variables used to measure each theme. Independent sample t-tests were conducted to assess statistical differences in means between the control and experimental groups at baseline and endline. The results of the in-depth interviews and group discussions were coded and analysed manually by theme.

References

Barker, Gary, Christine Ricardo, and Marcos Nascimento (2007) *Engaging Men and Boys in Changing Gender-based Inequity in Health: Evidence from Programme Interventions*, Geneva: World Health Organization

Bista, Dor Bahadur (2008) *Fatalism and Development: Nepal's Struggle for Modernization*, Kolkata: Orient Longman

Centre for Development and Population Activities (2010) 'Early Marriage and Dahej in Nepal's Central Terai', Draft report for United States Agency for International Development

Chong, Erica, Kelly Hallman, and Martha Brady (2006) *Investing When it Counts: Generating the Evidence Base for Policies and Programmes for Very Young Adolescents*, New York: UN Population Fund and the Population Council

Dell Clark, Cindy (2011) *In a Younger Voice: Doing Child-centered Qualitative Research*, New York: Oxford University Press

Dixon-Mueller, Ruth (2011) *The Sexual and Reproductive Health of Younger Adolescents: Research Issues in Developing Countries*, Geneva: World Health Organization

Greene, Margaret and Gary Barker (2011) 'Masculinity and its public health implications for sexual and reproductive health and HIV prevention', in R. Parker and Marni Sommer (eds.) *Routledge Handbook of Global Public Health*, New York: Routledge

Hergenrather, Kenneth C., Scott D. Rhodes, Chris A. Cowan, Bardhoshi Gerta, and Sara Pula (2009) 'Photovoice as community-based participatory research: a qualitative review', *American Journal of Health Behavior* 33(6): 686–98

Interagency Gender Working Group (2011) 'A Summary Report of New Evidence that Gender Perspectives Improve Reproductive Health Outcomes', Washington, DC: Population Reference Bureau

International Center for Research on Women (ICRW) (2010) 'The Girl Effect: What Do Boys Have to Do with It?', Briefing note for an Expert Meeting and Workshop, Washington, DC, 5–6 October

Marston, Cicely, and Eleanor King (2006) 'Factors that shape young people's sexual behavior: a systematic review', *Lancet* 368: 1581–6

Powers, Jane L., and Jennifer S. Tiffany (2006) 'Engaging youth in participatory research and evaluation', *Journal of Public Health Management Practice* November (Suppl) S79–87

Soley, Lawrence C., and Aaron Lee Smith (2008) *Projective Techniques for Social Science and Business Research*, Milwaukee, WI.: Southshore Press

University of Chicago (2008) 'Children are naturally prone to be empathic and moral', *ScienceDaily*, 12 July, www.sciencedaily.com (last checked by the author 8 October 2012)

Abouit the authors

Rebecka Lundgren is the Director of Research for the Institute for Reproductive Health at Georgetown University. Email: lundgrer@georgetown.edu

Miranda Beckman is currently a Health, Population and Nutrition Officer with USAID's Global Health Bureau. Email: mbeckman@usaid.gov

Surendra Prasad Chaurasiya is a programme specialist on child protection and gender for Save the Children in Nepal. Email: surendra.chaurasiya@savethechildren.org

Bhawana Subhedi is the Gender and Programme Operation Adviser for Great Himalaya Trail Development Program (GHTDP), SNV Netherlands Development Organisation. Email: bhawana@thegreathimalayatrail.org

Brad Kerner is Senior Director, Global Sponsorship Programs at Save the Children. Email: bkerner@savechildren.org

Where the boys are: engaging young adolescent boys in support of girls' education and leadership

Stephanie Baric

Abstract

The Power to Lead Alliance (PTLA) is a three-year (2008–2011) project implemented by CARE in six countries: Honduras, Yemen, India, Malawi, Tanzania, and Egypt. PTLA was part of a larger girls' education programme, focusing on basic education (access and quality), and gender equality. The programme aimed to promote leadership skills among girls aged between 10 and 14 from vulnerable communities. It used extracurricular activities, social networks, and civic action. In practice, more than 30 per cent of project participants were male. Working with younger adolescent boys provided an opportunity to pilot activities aimed at changing gender norms and attitudes early in their lives.

Key words: leadership skills; extracurricular activities; youth; girls' education; masculinities; gender norms

Introduction

Support for girls' education is often described as the best return on investment in developing countries, as countless studies show that getting and keeping girls in school has a positive impact on development, including reducing maternal and child mortality; delaying the age of marriage; lowering fertility rates; enhancing political participation; and increasing economic growth.[1] Despite a clear link between girls' education and improved development outcomes, gender disparity in education remains a challenge globally as rates for enrolment, retention, and completion are lower among girls. While the past several years have seen a surge in the international development community's focus on girls' education, the engagement of men and boys must not be overlooked in addressing the root causes of gender discrimination and poverty.

This chapter examines the Power to Lead Alliance (PTLA), a three-year (2008–2011) project funded by the United States Agency for International Development (USAID). PTLA was implemented by CARE in six countries: Honduras, Yemen, India, Malawi, Tanzania, and Egypt. In each country, PTLA

http://dx.doi.org/10.3362/9781780448664.010

activities were implemented as part of a larger girls' education programme focusing on basic education (access and quality), and gender equality. The PTLA aimed to promote leadership skills among girls aged between 10 and 14, in vulnerable communities, using extracurricular activities, social networks, and civic action. However, while the project specifically targeted young adolescent girls, we found as the project progressed that in fact more than 30 per cent of project participants across the six countries were boys. Working with younger adolescent boys provided an opportunity to pilot activities aimed at changing gender norms and attitudes early in their socialisation process.

This chapter draws on the findings of the final evaluation of the project. It begins with a section providing the context of the PTLA project. It focuses on CARE's work on girls' leadership, education, and empowerment. The involvement of men and boys in leadership and empowerment programmes is briefly discussed, together with the cost to children of both sexes of gender stereotypes and harmful social practices.

The chapter then moves to discuss the PTLA project, and discusses the findings of the final evaluation. These findings suggested that boys who participated in the PTLA project ended up with stronger perceptions of equality of rights and understanding of gendered social norms. They also revealed that behaviour change is especially challenging, and requires more time and stronger messages to counter the powerful influences on boys from wider society.

The context: girls' education, empowerment, and leadership development

Advancing girls' education and leadership skills

Girls' education has emerged over recent decades as one of the top priorities of the international development community, and is recognised as a cornerstone of development. In 2000, 189 countries signed up for the Education for All (EFA) initiative, pledging to eliminate gender disparities in education by 2005 (see UN Girls' Education Initiative 2002). Additionally, in support of the gender-related EFA goals, the second United Nations' Millennium Development Goal (MDG) strives to achieve universal and primary education, and MDG 3 to promote gender equality and empower women by 2015. There is recognition globally that access to the intellectual and social benefits of basic education ensures the protection and fulfilment of the rights of girls and increases the range of life choices available to them as women. Girls' education is also one of the most important and powerful steps towards challenging gender discrimination and ending poverty.

As an organisation, CARE has been supporting education programmes for more than 50 years, with a focus on addressing gender parity in basic education since 1994. The organisation has drawn on its experience implementing education programmes in more than 40 countries to realise the importance of engaging men and boys in support of girls' education, and gender equality more broadly. In 2008, CARE launched the 'Power Within – Learning to Lead' programme (PW) with the goal of providing support to girls to complete their primary education and develop leadership skills. PW targeted girls between the ages of 10 and 14, as this is the period of early adolescence when puberty brings about physical changes and gender roles become more defined as girls begin the transition to adulthood. It is also the age range when most girls drop out of primary school in developing countries. The programme's three key change domains addressed some of the most fundamental challenges to girls' education, and provided vulnerable and marginalised girls with the opportunity to complete primary education, and to cultivate their leadership skills through a range of opportunities. The programme also included activities designed to foster an enabling environment for girls' education.

Empowering girls through leadership development

The emphasis on leadership skills development stems from identifying ways to support girls to better articulate their needs, protect their personal assets, participate in decision-making, and, overall, shape their futures. Following secondary literature review and technical consultations with experts, CARE defined girls' leadership as 'an active learner who believes that she can make a difference in her world, and acts individually and with others to bring about positive change' (Baric *et al.* 2009, 10). These characteristics of a girl leader emerged in a study commissioned by CARE.

This CARE description of a girl leader is comparable to descriptions of positive youth development adopted by other organisations, such as the International Youth Foundation's model: 'Many girls may show voice, decision-making, confidence, and organization, but a more limited number will show the characteristic we have called vision and have the ability and desire to motivate others to follow' (Baric *et al.* 2009, 9). The competencies or characteristics of a girl leader identified in the CARE study included:

1. *Confidence:* a confident girl, who is aware of her opinions, goals, and abilities, and acts to assert herself in order to influence and change her life and world.
2. *Voice/assertion:* a girl who has found her voice, is comfortable sharing her thoughts and ideas with others, and who knows she has the right to do so.
3. *Decision-making/action:* a girl who demonstrates sound decision-making, and understands that her own decisions matter for herself, for her future, and, often, for others.
4. *Organisation:* a girl with organisational skills, who is able to organise herself and her actions in order to accomplish a goal, and to take an idea and realise it.
5. *Vision and ability to motivate others:* a girl with a strong and clear vision, who is able to motivate others, and brings people together to accomplish a task.

While girls are the impact group under PW, recognising the position of power and influence men hold in most societies, men and boys are a target group as potential agents of community change who also benefit from improved education access and quality, and more equitable gender relations.

CARE's work with men and boys began with increasing awareness of the importance of engaging them if the goals of gender equality and women's empowerment are to be attained. CARE's awareness of the importance of engaging men and boys stemmed from research conducted by CARE over three years, beginning in 2005, through its 'Strategic Impact Inquiry on Women's Empowerment' (Martinez 2006) which attempted to answer the critical question: were CARE programmes having an impact on the underlying causes of poverty and rights denial, and if so, how? The research into CARE's programmes in different country contexts focused on gender and power, and the question of CARE's contributions to women's empowerment and gender equality. Across the nearly 30 countries that were featured in the three-year study, CARE gained key insights on how to work with greater impact toward women's empowerment.

CARE's *Strategic Impact Inquiry on Women's Empowerment* emphasised the importance of three actions. First, it is critical to understanding the complexities of male–female relations, acknowledging that these contain binding as well as divisive forces, which people value in ways which are not necessarily allowed for in development approaches which stereotype gender relations. Second, men need to be taken seriously as central players in processes of transformation to gender relations, and time needs to be invested in supporting them to open up to the idea of more gender-equitable ways of being and doing. Thirdly, development programmes need to create valuable entry points and safe staging grounds for men and women to grow into change. The same study also prioritised defining women's empowerment.

In line with this, following a literature review among practitioners and academics, CARE duly developed a Global Framework for Women's Empowerment. The Global Framework has been critical in exploring the links between education, leadership, and empowerment for girls. It addresses three interconnecting aspects of social change: agency, structures, and human relationships. All of these aspects are considered key factors in the construction and entrenchment of poverty and gender discrimination. Change – in this case, improvement in the physical, economic, political, or social wellbeing of girls and women – will not be sustained unless all three components of the framework change – individuals, structures, and relations.

The three components of women's and girls' empowerment are defined in the Global Framework as follows:

1. *Individuals change:* poor women become *agents* of their own development, able to analyse their own lives, make their own decisions and take their own actions. Women (and men) *gain agency* by gaining skills, knowledge, confidence, and experience.

2. *Structures change:* women, individually and collectively, challenge the routines, conventions, laws, family forms, kinship structures, and taken-for-granted behaviours that shape their lives – the 'social order', accepted forms of power and how these are perpetuated.
3. *Relations change:* women form new relations with other social actors, build relationships, form coalitions, and develop mutual support; in order to negotiate, be agents of change, alter structures, and so realise rights and livelihood security.

Empowerment is not the only precondition for leadership development, but it is a critical one, and if leadership development work is to be accomplished, programmes must have a full understanding of how empowerment of girls may be accomplished. This involves moving from a focus on the first component of empowerment laid out in the Global Framework (that is, individual change which enables girls to exercise more agency and control over their own lives), to the second and third components. In essence, this means that development programmes need also to promote and support changes in structures which constrain girls' agency, and to promote supportive relationships for girls.

Working with men and boys is a critical component in this work. Men and boys are required to support changes in social relations in the household and community, and changes in the institutions whose workings structure women's lives and provide the framework for their choices. Men and boys can support positive change in their capacity as both formal and informal leaders (e.g. religious leaders, clan heads, and teachers, among others). They can also act as community role models, changing their peers' perceptions of gender, as well as acting as agents of change in their own right, supporting and enforcing gender-sensitive policies and laws. Engaging men and boys helps create awareness of the damage caused to both sexes by gender stereotypes, norms, and attitudes, which limit choices and behaviour, and penalise individuals who refuse to conform to particular societal standards.

Children are often constrained by social expectations and practices which not only limit their vision of the future, but also cause emotional or physical harm. For example, girls may face such practices as early (that is, child) marriage, and female genital cutting. Boys can face violent initiation ceremonies. For both sexes, exploitative child labour is a reality – though the nature of the work is very gender-specific (e.g. boys may be employed as heavy labourers or herd-boys, while girls may face exploitation as domestic workers). All these gendered experiences can deeply affect a child's future aspirations as well as his or her social and physical mobility. Furthermore, conceptualisations of masculinity and femininity can place burdens on both genders that inhibit equitable relationships. A key consideration in the design of PW is the varied roles that men and boys, more specifically young peer adolescent boys, play in shaping a supportive environment, including renegotiating traditional gender roles, for girls to become leaders and access their rights, including an education, and substantive freedoms.

The Power to Lead Alliance project

Acting as a core initiative of CARE's PW programme, the PTLA project sought to create and strengthen different kinds of leadership opportunities for girls in vulnerable communities in the following six countries: Egypt, Honduras, India, Malawi, Tanzania, and Yemen.

The project's three objectives were as follows:

- *Objective 1:* To cultivate opportunities for girls to practise their leadership skills through a combination of extracurricular activities, social networks, and opportunities to participate in civic action.

Leadership skills were developed and practised through 13 categories of activities. These were: music; debate; sports; arts and drama; youth councils; parliaments and boards; health; life skills groups; awareness campaigns; classroom support; academic clubs; scouts; and environment work. According to the final evaluation of the project, sports and arts and drama had the strongest involvement across all countries for project participants. Through participation in social networks, girls were given an opportunity to socialise with peers and the networks served as a 'safe space' for girls to explore challenging life issues, such as safe sex or early marriage. The third key activity under this objective, participation in civic action, facilitated a variety of collective actions through initiatives in the surrounding community. PTLA activities were developed based on consultation with the Girl Scouts of the USA for empowering girls and developing girls' leadership skills.

- *Objective 2:* To create partnerships to promote girls' leadership that not only bring in financial and technical resources to support this work, but also engage in advocacy work to advance girls' rights.

Under this objective, country offices and headquarters developed partnerships with non-government organisations (NGOs) and the private sector. NGOs implemented activities in the six countries and the US partnerships with NGOs were often linked to advocacy initiatives around adolescent girls' rights. Since the project was funded under USAID's Global Development Alliance, which promotes public–private partner-ships, private-sector funding was leveraged to support the girls' education programmes.

- *Objective 3:* To enhance knowledge to implement and promote girls' leadership programmes by learning and sharing lessons learnt about barriers to, and openings for, girls' leadership.

At the time of the design of PTLA in 2008, a review of relevant literature showed that research and learning around girls' leadership had been restricted, for the most part, to the developed North (Baric *et al.* 2009). PTLA provided an opportunity to see how girls' leadership is developed and expressed in six different developing countries with considerable social and cultural differences. Each country involved in the work presented a unique combination of gender norms and attitudes, policies and programmes for girls, type of governance, educational systems, and economic environments.

The Power to Lead Alliance and the involvement of boys in its work

As highlighted, PTLA aimed to target young adolescent girls. However, a demographic analysis of participants during the start-up phase of the project revealed that approximately 30 per cent of participants were actually boys, across the six countries. The PTLA developed its work accordingly to respond to these male participants. It aimed to change perceptions among male project participants around issues such as caregiving and domestic roles, education, work and leadership, violence, and reproductive health decision-making. The approach was largely based on the work of Instituto Promundo's Program H[2] which has focused on sexual and reproductive health, in contrast to PTLA's focus on girls' education and leadership.

Working with peer boys presented an opportunity to look at the role they could play in spurring change in the area of gender equality by implementing activities intended to challenge the 'social order' which perpetuates accepted forms of power and discrimination. With joining in extracurricular activities and civic participation alongside girls in some of the countries through structured activities supervised by adults, they witnessed girls stepping out of traditional gender roles, and did the same themselves. The project also exposed them to messaging around the importance of behaving in ways which encourage gender equality. The social networks were intended to be 'safe spaces', and were run as gender-exclusive spaces (that is, as boys-only and girls-only) which gave the children the opportunity to socialise with their peers and freely explore many of the life challenges they face as early adolescent boys or girls.

As a key component of the leadership activities, participation in civic action introduced adolescents to concepts of governance, and more active and engaged citizenry. Again, boys and girls participated – this time, together – in activities that were intended to expose children to the basics of governance – and to be more specific to development processes. They learnt about the steps of identifying an issue in the community, developing a plan for addressing the issue, and then working collectively to implement the plan. In most countries where PTLA ran, the civic action component included activities such as student government and community service. Through enabling children to learn about and explore these processes of active citizenship, PTLA reinforced the importance of bringing different perspectives (in this case, perspectives which differ by gender) to social action and processes of change.

The Gender Equitable Index: assessing boys' perceptions

As PTLA sought to change the ways in which both girls and boys thought about concepts of gender, this required understanding gender perceptions that contribute to gender inequality. The project developed the 'Gender Equitable

Index' (GEI) as a tool for assessing the success of PTLA in changing boys' perceptions about gender equality.

Following the Gender Equitable Attitudes in Men Scale (GEM Scale) model, a series of statements were developed with which respondents would either agree or disagree. While the GEI tool is based on the GEM Scale, when comparing the two evaluation models, the GEI has 48 statements and the GEM Scale includes 34. During the process of developing gender-equitable statements for PTLA, consultations were made with all six countries under the project, with field testing carried out in Egypt and Tanzania. GEM Scale statements were selected or adapted based on age and cultural appropriateness. Additional statements were included (hence the higher number of statements under PTLA) as well as a grouping of the statements under domains such as 'work and leadership' or 'violence'. The following three statements were adopted from the GEM Scale without change:

- Changing nappies, giving the kids a bath, and feeding the kids are the mothers' responsibility.
- It is important to have a male friend that you can talk about your problems with.
- If a man sees another man beating a woman, he should stop it.

Statements were developed to monitor and evaluate boys' perceptions and opinions. The statements below in *italics* are considered to be equitable statements. That is, the statement reflects a condition in which boys and girls are treated the same. For example, all of the statements under the category of 'Work and Leadership' are equitable statements. Girls or women are compared to men similarly. In contrast, inequitable statements reinforce the superiority of boys to girls.

Provided below are examples of statements that were adopted by PTLA for the GEI from the GEM Scale but where the wording of the statement was changed:

- A man should have the final word about decisions in his home.
- The father is the final decision-maker in the family.
- There are times when a woman deserves to be beaten.
- I think it is acceptable that a husband beats his wife if she disobeys him.
- It is a woman's responsibility to avoid getting pregnant.
- If a girl gets pregnant by a male teacher, it is her fault.

Additional statements were developed to reflect PTLA's focus on girls' education and leadership:

Education

- Boys have more opportunities than girls to go to university.
- When the family cannot afford to educate all children, only boys should go to school.

- *Girls have the same right as boys to be educated.*
- A man should be better educated than his wife.
- Boys are more intelligent than girls.

Leisure and Social Networking

- *Boys should ask their parents for permission to go outside just like girls.*
- *There should be places where girls can practise social, cultural, and sports activities, just like there are places for boys.*
- Boys are better than girls in sports.
- *Girls have the right to select their female friends just as boys select their male friends.*
- *It is OK for girls to play sports like football.*

Work and Leadership

- *A woman could be a President or Prime Minister and be as good as a man.*
- *Women should have equal access to leadership positions at the village, district, and state government level.*
- *Women can be engineers or scientists like men.*
- *A woman has the same right as a man to work outside the village.*
- *Girls have the same right as boys to express their opinions.*

While PTLA drew heavily from the GEM Scale, the GEI is broad in scope socially and affects multiple social spheres (e.g. includes statements around education or work and leadership); and the GEI is about present and future interactions between boys and girls.

Provided below are some of the baseline findings from India and Egypt based on the GEI. In India, the statements were presented to boys in school and out of school, whereas in Egypt the GEI was only applied to boys in school.

Example of baseline findings from India:

- Caring for her children and husband, and doing the household chores and cooking, are the most important roles in a woman's life. (in school boys 78.3 per cent/85.7 per cent out of school boys)
- Only girls should help with household chores. (21.7 per cent/71.4 per cent)
- Boys have more opportunities than girls to go to university. (68.9 per cent/78.6 per cent)
- Boys are more intelligent than girls. (54.7 per cent/85.7 per cent)
- Women should have equal access to leadership positions at the village, district, and state government level. (80.2 per cent/50 per cent)
- It is OK for girls to play sports like football. (45.3 per cent/64.3 per cent)
- If I see a man beating his wife, I should try to stop him. (99.1 per cent/100 per cent)
- I think it is acceptable that a husband beats his wife if she disobeys him. (58.5 per cent/71.4 per cent)

The baseline findings from India reveal contradictions in gender perceptions among boys. While almost 100 per cent of boys in and out of school would stop a man from beating his wife, 58.5 per cent of boys in school and 71.4 per cent of boys out of school found it acceptable for a husband to beat his wife if she disobeys him, implying that violence against women is condoned in the household. It is also worth noting the number of boys who agreed that boys have more opportunities to attend university than girls but also agree that boys are more intelligent than girls.

Examples of baseline findings from Egypt:

- Caring for her children and husband and doing the household chores and cooking are the most important roles in a woman's life. (27 per cent)
- Only girls should help with household chores. (29 per cent)
- Boys have more opportunities than girls to go to university. (11 per cent)
- Girls have the same right as boys to be educated. (64 per cent)
- A man should be better educated than his wife. (45 per cent)
- Women should have equal access to leadership positions at the village, district, and state government level. (40 per cent)
- If I see a man beating his wife, I should try to stop him. (79 per cent)
- I think it is acceptable that a husband beats his wife if she disobeyed him. (50 per cent)

In Egypt, as in India, a higher percentage of boys agreed they would stop a man from beating his wife whereas half of the boys surveyed found it acceptable for a husband to beat his wife if she disobeys him. Another finding worth noting is the relatively low number of boys who think household work is primarily the role of a woman or that only girls should help with household chores and yet only 64 per cent believe girls have the same right as boys to be educated.

As previously discussed, the findings were supposed to be used in promoting gender equity as well as targeting issues that need to be addressed in social networks with boys through activities that explore definitions of gender, reversing gender roles, labelling or stereotyping, power relationships, relating to peers, gender roles in the family, household duties and gender stereotypes, and what is violence.

Findings from the Power to Lead Alliance's final project evaluation

Following three years of implementation (September 2008 to September 2011), a final evaluation of the project was conducted and data collection included focus groups, semi-structured interviews, activity observations, and the GEI and Girls' Leadership Index (GLI). The GLI is a monitoring tool developed under PTLA that not only gathers data about girls' perceptions of their leadership skills and behaviours but was also designed as a means of initiating reflection and self-awareness about leadership competencies among girls.

Given that the baseline data collection in most countries was not structured to track respondents, as a result, it was difficult to assess individual change among girls and boys, and determine which activity was more effective at building leadership skills or promoting more gender equitable relations. However, the final evaluation was able to draw a varied range of conclusions about the impact of the project, which included many very positive and encouraging findings. These included the following:

- All countries achieved or were at least close to achieving the 70 per cent target of possessing leadership skills and competencies.
- Girls throughout the six countries, with the exception of Honduras, met the 70 per cent target of taking leadership action.
- While the 70 per cent targets for leadership skills and competencies and for leadership action in homes, schools, or communities were not met, at least 50 per cent improved in these areas as well.

Sports, theatre and art groups, debate clubs, scouting, and civic action opportunities were the most popular among project participants. It is worth noting that girls identified community attitudes and norms as the most common barrier for participation in PTLA activities. Focus group discussions revealed that the majority of girls felt they were leaders or were developing as leaders with boys sharing a similar perception about their own leadership development. Overall, with the exception of Malawi, all countries showed a statistically significant difference in leadership skills development between the active participant group and the comparison group.

Results from the GEI led the project evaluators to conclude that girls and boys from PTLA sites 'had stronger perceptions of equality or rights and understanding of gendered social norms than girls and boys from comparison sites; and the difference between groups is notable' (Miske Witt & Associates Inc. 2011, 40). The evaluators commented:

> *some girls in Malawi and Tanzania noted increased opportunities to interact with boys and the girls said they felt free to talk to boys whereas before they were not allowed to even sit next to them. In Yemen, the girls noted that attitudes appeared to be changing as the boys began treating them with more respect. In India, a community leader stated boys and girls appeared to be more comfortable with each other ... Following a year of project implementation, staff observed boys' changed attitudes and were interested in learning how to stitch, roll chapattis, and help with household chores, activities that are generally considered 'female'.* (Miske Witt & Associates Inc. 2011, 40, 52)

Relationships between boys and girls appeared to have improved. The evaluation noted that supportive relationships could be discerned among participants in the project:

> *friendly relationships between girls and boys appeared to be present to a greater extent in active sites than comparison sites. For example, in Honduras boys and girls were observed interacting with one another in various activities. In India, both boys and girls commented on improved relationships with each*

other. This was also evident in Malawi and Tanzania. Egypt and Yemen have fewer examples of interactions between boys and girls, likely due to the cultural norms around male and female interactions in Muslim countries. (Miske Witt & Associates Inc. 2011, 32)

However, data from focus groups also revealed the discrepancies that exist between attitudes and behaviour. While the majority of boys in focus groups agreed that girls have the same right as boys to express opinions and the right to be educated, statements from girls did not always align with boys' responses. In Malawi, girls observed that boys who participated in the *gule wamkulu* ritual (a traditional dance usually performed by boys) became rude because they felt superior to girls in their male-only role. Another example was girls in Honduras, who said boys did not support them in playing football (Miske Witt & Associates Inc. 2011).

Conclusion

PTLA was an innovative and ambitious intervention which may be unique, in working with young adolescent boys to challenge gender norms and attitudes in support of girls' education and leadership development. Given that young adolescence (ages 10–14) is the period when puberty brings about physical changes and gender roles become more defined, it presents an opportune time to promote gender-equitable norms and behaviours.

While PTLA presented promising results in engaging peer boys, including changes in attitude that were sustained and documented following the end of the project, a key lesson that emerged is that three years is not enough time to support changes in behaviour on the part of the adolescent boys who participated, especially when it comes to gender norms that are so deeply entrenched in a society. In addition to the short timeframe, the project points to the need for stronger social messaging and trained mentors to work with boys to facilitate a structured process for surfacing and unpacking prevailing gender social norms that lead to gender discrimination.

The findings of PTLA, including the activities piloted, and the GEI as a tool for understanding and critically reflecting on gender perceptions, can potentially be used as a basis for designing future programmes for girls' education and leadership development in working with younger adolescent boys whose gender norms and attitudes are still being developed and where there is an opportunity to affect positive change.

Notes

1. Studies have been conducted by the World Bank (Psacharopoulos and Patrinos 2004) and UNICEF (2005).
2. Program H helps young men to reflect upon and question the traditional norms of what defines 'manhood' through two elements: a curriculum that includes manuals and educational video for promoting attitude and

behaviour change among young men; and a lifestyle social marketing campaign for promoting changes in community or social norms related to what it means to be a man (Nascimento 2006). Program H also includes an evaluation model, the Gender Equitable Attitudes in Men Scale (GEM Scale), for measuring changes in attitudes and social norms around manhood to measure outcomes of the initiative (*ibid.*). The Program H Initiative promotes gender-equitable norms and behaviours, as defined by four principles. First, it promotes the idea that intimate relationships should be based on respect, equality, and intimacy rather than sexual conquest; second, it offers men a perspective on fatherhood which stresses that men should take financial and caregiving responsibility; third, it supports men to assume some responsibility for their own and their partners' reproductive health and disease prevention issues; and finally, supports men to oppose violence towards their female partners (*ibid.*). Program H seeks to 'positively influence safer sexual behaviours (including increased condom use in those sexually active, reducing gender based violence), fewer unplanned pregnancies, improved partner negotiation skills, and increased utilization of health services' (*ibid.*, 1). For more information, visit http://www.promundo.org.br/en/about-us/introduction/.

References

Baric, Stephanie, Sarah Bouchie, Peter Cronin, Archer Heinzen, Geeta Menon, and Cynthia Prather (2009) 'The Power to Lead – Unleashing Potential and Participation for Adolescent Girls', CARE, http://www.care.org/campaigns/2009/downloads/sigprog_pw_leadership.pdf (last checked by the author January 2013)

Martinez, Elisa (2006) 'The Courage to Change: Confronting the Limits and Unleashing the Potential of CARE's Programming for Women. Synthesis Report: Phase 2, Strategic Impact Inquiry on Women's Empowerment', CARE International, http://expert.care.at/downloads/careexpert/CARE_TheCourageToChange.pdf (last checked by the author February 2013)

Miske Witt & Associates Inc. (2011) 'The Power to Lead Alliance (PTLA): Empowering Girls to Learn and Lead, Final Evaluation Report for CARE USA', St Paul, MN.: Miske Witt & Associates Inc.

Nascimento, Marcos (2006) 'Working with Young Men to Promote Gender Equality: An Experience in Brazil and Latin America', www.eldis.org/fulltext/working-with-young-men-Jan2006.pdf (last checked by the author February 2013)

Psacharopoulos, George and Harry Anthony Patrinos (2004) 'Returns to investment in education: a further update', *Education Economics* 12(2), August, http://siteresources.worldbank.org/INTDEBTDEPT/Resources/468980-1170954447788/3430000-1273248341332/20100426_16.pdf (last checked by the author February 2013)

UN Girls' Education Initiative (2002) 'The Millennium Development Goals and the United Nations Girls Education Initiative: A Guidance Note to UN Country Teams', April, http://www.unesco.org/education/efa/know_sharing/flagship_initiatives/ungei_guidance.pdf (last checked by the author February 2013)

UNICEF (2005) 'Progress for Children: A Report Card on Gender Parity and Primary Education', No. 2, April, www.unicef.org/media/files/pfc2.pdf (last checked by the author February 2013)

About the author

Stephanie Baric is an international development consultant with expertise in gender, education, and governance programmes. Her experience includes working in Africa, the Middle East and Eastern Europe for UNICEF, ChildFund, and CARE. She served as Senior Technical Advisor at CARE USA in the Basic and Girls' Education Unit and Project Manager for PTLA from 2008 to 2011. Email: stephaniebaric13@gmail.com

CHAPTER 11

Men's involvement in gender equality – European perspectives

Sandy Ruxton and Nikki van der Gaag

Abstract

This chapter is based on a study that was commissioned from the Swedish non-government organisation, Men for Gender Equality, by the European Institute for Gender Equality (EIGE). The aim of the research was to map stakeholders – including public authorities, research centres, civil society organisations, social partners, and individual experts – working to engage men in gender equality work in all 27 Member States and at European level. Drawing on existing scholarship in the field of men and masculinities, the chapter outlines the current regional and national context, and the main findings of the research that were published as a report by the EIGE. The chapter examines the extent and nature of the work, identifying 241 organisations working on themes such as gender equality, violence prevention, fatherhood/caregiving, health, gay/bisexual and transgender issues, and education and learning. The greatest number were found in Sweden and the UK, and the fewest in Central and Eastern Europe. The chapter highlights different perspectives on the benefits of involving men in gender equality initiatives and examines stakeholder views of the obstacles to this work. It concludes with some observations on ways forward.

Key words: men; masculinities; women; gender equality; Europe; European Union

Introduction

Equality between men and women is a fundamental principle of the European Union (EU), which has a long tradition of support for measures to promote gender equality.[1] In recent years, the role of men in this work has received growing attention, both at European level and within the Member States.[2] The European Commission's current 'Strategy for Equality Between Women and Men 2010-2015', for example, states that 'gender equality needs the active contribution, support and participation of men' (European Commission 2011, 32). But although it is widely accepted that some focus on men's participation is important if gender equality is to be achieved, very little EU-wide information and data have been available relating to projects and initiatives working with men at local, national, and European levels.

http://dx.doi.org/10.3362/9781780448664.011

This chapter is based on a study conducted in 2011 by the authors on behalf of the Swedish non-government organisation (NGO), Men for Gender Equality,[3] and represents one of the first attempts to close this gap. It was commissioned by the European Institute for Gender Equality (EIGE), a regulatory agency of the European Union based in Lithuania.[4] The study mapped relevant stakeholders active in engaging men in gender equality work in all 27 Member States, and at European level, between 2007 and 2010. These stakeholders included public authorities, research centres, civil society organisations, social partners, and individual experts.

The study was based on research and reports by a network of national experts across 23 Member States. As part of their activities, the national experts conducted more than 70 interviews across 23 Member States (either face-to-face or on the phone).[5] Just over a third of the interviewees were linked to NGOs working in the field, just under a third were academics, around a quarter worked for government bodies, and the remainder were politicians, journalists, or members of men's groups. The bulk of the quotations throughout this chapter come from these interviews, and are drawn from the notes of the interviewers. The Country Reports compiled as part of the study remain unpublished and are not publically available.

One important outcome of this work was the compilation of an online database of the stakeholders and their activities, based on questionnaires, internet searches and personal contacts; this can be found at the EIGE Documentation Centre (www.eige. europa.eu/internal/csr/search). Another was a report providing an analysis of the various organisational forms, working methods, tools, and materials identified by the national experts (www.eige.europa.eu/content/document/the-involvement-of-men-in-gender-equality-initiatives-in-the-european-union).

The chapter begins with a brief discussion of the theory behind the approach we took in this research. It then goes on to look at some of the broad factors in the context of the different countries in the EU which are currently affecting public attitudes and institutional responses to gender issues, and in particular men's involvement in activities intended to promote gender equality. Although there are some common themes, they may play out differently in different regional, national, and local contexts. The article explores the opinions and attitudes of participants in the research about the obstacles to involving men further in gender equality work, and their perceptions of the benefits of involving men. Finally, the article outlines interviewees' views of possible ways to take this work forward.

Theoretical framework

The research project was informed by social science theories and research into men and masculinities. We particularly drew on insights from an interdisciplinary field of study known as 'Critical Studies on Men' (CSM). Building on insights from the work of theorists (see, for example, perspectives in the edited collection of Michael Kimmel, Jeff Hearn, and Raewyn Connell (2005), our research was founded on a view of 'masculinity' – of what it is to be a man – as socially constructed and produced, rather than 'natural'. Masculinity is more properly expressed as 'masculinities' – that is, as a plural rather than a singular concept. This is because ideas about what it is to be a man and appropriate male behaviour vary, changing across time and between and within different societies, and through individual men's life-courses. However, 'masculinities' are collective as well as individual, and are reflected in institutional regimes (for example, in schools, sports clubs, and workplaces), as well as in personal relations. Finally, men and masculinities are rooted in complex, and sometimes contradictory, gendered power relations which advantage men over women. This dominance is built into social relations and structures, which maintain male superiority, and make it appear 'natural'.

Men are generally brought up to see being powerful as part of masculine identity, and to take this power for granted. As Jeff Hearn, a researcher well-known for his work on men and masculinities, argued in one of the interviews for this research: 'Being brought up to become a man still includes expectations and promises of power, even though this may be unrealistic in some contexts' (interview, 12 April 2011). The advantages conferred on men by unequal gender power relations are not shared equally among individual men. This is because, 'masculinities' – that is, the many possible ways of 'being a man' – intersect with other social divisions (including age, race, ethnicity, faith, class, disability, and sexual orientation) in a dynamic way. Some groups of men – often those who are white, university-educated, and on higher incomes – establish and wield significant economic, social, and political power over other men, women, and children. Other groups of men may be marginalised by aspects of their identities which play out in a particular context to result in considerable disadvantage. For example, older men can suffer from social isolation, and are less likely than women to use existing services (Ruxton 2007); men with disabilities are often unwilling, or feel unable, to live up to 'ideal' models of masculinity based on bodily strength and performance (Gerschick 2005; Shakespeare 1999); and the lives of gay, bisexual, and transgender men are structured by their experiences within a dominant heterosexual culture, and in particular by homophobia.

It is therefore important for policymakers and researchers to address both the social problems that men cause, *and* the problems that some men experience. This approach goes beyond the simplified focus of much previous research and policy, which has tended to regard men and boys either as in need of control or punishment, or in need of help or support. Instead, it addresses both perspectives, and the interconnections between them (Hearn and Pringle 2006).

The importance of context

Key economic and social changes in the EU: a gender analysis

A wide variety of social, economic, political, and cultural changes have taken place in recent years that have affected gender equality policies and gender relations within the EU. These also affect the many ways in which masculinities are lived out and experienced by men in different regional, national, and local contexts.

Some trends are common across most, if not all, EU countries. In all countries (but to differing extents), economic and financial crisis since 2007/8 has generally led to a significant decline in employment and social support, both in specific sectors and between and within countries and regions. This has affected both men and women, but in different ways. For example, job losses in sectors such as construction and manufacturing impact are mostly concentrated among working-class men, while job losses in sectors such as services and retail mostly affect working-class women. Dramatic cuts in public spending (in some countries imposed by external bodies such as the International Monetary Fund and the European Central Bank), are also having a very negative impact on family incomes – and particularly women's incomes – and on the users of public services (again, predominantly women).

The Irish National Report provides a graphic description of the impact of boom and bust on men and masculinity; whilst the context is specific, many of the effects are echoed elsewhere in the EU:

> *The boom was construction-led and provided high earning for traditional male skilled and unskilled labour. It was a good time to be a man. The traditional provider role based on hard graft and physical labour was rewarded and the role affirmed – if you were in employment. If you were not, it left a sense of failure and shame – not even in this boom when everything was going well, could he deliver. When the bubble burst this consensus about performance of the traditional role also burst. Unemployment among men, especially in the construction industry rocketed. All of the success that affirmed that role melted, the wealth that was earned was no longer there to sustain the lifestyle that had grown up on its back. Many men were left bereft as they could no longer rely on their labour or indeed on their traditional resilience, they were now living in a time and a context over which they had no control.* (Irish National Report)

Significant demographic changes have also taken place across the EU, including declining fertility, population ageing, falling marriage rates, an increase in relationship breakdown, and increasing migration (both rural to urban, and transnational).

Shifts in attitudes to feminism and gender relations: fatherhood and 'men's rights'

All these social and economic changes have an impact on men's – and women's – lives, roles, and ideas about gender roles, relations, and identities. In many countries, fathers' attitudes have shifted, although debate remains as to the extent of change in their practices. The UK National Report argues that: 'Fathers show a growing interest in being "involved" at home, and some movement away from the traditional "breadwinner" role (although this remains central to the identity of many)'.

Probably the most important initiatives have been in Scandinavian countries, where since the 1970s there has been increasing emphasis on encouraging men to become more active fathers (for example, by getting them to take paternity and parental leave), facilitating women's entry into the labour market.

However, support for traditional family values remains strong in many countries. The National Report for Cyprus states that, although family relations are changing, 'traditional gender roles in the family are re-enforcing traditional gender stereotypes, with a patriarchal male stereotype prevailing, particularly in the rural areas'. The position is similar in Greece and Malta, with Malta being in 2011 the last EU country to legalise divorce. In Italy there remains a family-orientated culture, with traditional gender roles supported by the Catholic Church.

In many former socialist countries in Central and Eastern Europe, EU accession (that is, entry into the EU) initially led to an increase in attention to policies supporting the aim of greater gender equality, in line with EU priorities and supported by EU funding. However, in the longer term, this initial trend has been followed by a resurgence of conservatism among political elites, and a renewed emphasis on policies which support the traditional family, rather than gender equality. The Catholic Church has often intervened actively in public policy debates, and governments have been increasingly wary of intervening in what they widely continue to perceive as the 'private' sphere of the family and household. For instance, the National Report on Slovakia states that: 'conservative politicians who explicitly rejected influences or inspirations from the European Union warned of dangerous "social engineering" that – in their eyes – threatened to undermine Slovakia's traditional Christian values.'

In Lithuania, similar trends are at work:

> the issues of the prohibition of abortion, the definition of family (according to a new proposal by the Ministry of Labour and Social Affairs, family equals only a married couple with children) and even administrative fines for expressing non-normative sexual orientations in public are constantly discussed. (National Report)

Often this shift to a conservative approach to the family and gender relations has been allied with the emergence of 'men's rights' and 'father's rights' groups. Although they embrace a variety of points of view (Clatterbaugh 2007), these groups tend to come together around core arguments that men are as powerless relative to women as women are to men, that women or feminism are to blame for men's plight, and that men are now the real victims within current gender relations. In Poland, for instance, it is widely suggested that 'responsibility for the apparent "crisis of fatherhood" should be borne mainly by women'. In Estonia, 'men think that men's rights are less protected than women's rights' (National Report). This trend toward anti-feminist analysis and action is also visible in Western European countries. In Denmark, as one example, 'Facebook groups and websites are increasingly used to oppose (academic and/or elite) feminists' critique of the lack of gender equality from a female perspective'.

Nevertheless, the research highlights the fact that in some countries, particularly in Western Europe, there is simultaneously a renaissance of interest in feminist ideas. In France and Italy, for example, recent sex scandals involving male politicians have helped to put the sexual exploitation of women on the public agenda. Franc,ois Hollande's government in France has emphasised the importance of gender equality, with equal numbers of women and men in the Cabinet for the first time; one of its first initiatives was new legislation on sexual harassment. In the UK, feminist activism is growing, particularly among young women, with increasing focus on tackling male violence and the sexual objectification of women. Although on a small scale, men are also getting involved in pro-feminist groups in countries such as Finland, Sweden, and Spain.

Homosexuality is another key issue to which country responses differ widely. As outlined earlier, men whose sexuality differs from the heterosexual norm are still widely seen as deviating from the social and cultural ideals of masculinity. Although same-sex relationships are legal in all EU countries, progress towards this has been highly uneven historically. Recognition of the existence and legitimacy of same-sex relationships is still relatively recent in many EU states – particularly, but not exclusively, in Central and Eastern Europe. In Latvia, for example, the first Pride March (2005) provoked negative changes to the Constitution, defining marriage as a union between a man and a woman (to avoid the possibility of same-sex marriage). With a heavy police presence, Baltic Pride 2010 took place in Vilnius, Lithuania, accompanied by violence from opponents of gay rights. In contrast, in many other EU countries (with the Netherlands perhaps being the outstanding example), gay relationships are widely accepted, civil partnerships are legal in some, including the Netherlands and the UK, and lesbian, gay, bisexual and transgender (LGBT) groups are active in a number of ways. The activities of LGBT groups range from lobbying for political representation, through to awareness-raising, education, provision of health advice (mental and physical), individual counselling, research, and social events.

Contextualising the research

An earlier attempt to analyse the social position of men across Europe is provided by the work of the CROME network (Hearn and Pringle 2006). Their simple categorisation suggests that among European countries, there is considerable difference in approaches to gender equality law and policy, and in the extent to which they have explored the issues of men and masculinity. CROME categorises countries into three broad groups, whilst acknowledging the importance of more nuanced analysis of the specific variations between and within them. The categories are: former Eastern bloc countries (e.g. Bulgaria, the Czech Republic, Estonia, Latvia, and Poland) that are in the process of developing their gender equality strategies, but with very little specific emphasis on men; established EU Member States (e.g. Ireland, Italy, Germany, and the UK) that have developed equal opportunities and gender equality policies within the EU framework, with some specific emphasis on men; and the Nordic nations (including Denmark, Finland, Norway, and Sweden) that have, since the 1980s, developed gender equality mechanisms and some focused policies in relation to men (especially within the context of the Nordic Council of Ministers).

Our research discussed in this article complements this earlier work by analysing the current state of play across the EU in relation to work with men to promote gender equality. Our study found 241 organisations involved in this work. The level of involvement varied considerably from country to country, with Sweden and the UK having the greatest number of organisations (followed by Finland, Germany, the Netherlands, and Spain), and the newer Member States in Eastern Europe having the fewest.

Our analysis of the main forms of involvement of the organisations, identi-fied both through questionnaires they filled in and/or information from their websites, found that the largest number (33 per cent) were working broadly on gender equality with a sub-focus on men.[6] Sixteen per cent worked on vio-lence prevention, followed by 'fatherhood/caregiving' (14 per cent), 'health' (10 per cent), 'gay/ bisexual/transgender issues' (9 per cent), and 'education and learning' (9 per cent).

Interestingly, the countries with the highest levels of activity around men and gender equality also came near the top in the 2010 World Economic Forum's (WEF) ranking of gender gaps,[7] and those countries near the bottom of the WEF ranking had the fewest organisations working on men and gender equality.[8] We tentatively suggest, allowing for other factors such as population size, that there is more work on gender equality with men in countries with greater gender equality. This would make sense; where gender equality is more central to public discourse and government action, this is likely to make issues relating to men's involvement in gender equality more visible, and therefore stimulate more policy and programme interventions on this theme.

Emerging issues

The study, in the course of the interviews conducted by the various research-ers, identified some common themes: what prevents men becoming involved in this work, the benefits of involving men in gender equality, and some pos-sible ways forward.

So what prevents men becoming involved in gender equality? It was sig-nificant that the term 'gender equality' itself was not well-understood by research participants in a number of countries, particularly in Eastern and

Central Europe. Jivka Marinova, Director of the Gender Education, Research and Technologies foundation (GERT), who was the researcher in Bulgaria, noted in her background study that:

> *Gender equality has been introduced as a term in public discourse, but it is still an empty term, not well and properly understood by either women or men. When the terms 'gender' and 'gender equality' were introduced they sounded completely alien. Outside women's NGOs, gender organisations and some academic circles, they still sound alien.*

Other research participants pointed out that gender equality as an issue is simply not on the public agenda in their countries. Krassimira Daskalova, Professor of Feminist History at the University of Sofia in Bulgaria, said that, 'the entire culture is patriarchal and gender blind'. In Hungary, Miklos Hadas, from Corvinus University of Budapest, noted that the emphasis on a conservative 'familialism' makes discussion about gender very difficult. Tatyana Kmetova, from Gender Work, Bulgaria, noted that this makes it hard for men – even those who are interested and potentially supportive – to publically demonstrate their support.

In addition, gender equality continues to be seen by many people as a 'women's issue'. For example, Ovidiu Anemtoaicei, from the Central European University, Budapest, the researcher in Romania, noted that: 'at the level of the state policies, academic and activist spheres, gender equality was conceived of as having generally women as the main target group'. This was not just true in some countries, but in most. An Irish interviewee noted that 'gender is for women, it's not for men or about men'.

The consequences of this are not only that many men think gender equality is nothing to do with them, but that they also think it has nothing positive to offer them. They may even be overtly hostile, believing that feminist approaches to gender equality seek to 'take rights away from men and give them to women', as Jari Hautama¨ki, of Lyo¨ ma¨to¨ n Linja Espoo, Finland, noted.

Other interviewees remarked on the considerable pressure on men to conform to traditional roles and stereotypes. Anna Karamanou, former chairperson of the Committee on Women's Rights and Gender Equality of the European Parliament, from Greece, argued that: 'The expression of feelings is not allowed in this masculine model ("Men don't cry"). Men are scorned if they are interested in gender equality issues or if they are involved in housework'. Interviewees said that traditional masculine attitudes can also make it hard for men to recognise any problems which suggest vulnerability. The Men's Health Forum, UK, stated that it is 'difficult for many men to acknowledge their vulnerability to health problems'.

If a man displays any kind of weakness, this can also be denigrated – including by men themselves – as 'feminine' or 'gay'. There still seem to be strong homophobic sentiments, even in countries which are ostensibly in favour of gay rights. Henk DeSmaele, from the University of Antwerp, Belgium, perceived there to be 'an 'absolute terror in individual men of coming across as gay, and female, and so on'.

Other interviewees noted the lack of positive male role models in society and the media. In relation to Lithuania, for instance, Margarita Jankauskaite', from the Centre for Equality Advancement, suggested in her interview that: 'If a famous basketball player publicly shows that he takes care of his daughter and changes her nappies he sends a politically correct message to his fans, especially to younger ones, that it is normal to do so. However, in Lithuania publicly seen and admired men are essentially chauvinist and sexist'. She concluded that different male examples are desperately needed, and that authoritative men or men in power should be the main target of gender work because everyone pays attention to what they say in public.

Timo Honkasalo, from Profeministimiehet, Finland, noted that even men who are sympathetic to gender equality as a goal may opt not to work on the issue: 'The biggest barrier is apathy, or at least reluctance. Even for men who in principle support gender equality, practical work to promote it seems to be an insurmountable barrier'. For other men, he pointed out, gender equality work is resisted, because it is seen as against men's interests: 'In addition to such reluctance, there is active resistance. Activists who engage in gender equality work may even be considered traitors'.

Another obstacle that was mentioned is the concern that the project of gender equality will be derailed by attempts to engage men in gender equality strategies, which could be a distraction from the task of empowering women. There is also a risk of diverting resources away from support for women, in a context where such resources (e.g. for refugees or rape crisis centres) are already under threat. In addition, men's socially condoned public leadership roles can lead to encroachment into fields which were formerly led by women. As Marceline Naudi, from the University of Malta, said: 'if men join in the struggle, they will take over'. Engaging men in gender equality should not involve abandoning support for projects and strategies that focus on women.

Finally, interviewees and researchers said that in many countries this work with men on gender equality was still very new, and often depended on a few individuals. Oana Ba˘lu̜ta˘, Chairwoman of FILIA, the Centre for Curricular Development and Gender Studies in Romania, said: 'We are still at the beginning of the story in a way, and we can only talk about individual men who express their support and solidarity for our struggles and efforts'.

For the well-being of society: perceptions of the benefits of gender equality for men

The benefits of involving men and boys in gender equality have been articulated in a range of documents and reports (e.g. Connell 2003; Kaufman 2003; Ruxton 2009). Strategies need to be identified to achieve men's commitment to such equality. At European level, the Council of Ministers has stated that:

> in order to improve the status of women and promote gender equality, more attention should be paid to how men are involved in the achievement of equality, as well as to the positive impact of gender equality for men and for the well-being of society as a whole. (Council of the European Union 2006, 38)

Respondents in this study endorsed or suggested various benefits of men becoming involved in gender equality work. First, gender equality holds the promise of improvements in men's and boy's relationships – not only with women and girls, but also in the relations they have with their male peers. Colin Fowler of the Men's Health Forum, in Ireland, stated: 'An involved and aware man is good for himself, his partner and his children; a healthy man is more of a contributor to his family and his community'.

A second benefit identified by interviewees relates to the damaging effects that stereotyping about men and masculinities can have on the health and well-being of men who for some reason fail to live up to the ideals of masculinity in their particular context. (Of course, these also have a damaging effect on women, though in different ways.) Men and boys face gender-specific health problems, such as higher rates of premature death through accident or suicide, and higher levels of drug and alcohol abuse. Many of these are linked to attempts by men to live up to dominant notions of masculinity ('be tough', 'compete', 'take risks'). Promoting and nurturing alternative models of being a man, and healthier and more equal relations between women and men, can do much to improve men's health and well-being, and reduce the negative impact of their actions – both on themselves and on other people. Margarita Jankauskaite, Project Manager at the Centre for Equality Advancement, Vilnius, Lithuania, stated: 'If men understood the importance of gender equality and were involved in gender equality practices, their lives could change significantly. There would be less self-destructive male behaviour in Lithuania'.

Interviewees also pointed out that involving men in gender equality programmes can also have positive benefits for the whole community, because reducing the pressures on men to conform to damaging and rigid forms of masculinity is likely, for example, to reduce men's violence, and so improve community and the safety of both women and men. It would also contribute to raising the next generation of boys (and girls) in a more egalitarian and violence-free way. In addition, it would also benefit men, especially those who are gay or transgender, who do not conform to traditional gender norms.

Henk DeSmaele, the researcher for the Flemish part of Belgium, who teaches history at Antwerp University, said:

> Having more open categories of masculinity means that men do have not to conform to a particular view on masculinity. It weakens the hegemonic discourse of masculinity and has a positive effect on perceptions of male identity'.

It takes courage: ways forward

Many interviewees felt that addressing apathy or resistance among many men must also be accompanied by efforts to address the real problems that some men experience. They said that it is important to be able to demonstrate, through practical examples, that the goal of gender equality work is just that – sharing power equally. It is not about women taking power from men, but about both sexes relating in a way which has considerable potential benefits for men themselves, as well as for women.

A number of interviewees said that they think this meant it was important to ensure that men feel they are listened to.

Jouko Huttunen, a fatherhood researcher from the University of Jyväskylä in Finland, said: 'As a starting point, the most important thing is to access men's point of view, so that they understand the advantages of equality as beneficial for men as for women'.

In the vast majority of cases, it is likely that encouragement will work better than attempts to cajole men to act in favour of gender equality. Gabriel Bianchi, from the Institute for Research in Social Communication in Slovakia, said:

> *The topic needs more positive image, i.e. as it happened with smoking and healthy lifestyle. It should be more discussed and promoted the positive impact of the life of men themselves, to encourage men to behave differently, breaking the gender stereotypes and prejudices still prevailing in the society. There should be a message like 'it is great to be a "new man"'.*

Targeting men, especially those who have a powerful role within institutions, and persuading them to be role models for progressive modes of masculinity, may help to encourage other men to participate in actions for gender equality. Judit Takács, from the Hungarian Academy of Sciences, Budapest, considered that:

> *Making these men visible for other men and the whole society has also a strong awareness-raising role, and can make other people believe that it is not awkward to deal with gender equality issues as a man.*

Jouko Huttunen (University of Jyva"skyla", Finland), proposed that the best known male politicians and male heads of influential corporations, trade unions, etc., should be obliged to support gender equality initiatives (e.g. by taking parental leave).

On the basis of their grassroots contact with men, White Ribbon UK argued that 'when we do engage with men, they are almost always actively supportive'. It may also be that in some situations, men will be compelled to reassess their options. For instance, Maria Strategaki, General Secretary for Gender Equality, Ministry of Interior, Decentralisation and E-Government, in Athens, argued that men in Greece 'will be forced to change due to the changing circumstances and the economic crisis: they will be forced to take up traditionally "female" jobs such as carers'.

Finally, the risks of *not* engaging with men should be taken into account. As the UK Coalition on Men and Boys argued:

> *Focusing exclusively on women can leave them with even more work to do and may entrench static definitions of women (e.g. as 'carers') and men (e.g. as 'breadwinners'). Moreover, the vast majority of decision-makers (most of whom are male) will continue to ignore the relevance of gender issues; as a*

result, gender will remain a peripheral issue and will not be integrated effectively into policy and programmes. (Ruxton 2009, 27)

Conclusion

Our research for this report identified a considerable amount of work in the area of men working for gender equality and men and masculinities in many EU Member States. However, this area is very much in its infancy and is also patchy compared with work on gender equality from women's perspectives.

The research suggests a number of further steps that should be taken to develop this work. First, there is a need to take evaluation and monitoring forward, spreading knowledge across EU Member States and providing technical assistance on how to perform impact evaluation of programmes, projects, and organisations that could be adapted for different country contexts. The latter could be part of a larger effort to provide toolkits on engaging men and boys in gender equality adapted to an EU context.

Second, European institutions involved in work on gender equality should be encouraged to also pay attention to men and masculinities. As the study found that most work on men and masculinities is being carried out at NGO level, it is particularly important to broaden the work to include the public sector, local, national, and regional governments, and business organisations. A significant challenge is to make masculinity issues and responses to them explicit rather than implicit within existing policymaking.

Third, it is essential to bring people together who are working on this issue to share ideas and practices, for example at conferences and seminars or through mentoring arrangements. Many are not aware of the innovative work on this theme in other countries, and the links between men and masculinities and broader work on gender equality are also not clear.

Finally, we believe that opportunities at EU and national levels available to NGOs and other actors to develop the field would be a strategic contribution at this stage. It is essential to keep in mind, however, that funding for work of this kind should not detract from funding for the crucial work being done with women's organisations on gender equality.

Notes

1. Equality between women and men is enshrined in Article 2 of the Treaty on European Union and in the EU's Charter of Fundamental Rights. In particular, the EU has focused on combating sex discrimination in employment, social security, and access to goods and services, and more recently, on gender mainstreaming.
2. For example, in 2006, Finland's EU Presidency organised a European-wide expert conference on men and gender equality, which informed the development of Council 'Conclusions on Men and Gender Equality' later that year (see Council of the European Union 2006).

3. Men for Gender Equality is the co-ordinator of the European section of MenEngage, a global alliance of more than 400 NGOs and UN agencies that seeks to engage boys and men to achieve gender equality (see www.menengage.org/, last checked by the author 31 December 2012).
4. The EIGE aims to: collect, analyse, and disseminate objective, comparable, and reliable information; develop, analyse, evaluate, and disseminate methodological tools; co-ordinate a European Network on Gender Equality; organise *ad hoc* meetings of experts; disseminate information on positive examples of non-stereotypical roles for women and men; develop dialogue and co-operation; and set up documentation resources accessible to the public (see www.eige.europa.eu/).
5. In France, Latvia, Luxembourg, and Slovenia, the researchers either struggled to get potential interviewees to commit to participating in the time available, or found it impossible to identify appropriate candidates.
6. While many organisations working in this area were involved in a range of different activities, in order to develop overall statistics for the database, it was necessary to decide the main theme of activity for each. Where organisations covered more than one main theme, a more general 'gender equality' label was applied.
7. The WEF Global Gender Gap Index examines the gap between men and women in four fundamental categories: economic participation and opportunity, educational attainment, health and survival, and political empowerment.
8. Note that the EIGE is at present developing an EU-specific 'Gender Equality Index' intended to stimulate countries to pay more attention to gender equality and data collection on gender issues.

References

Clatterbaugh, Kenneth (2007) 'Men's rights', in M. Flood, J.K. Gardiner, B. Pease, and K. Pringle (eds.) *International Encyclopedia of Men and Masculinities*, London: Routledge

Connell, R.W. (2003) 'The Role of Men and Boys in Achieving Gender Equality', EGM/Men-Boys-GE/2003/BP.1, United Nations Division for the Advancement of Women, Expert Group Meeting, Brasilia, 21–24 October

Council of the European Union (2006) 'Conclusions on Men and Gender Equality', http://register.consilium.europa.eu/pdf/en/06/st15/st15487.en06.pdf (last checked by the author 31 December 2012)

European Commission (2011) 'Strategy for Equality Between Women and Men 2010-2015', Luxembourg: Publications Office of the European Union, www.ec.europa.eu/social/BlobServlet?docId=6568&langId=en (last checked by the author 11 January 2013)

Gerschick, Thomas J. (2005) 'Masculinity and degrees of bodily normativity in Western culture', in M. Kimmel, J. Hearn, and R. Connell (eds.) *Handbook of Studies on Men and Masculinities*, Thousand Oaks, CA: Sage

Hearn, Jeff and Keith Pringle (2006) *European Perspectives on Men and Masculinities: National and Transnational Approaches*, Basingstoke: Palgrave

Kaufman, Michael (2003) *The Aim Framework: Addressing and Involving Men and Boys to Promote Gender Equality and End Gender Discrimination and Violence*, New York: UNICEF

Kimmel, Michael S., Jeff Hearn, and R.W. Connell (eds.) (2005) *Handbook of Studies on Men and Masculinities*, London: Sage

Ruxton, Sandy (2007) 'Working with Older Men: A Review of Age Concern Services', London: Age Concern England, www.gohealthlive.com/files/images/AgeConcernoldermenservices.pdf (last checked by the author 31 December 2012)

Ruxton, Sandy (2009) 'Man Made: Men, Masculinities and Equality in Public Policy', London: Coalition on Men and Boys, www.xyonline.net/sites/default/files/COMAB,%20Man%20Made%20-%20Men,%20masculinities%20and%20equality%20in%20public%20policy%202009.pdf (last checked by the author 31 December 2012)

Shakespeare, Tom (1999) 'When is a man not a man? When he's disabled', in J. Wild (ed.) *Working with Men for Change*, London: UCL Press

About the author

Sandy Ruxton is an independent policy advisor and researcher, based in Oxford, UK. He is a member of the Steering Group of MenEngage Europe. Among his publications are 'Beyond male role models: Gender identities andwork with young men in the UK' (with Featherstone, B., Robb, M., and Ward, M.), in Kulkarni, M., Jain, R. (eds.) (2019) Global Masculinities, Routledge; 'Man Made: Men, masculinities and equality in public policy' (2009), Coalition on Men and Boys), and 'Gender Equality and Men: Learning from Practice' (Oxfam GB, 2004). Email: sandy.ruxton@googlemail.com

Nikki van der Gaag is an independent consultant and writer on gender issues, based in Oxford, UK. Until February 2019 she was Director of Gender Justice and Women's Rights at Oxfam GB. Relevant publications include 'The No-nonsense guide to Feminism' (New Internationalist 2017), 'Feminism and Men' (Zed Press, 2016), Co-authoring 'The State of the World's Fathers' (Men Care, 2015 and 2017, and 'Because I Am a Girl: So What About Boys?' (Plan International, 2011). Email: nikkivdg@yahoo.co.uk

Resources

Liz Cooke

Key words: Men and gender equality; Men and masculinities; Health; Gender-based violence; Organisations and websites

Men and gender equality

The Role of Men for Gender Equality. World Development Report 2012 Background Paper (2011), Lidia Farré, http://siteresources.worldbank.org/INTWDR2012/ Resources/7778105-1299699968583/7786210-1322671773271/Farre-role-of-men-on-gender-equality.pdf, 47 pp.

This interesting paper argues for the necessity of including men and boys in gender equality work in order for full gender equality to be realised. The paper discusses where and why men have, in the past, ceded power and accepted changes in the traditional gender order. In its discussion of the family and decision-making within it, and men's impact on the socioeconomic and health status of women, the paper incorporates a wide-ranging and valuable literature survey.

Perspectives of Men Working for Gender Equality – Part of the BRIDGE Gender and Social Movements Cutting Edge Programme (2012), www.youtube.com/user/ BRIDGE socialmovement

In this set of video interviews, five men who work with other men on gender equality issues reflect on, amongst other aspects of their work, their relationship, and that of their organisation, to the women's rights movement and feminism. The interviewees are as follows: Philip Otieno, Men for Gender Equality Now, Kenya; Jerker Edstro¨ m, Institute of Development Studies, UK; Dean Peacock, Sonke Gender Justice Network, South Africa; Abhijit Das, Centre for Health and Social Justice, India; and Simon Cazal, LGBT activist from Paraguay.

Evolving Men: Initial Results from the International Men and Gender Equality Survey (IMAGES) (2011), Washington, DC and Rio de Janeiro: International Center for Research on Women and Instituto Promundo, www.engagingmen.net/files/ resources/2011/xiano/Evolving-Men-Initial-Results-from-the-International-Men-and-Gender-Equality-Survey-IMAGES_0.pdf, 120 pp.

This paper reports on the results of a survey on men's attitudes and practices on a variety of topics relating to gender equality. The survey was conducted in

http://dx.doi.org/10.3362/9781780448664.012

Brazil, Chile, Croatia, India, Mexico, and Rwanda, and the paper is an initial, comparative analysis of results across the six countries. Part I of the paper introduces the IMAGES project itself, and sets out the methodology and limitations of the research, with Part II reporting the results of the survey, and Part III outlining the key findings.

Engaging Men in Gender Equality: Positive Strategies and Approaches – Overview and Annotated Bibliography (2006), Emily Esplen, BRIDGE Bibliography No. 15, www. bridge.ids.ac.uk/vfile/upload/4/document/1109/bb15%20.pdf, 51 pp.

This extremely useful and accessibly written document is divided into three parts – the first providing an overview of the topic, laying out the arguments for involving men in gender and development work; the second an annotated bibliography, which includes many items downloadable for free from the internet, and the third, further information, consisting of contact details for organisations working in the area, plus a list of Web resources.

Gender Equality and Men: Learning from Practice (2004), Sandy Ruxton (ed.), Oxford: Oxfam GB, ISBN: 9-780855-9851141, http://policy-practice.oxfam. org.uk/publications/gender-equality-and-men-learning-from-practice-133968

With contributions from both the global South and North, this book critically assesses programmes run by Oxfam GB and other organisations that sought to actively engage men in gender equality work. The programmes discussed fall within five different areas: reproductive and sexual health; fatherhood; gender-based violence; livelihoods; and working with young men. The concluding chapter to the book is particularly recommended. The whole book can be downloaded, at no cost, from the link above.

What Men Have to Do With It: Public Policies to Promote Gender Equality (n.d.), Washington, DC and Rio de Janeiro: International Center for Research on Women and Instituto Promundo, www.icrw.org/files/publications/What-Men-Have-to-Do-With-It.pdf, 64 pp.

This paper argues that while programme experience with men and boys in many countries around the world indicates that programmes can positively influence men's attitudes and behaviours in relation to gender equality, public policy has not yet addressed the engagement of men and boys in eradicating gender inequality. The paper first looks at the issue of gender and public policy, and then, in a series of country case studies, surveys men and boys in existing gender equality policies. Part III provides examples of what gender and social policies that pay attention to men and masculinities would look like, and an annex sets out paternity and maternity leave in a list of selected countries.

Mainstreaming Men into Gender and Development: Debates, Reflections, and Experiences (2000), Sylvia Chant and Matthew Gutmann, Oxfam Working

Papers, Oxford: Oxfam GB, http://policy-practice.oxfam.org.uk/publications/mainstreaming-men-into-gender-and-development-debates-reflections-and-experienc-121166, 66 pp.

Based on research conducted for the World Bank, this paper from 2000 contends that while women bear a disproportionate share of social and economic disadvantage, gender, race, and poverty also disadvantage certain categories of men as well, and that a consideration of the place of men in gender and development is therefore crucial. The paper stresses the need for men to be recognised as a heterogeneous group in the same way as women are in gender and development, and points to the fact that calls for the involvement of men into increasing numbers of gender and development projects often come from grassroots women themselves.

Men and masculinities

Men Who Care: A Multi-country Qualitative Study of Men in Non-traditional Caregiving Roles (2012), Rio de Janeiro and Washington, DC: Instituto Promundo and International Center for Research on Women, www.promundo.org.br/en/wp-content/uploads/ 2012/06/Men-Who-Care.pdf, 76 pp.

This paper reports on the findings of qualitative research conducted in five countries – Brazil, Chile, India, Mexico, and South Africa – that set out to answer the following questions: What hinders men's involvement in care work and what encourages it? Who are the men who are doing more than the average in terms of care work? How do men understand and describe their participation in activities that have traditionally been described as female roles, both in the home and in the workplace? Based on the findings of the study, the paper offers a set of recommendations for action, and in an annex, sets out the interview protocol used during the research.

Masculinities, Social Change, and Development. World Development Report 2012 Background Paper (2011), Margaret E. Greene, Omar Robles, and Piotr Pawlak, http://siteresources. worldbank.org/INTWDR2012/Resources/7778105-1299699968583/7786210-1322671773271/Greene-et-al-masculinities.pdf, 32pp.

An impressive and up-to-date literature survey, this clearly written paper looks at the impact of social norms, gender roles, and stereotypes, and the expectations placed on men and boys. Importantly, it discusses the processes of change – how change occurs in gender norms and behaviours, and lists policy changes likely to bring about positive results in attempts to achieve gender equality.

Men and Development: Politicizing Masculinities (2011), Andrea Cornwall, Jerker Edstro¨ m, and Alan Greig, London and New York: Zed Books, ISBN: 9781848139787, website: http://zedbooks.co.uk

This book aims to challenge the neglect of the structural dimensions of gendered power relations in current development policy and practice, placing it at the centre of its analysis, with colonialism, globalisation, poverty, heteronormativity, poverty, class, and racism all included in its examination of men and masculinities. The book provides a wide range of case studies from across the global South, and contributors are both academics and activists, who draw on theory and practice in their analyses. The book was developed from a symposium held at the Institute of Development Studies in the UK, the report of which – 'Politicising Masculinities: Beyond the Personal' (2007) – can be downloaded from www.ids.ac.uk/files/dmfile/Masculinities.pdf.

Marriage, Motherhood and Masculinity in the Global Economy: Reconfigurations of Personal and Economic Life, IDS Working Paper 290 (2007), Naila Kabeer, Brighton: Institute of Development Studies, www.ids.ac.uk/files/dmfile/Wp290.pdf, 69 pp.

Globalisation has seen rising rates of paid work undertaken by women, often in contexts where male employment is stagnant or declining. This 69-page paper examines how women and men are dealing with this feminisation of labour markets, amidst a general prevalence of male breadwinner ideologies, and the apparent threat to male authority represented by women's earnings, coupled with an almost unvaried resistance to changes in the domestic division of unpaid work within the home, and a continuing failure by policymakers to provide support for women's care responsibilities, despite the growing importance of their breadwinning roles, which results in many women effectively working a 'double shift'. The commodification of love and sex in the global economy is explored, as are changing notions of marriage, motherhood, and masculinity, within the context of what the author frames as a crisis in social reproduction. As well as being extremely well-written and argued, the paper serves as an invaluable literature review, with an extensive list of references.

Making Sense of Fatherhood: Gender, Caring and Work (2010), Tina Miller, Cambridge: Cambridge University Press, ISBN: 9780521743013, website: www.cambridge.org

In this book, the author examines, in a global Northern context, the experiences of fatherhood of a group of men as they anticipate and then experience becoming fathers for the first time. Their experiences are considered in the light of economic and social changes and employment patterns, and the way in which these affect family relationships. The book also reveals how historically determined ideas about gender and policy continue to shape the expectations and experiences of fatherhood. (The author has also written *Making Sense of Motherhood*, Cambridge University Press, 2005.)

Men of the Global South: A Reader (2006), Adam Jones (ed.), London and New York: Zed Books, ISBN: 9781842775134, website: http://zedbooks.co.uk

Providing a wide-ranging survey of men and masculinities and the lives of men and boys in the developing world, this book is organised into six sections: Family and Sexuality; Ritual and Belief; Work; Governance and Conflict; Migrations; and Masculinities in Motion. The Introduction gives an overview of the literature on men and masculinities in the developing world, within the broader context of the study of gender and development.

Baba: Men and Fatherhood in South Africa (2006), Linda Richter and Robert Morrell (eds.), Cape Town: HSRC Press, ISBN: 978-07969-2096-6, website: www.hsrcpress.ac.za

With contributions from authors from a range of disciplines and backgrounds, this extremely informative collection is divided into five sections. Conceptual and theoretical issues are examined in section one; the historical perspective – how race and class shaped fatherhood in the last half of the twentieth century – explored in section two; the depiction of fathers in the media discussed in section three; the realities of being a father in South Africa today, including the obstacles preventing men from developing their engagement with children are considered in section four; and local and international policies and programmes are reviewed in the final section.

Handbook of Studies on Men and Masculinities (2004), Michael S. Kimmel, Jeff Hearn, and R.W. Connell (eds.), Thousand Oaks, CA: Sage, ISBN: 9780761923695, website: www. sagepub.com

This book provides a wealth of perspectives on men and masculinities from contributors from a range of disciplines, though largely the social sciences, with a focus on both the global North and South. Organised into five sections, the book looks first at theory, and then at masculinities in global and regional contexts; the effects of structures, institutions and processes on masculinities, with class, crime, families, fatherhood, organisations, and media representation examined; embodiment and masculinities; and politics, in which masculinities are discussed in relation to the nation; terrorism; war and militarism; Islam, and anti-violence activism.

Gender & Development, Vol. 5, No. 2 (June 1997), Men and Masculinity, http://oxf.am/o8k

Although published some 16 years ago, this issue of *Gender & Development* still serves as a clear and accessible introduction to the subject of men and masculinity in the context of gender and development policy and practice. The editorial article, in particular, is ideal for those completely new to the subject, being free of much of the somewhat esoteric and academic language often encountered in literature on gender.

Health

Synchronizing Gender Strategies: A Cooperative Model for Improving Reproductive Health and Transforming Gender Relations (2010), New York: EngenderHealth, www.engenderhealth.org/files/pubs/gender/synchronizing_gender_strategies. pdf, 34 pp.

The authors of this paper argue the case for working with men and women, and boys and girls together, to challenge gender norms in the pursuit of improved health and gender equality. In addition to providing a definition for the new concept of 'gender synchronization', the paper gives examples of synchronised approaches that have worked first with women and girls, or first with men and boys, and describes interventions that have worked with both sexes from the start. It also provides examples of new and emerging programmes, the results of which should help to inform future strategies.

Engaging Boys and Men in Gender Transformation: The Group Education Manual (2008), New York: The ACQUIRE Project/EngenderHealth and Promundo, www.acquireproject.org/archive/files/7.0_engage_men_as_partners/7.2_ resources/7.2.3_tools/Group_Education_Manual_final.pdf (also available in French), 357 pp.

This manual, designed for trainers, provides a range of participatory exercises aimed at men (and their partners), exploring ideas about gender, and their impact on HIV prevention and care. The manual was piloted in Ethiopia, Namibia, South Africa, and Tanzania, in order to assist trainers in developing curricula to work with men and boys on gender, HIV and AIDS issues. After a short background discussing the scientific rationale, chapter topics include: Gender and Power, Sexuality, Men and Health, Substance Use, Healthy Relationships, STI and HIV Prevention, Living with HIV, Fatherhood, Violence, and Making Change-taking Action.

Engaging Men and Boys in Changing Gender-based Inequity in Health: Evidence from Programme Interventions (2007), Gary Barker, Christine Ricardo, and Marcos Nasci-mento, Geneva: World Health Organization, www.who.int/gender/documents/Engaging_men_boys.pdf, 70 pp.

This paper reviews the effectiveness of 58 programmes in countries in both the global South and North engaging men and boys in achieving gender equity in health in the following areas: sexual and reproductive health; HIV prevention, treatment, care, and support; fatherhood; gender-based violence; and maternal, newborn, and child health. The aim was to assess the extent to which the programmes moved beyond addressing knowledge and attitudes in the specific health-related area, to changing the social construction of masculinity, and were, therefore, gender transformative. Among the findings of the survey was that those programmes assessed as being gender transformative had more effective outcomes. The paper concludes with a discussion on proposed steps forward and annexes summarise the interventions looked at in the study.

Gender-based violence

Engaging Men to Prevent Gender-based violence: A Multi-country Intervention and Impact Evaluation Study (2012), Rio de Janeiro: Instituto Promundo, www.promundo.org.br/wp-content/uploads/2012/04/UNT_Eng_10-1.pdf, 47 pp.

This paper discusses a United Nations (UN)-backed project which sought to evaluate a variety of programmes working with men to prevent gender-based violence. The programmes were: a community-based programme in India; a sports-based programme in Brazil, a health-based programme in Chile, and a work-place programme in Rwanda. All included workshops on gender equity and gender-based violence prevention training. The evaluation found a significant change in attitudes related to the use of violence against women, a self-reported decrease in the use of violence against female partners, along with a decrease in support for attitudes encouraging men's use of violence against women.

Mobilising Men in Practice: Challenging Sexual and Gender-based Violence in Institutional Settings: Tools, Stories, Lessons (2012), Alan Greig with Jerker Edströ m, Brighton: Institute of Development Studies, www.ids.ac.uk/files/dmfile/MobilisingMeninPracticeonlinefinal.pdf, 107 pp.

Recognising that 'gender inequalities and the violence that maintains them are not simply a matter of individuals and their behaviours; they are maintained by the social, economic and political institutions that structure all our lives', this excellent guide brings together stories and lessons, plus some of the tools used, from the Institute of Development Studies and UN Population Fund Mobilising Men programme, begun in 2010. This programme has seen partner organisations in India, Kenya, and Uganda identifying, recruiting, training, and supporting teams of male activists to work with women in developing campaigns to challenge and change the policies and cultures of specific institutional settings that enable and perpetrate violence against women.

Engaging Boys and Men in GBV Prevention and Reproductive Health in Conflict and Emergency-response Settings: A Workshop Module (2008), New York: The Acquire Project, www.engenderhealth.org/files/pubs/gender/map/conflictmanual.pdf, 53 pp.

Aimed at practitioners, this two-day participatory module is designed to build the skills of participants working to engage boys and men in the prevention of gender-based violence and in the promotion of reproductive health in conflict, and other emergency-response settings. It provides a framework for discussing strategies for male engagement, based on the phases of prevention and response in the contexts of conflict and displacement.

Organisations and websites

EngenderHealth, 440 Ninth Avenue, New York, NY 10001, USA, tel: +1 212 561 8000, email: info@engenderhealth.org, website: www.engenderhealth. org/our-work/gender

With offices and programmes in many countries around the world (including the USA), non-government organisation (NGO) EngenderHealth works on the issues of: family planning; maternal health; HIV and AIDS and STIs; and improving clinical quality; all with a gender equity focus. Of particular interest is their work on 'Engaging Men as Partners in Reproductive Health' and its 'Men As Partners' programme, which began in 1996, the components of which are: challenging traditional gender roles and attitudes about masculinity; enhancing men's awareness of and support for their partners' reproductive health; increasing men's access to and use of reproductive health services; and mobilising men to promote gender equity and end violence against women. EngenderHealth produces many useful publications, some of which are summarised in the resources sections above, and which are downloadable from their website.

The Fatherhood Institute, Unit 1, Warren Courtyard, Savernake, Marlborough, Wiltshire SN8 3UU, UK, tel: (from the UK) 0845 634 1328, email: mail@fatherhoodinstitute.org, website: www.fatherhoodinstitute.org

The Fatherhood Institute is a UK-focused research, advocacy, and training organisation. It concentrates its activities on three areas: work, education, and supports to family life. In the field of work, the Fatherhood Institute wants changes, such as more flexible and part-time working for fathers, so that they can be more available to care for their children. In terms of education, the organisation lobbies for boys being prepared for future caring roles, and the discussion by children and young people of gender inequalities and the pressure to conform to gender stereotypical roles. In terms of supports to family life, the organisation is calling for laws, policies, and public services to encourage and enable fathers to invest more of their time and energy in the direct care of their children, calling for 'all health, education, family and children's services to be "father-inclusive" – that is, to support fathers in their caring roles as seriously as they currently support mothers', although the Institute makes clear that it is not a 'fathers' rights' organisation.

Instituto Promundo, Rua México, 31/1502 – Centro, Cep. 20031-904, Rio de Janeiro, Brazil, tel: +55 (21) 2215-5216, email: contactdc@promundo.org. br, website: www. promundo.org.br/en

Instituto Promundo is a Brazilian NGO that seeks to promote 'caring, non-violent, equitable masculinities and gender relations in Brazil, and internationally'. Founded in 1997, and something of a pioneer in the field, Promundo's work falls into three categories: research (some of the findings of which are included in the resources section above), programme, and advocacy. Programme work includes 'Program H', in which young men are encouraged to reflect on inflexible gender norms and their effects on sexuality and reproductive health, intimate and family relationships, fatherhood and caregiving, violence prevention, and emotional health; and 'Program M', which aims to raise young women's awareness of gender inequality and their rights, and seeks to develop skills to enable them to act in more empowered ways. The publications section of the website contains many valuable resources – educational materials, reports, and articles. Founded in 2011, Promundo-US, based in Washington, DC, and a separate organisation, collaborates with Instituto Promundo on international advocacy, international programme development and communications work, and coordinates the work of the MenEngage Alliance.

Men Can Stop Rape, 1003 K Street NW, Suite 200, Washington, DC 2000, USA, tel: +1 202 265 6530, email: info@mencanstoprape.org, website: www.mencanstoprape.org

Founded in 1997, Men Can Stop Rape works in the USA to prevent men's violence against women and other men by encouraging young men to create their own, positive definitions of masculinity. The organisation's work falls into three categories – development programmes with young men in schools and universities; public awareness campaigns; and training and workshops for agencies and NGOs. The description on the website of what motivated the founders of Men Can Stop Rape states their ambitious goal: 'Though the majority of violent acts against women are committed by men, the vast majority of prevention efforts are risk-reduction and self-defense tactics directed at women. The founders wanted to shift the responsibility of deterring harm away from women by promoting healthy, nonviolent masculinity.'

MenCare, email: j.kato@promundo.org.br, wessel@genderjustice.org.za, website: www.men-care.org

MenCare is a global fatherhood campaign that aims to promote men's involvement as equal and non-violent fathers and caregivers, and to advance a vision in which one of the elements of 'being a man' is taking care of others. The campaign is co-ordinated by Promundo and Sonke Gender Justice (see above and below for more information on these organisations). The MenCare website provides access to advocacy and campaigning materials; relevant resources in the form of reports and research findings; and technical assistance and training, all aimed at supporting local NGOs, women's rights organisations, and government departments in their efforts to engage men and boys in care work.

MenEngage Global Alliance, email: via the website, website: www.menengage.org

A global alliance of international and national NGOs and UN agencies, MenEngage seeks to involve boys and men in achieving gender equality, promoting health, and reducing violence, and fulfilling the Millennium Development Goals, particularly those focusing on gender equality. At a national level, more than 400 NGOs from Sub-Saharan Africa, Latin America and the Caribbean, North America, Asia, and Europe are members of the Alliance, which began in 2004. MenEngage carries out advocacy and campaigning work, and aims to act as a collective voice in the promotion of a global movement of men and boys working towards the achievement of gender equality. The publications page of the MenEngage website provides many useful resources.

Partners for Prevention, 3rd Floor UN Service Building, Rajdemnern Nok Avenue, Bangkok, Thailand 10200, tel: +66 (0) 2304 9100 ext 2743, email: via website, website: www.partners4prevention.org

Partners for Prevention (P4P) is a UN Development Programme, UN Population Fund, UN Women and UN Volunteers regional joint programme in Asia and the Pacific, working to generate and disseminate knowledge, and provide technical support to national partners in order to prevent gender-based violence in the region. P4P is currently co-ordinating The Change Project, which is a multi-country regional research project that will provide cross-country comparable data on gender-based violence from the perspective of men. The P4P website provides research, capacity development, and communications resources derived from P4P programme work.

Sonke Gender Justice Network, 4th Floor Westminster House, 122 Longmarket Street, 8001, Cape Town, South Africa, tel: +27 (0) 21 423 7088, email: info@genderjustice.org.za, website: www.genderjustice.org.za

Based in South Africa, but working across the continent, Sonke Gender Justice Network supports men and boys in taking action to promote gender equality, prevent domestic and sexual violence, and reduce the spread and impact of HIV and AIDS, seeking to strengthen government, civil society, and individual capacity in order to do this. Current areas of work include: policy advocacy; opposing, together with other South African human rights organisations, the Traditional Courts bill, being considered (at the time of writing) by the South African parliament; and the Brothers for Life Campaign, aimed at addressing the risks involved with having multiple sexual partners, men's limited involvement in fatherhood, and issues around HIV status.

UN Population Fund (UNFPA), 605 Third Avenue, New York, NY 10158, USA, tel: +1 (212) 297 5000, email: hq@unfpa.org, website: www.unfpa.org/gender/men. htm

UNFPA's goals are to achieve universal access to sexual and reproductive health (including family planning), to promote reproductive rights, to reduce maternal mortality, and speed up progress on the International Conference on Population and Development (1994) agenda, and Millennium Development Goal 5 (improving maternal health). UNFPA also focuses on improving the lives of young people and women by advocating for human rights and gender equality, and by promoting the understanding of population dynamics. As part of this work, UNFPA seeks to engage men and boys, supporting many projects that emphasise men's role in reproductive health, for example, in HIV prevention, and greater male involvement in family life. The website provides more information on UNFPA programme work in this area, plus links to related UNFPA publications.

White Ribbon Campaign, websites: www.whiteribbon.ca, www.whiteribbon campaign.co.uk, www.whiteribbonscotland.org.uk, www.whiteribbon. org.au, www.whiteribbon.org.nz

Starting in Canada in 1991, the White Ribbon Campaign is a men's movement working to end violence against women and girls, and to promote gender equality, and a new vision of masculinity. Now active in other countries, the Campaign's White Ribbon Day takes place every year on 25 November, which is UN Day for the Elimination of Violence Against Women.

XY Online – Men, Masculinities, Gender Politics, email: via the website, website: www.xyonline.net

As its name suggests, this website is an online resource focusing on men and gender issues. It is also pro-feminist, stating that 'XY is intended to advance feminist goals of gender equality and gender justice'. The website serves as a space for debate and discussion, a resource library, and 'a toolkit for activism, personal transformation, and social change', and welcomes submissions from users.